# SEX FOR SALE

Studies in Theatre History and Culture

EDITED BY *Heather S. Nathans*

Katie N. Johnson

# Sex for Sale

## SIX PROGRESSIVE-ERA BROTHEL DRAMAS

UNIVERSITY OF IOWA PRESS
IOWA CITY

University of Iowa Press, Iowa City 52242


Printed in the United States of America

Design by Omega Clay

www.uiowapress.org



The University of Iowa Press is a member of Green Press Initiative and is committed to preserving natural resources.
Printed on acid-free paper

---

Sex for sale : brothel drama in U.S. culture / [edited by] Katie N. Johnson.
pages cm. — (Studies in theatre history and culture)
Includes bibliographical references and index.
ISBN 978-1-60938-313-8 (pbk), ISBN 978-1-60938-314-5 (ebk)
1. American drama—20th century. 2. Prostitutes in literature.
I. Johnson, Katie N., editor.
PS627.P76S49 2015
812'.5209355—dc23 2014026042

*For Hugo and Sally Nadine,*
*and for Timothy and Liam*

# CONTENTS

# ACKNOWLEDGMENTS

THIS BOOK has been long in the making. Miami University graciously awarded me a Faculty Summer Research Grant and an Assigned Research Leave to work on this project. Miami's College of Arts and Science also awarded me a Small Research Grant to travel to the Library of Congress and verify copyright dates. The Office for the Advancement of Research & Scholarship supported this project as well. Miami's English Department, under the helm of J. Kerry Powell, nurtured this project in incalculable ways. Karen Schilling provided amazing support and vision as dean of the College of Arts and Science. Debra Morner made everything happen in the front office. And Lu Ming Mao supported every move on this project and beyond.

Beyond the generous institutional support, I have been blessed with a supportive and amazingly smart reading group consisting of Mary Jean Corbett, Madelyn Detloff, Elisabeth Hodges, Timothy Melley, and Peggy Shaffer. Their insights into how to shape this project—and readings of numerous drafts—have been heroic. Matt Levy, as editorial associate, injected energy into the final phase of the project, helping with vital research and editing. Andrew Hebard and members of the American Cultures reading group gave excellent insights into this project. John Millard, and Elias Tzoc from the Digital Media Center, along with Tyler Grof and Tory Lowe, helped launch the digital aspect of this project. I thank Marlis Schweitzer for her insights into Progressive-Era theatre. David Shields shared his Fay Bainter production photos with me. Thanks to Lesley Moore for inspiration. I thank my students for their insights into this project.

I can never offer enough thanks for the tireless work of archivists and librarians, but I would especially like to thank those working at the Library of Congress Manuscript Division, Harvard Houghton Theatre Collection, New York Public Library for the Performing Arts, the Theatre Collection at the Museum of the City of New York, Sherman Theatre Collection at Southern Illinois University Special Collections Research Center as well as those at Illinois State University Library and the Bloomington Public Library. Thanks also to Weatherly Stephen at the Manuscripts and Archive Division, New York Public Library; Lisa Darms at Fales Library and Special Collections at New York University; Reagan Fletcher at the Shubert Archive; Tom Lisanti at the New York Public Library's Permissions and Reproductions; and Nancy Shawcross at the Rare Book and Manuscript Library, University of Pennsylvania. I thank Clara Goldman from the Whitney Museum of American Art and Hannah Rhadigan from the Artists Rights Society for securing John Sloan's artwork for this volume. Thanks to Angela Bruce from the Independent Age for granting rights for Elizabeth Robins's *My Little Sister*. A special shout-out to Heather Nathans and Catherine C. Cocks from the University of Iowa Press.

Mostly, it is Timothy D. Melley who has made this work a reality, with his vision and love.

# SEX FOR SALE

# Introduction

In early twentieth-century American theatre, sex was for sale. In some ways this was nothing new. Sex has always been for sale in the theatre, just as it has been in U.S. culture more generally. But at the turn of the twentieth century plays *about* sex for sale—that is, about prostitution—began to take Broadway by storm. Expanding upon the popular nineteenth-century fascination with the so-called fallen woman, Progressive-Era culture was obsessed with the figure of the prostitute, and U.S. theatre became a major site of this fascination. As a locus of enthrallment and revulsion, the underworld took center stage as early twentieth-century theatre performed cultural discourses of sexuality, women's suffrage, eugenics, prostitution reform, birth control, immigration legislation, urbanization, and women in the workforce.

*Sex for Sale* recovers this vital moment in U.S. history and brings to print six Progressive-Era plays about prostitution. Largely forgotten by historians, these "brothel dramas" played a crucial role in shaping early twentieth-century U.S. culture.[1] The prostitute was a "quintessential object of modernist fascination," to use Rebecca Schneider's formation, scrutinized relentlessly by a range of modern philosophers and artists, including Charles Baudelaire, Walter Benjamin, Edouard Manet, and John Sloan.[2] From essays about prostitution in the *Masses*, to short stories and novels about women who "fall" into a life of vice by Frank Norris, Stephen Crane, and others, to the Committee of Fourteen's reports on commercialized vice, U.S. culture was saturated with prostitution discourse. Many of these narratives contained a sense of impending catastrophe and danger, portraying an underworld that threatened to devour innocent young women. "Red-light districts," a typical 1912 pamphlet cautioned, "like a line of fire, are constantly engulfing unwary and unprotected girls."[3] Reformers and civic leaders warned that something had to be done. As they railed against the "social evil" of prostitution, many writers and performers turned to the theatre to portray the problem of commercialized vice on the stage.

Although no longer in our lexicon, the term "brothel drama" was widely used by cultural critics of the day to describe this popular subgenre of dramatic literature.[4] The term was synonymous with many others, such as red-light drama, white slave drama, vice drama, underworld drama, bawdy-house drama, and social evil drama. While these phrases were interchangeable, I use "brothel drama" as a way of capturing the larger cultural phenomenon of representing prostitution in U.S. Progressive-Era theatre. At the turn of the twentieth century, stories about prostitutes and fallen women flourished in both lowbrow popular entertainments (such as *Little Lost Sister* by Arthur James Pegler and Arthur Rose) and highbrow social problem plays (like the Pulitzer Prize–winning "*Anna Christie*" by Eugene O'Neill). Though popular and prevalent, brothel dramas suffered disparate fates. Some were censored; others had obscure regional runs; still others were Broadway hits. There were so many plays about prostitution on Broadway in the early twentieth century that critics complained about the number. In 1913 a *New York Herald* headline emblematized this vice-weary attitude, asking whether readers were "prepared to accept the new Red-Light Drama, with its sordid representation of vice for vice's sake, in all its hideousness?"[5] A critic from *Munsey*'s bemoaned in 1914 that Broadway "has nothing better than the vice theme to sustain it."[6] It was true: the vice theme very much sustained Broadway from the nineteenth century to the 1920s.

But why stage sex for sale? And why, during the height of antiprostitution reform, when prostitutes were being swept *off* the streets with increasing vigor if not malice, were prostitutes and white slaves hailed onto the stage as central characters? How could a brothel genre emerge—indeed flourish—precisely at the moment when regulatory efforts were closing brothels and red-light districts? The plays in this volume help to untangle this paradox, demonstrating the centrality of the theatre—and specifically the brothel drama—to American cultural production, especially in shaping attitudes regarding sexuality, gender, and the politics of women's work. This book therefore reads the selling of dramas about sex alongside actual practices of selling sex. The brothel drama exposes intense regulatory activity in regard to prostitution, or, as Kathleen Barry puts it, "female sexual slavery."[7] New York City—the City of Eros, as Timothy Gilfoyle calls it—was central to this enterprise. "To understand this seamy side of life," Gilfoyle writes, "is to understand how much of American society functioned."[8] The stage was a perfect venue for portraying the seamy side of Progressive-Era society. Brothel dramas therefore participated directly in the larger cultural project of regulating sexuality and gender in the modern American city. They represented, as Michel Foucault might say, a technology of sex.[9]

In short, brothel dramas became the performative platform for the Progressive Era's sexuality debates. The prostitute was relentlessly studied, regulated, incarcerated, and legislated in early twentieth-century U.S. culture. Historian Ruth Rosen has characterized the Progressive Era's reform efforts as "one of Western Society's most zealous and best-recorded campaigns against prostitution."[10] In 1900 the Committee of Fifteen was formed in New York City to study the "startl[ing] discoveries in regard to the spread of the Social Evil in certain districts, and . . . [the] flagrant offences against public morality and common decency."[11] Their first report, *The Social Evil, with Special References to Conditions Existing in the City of New York* (1902), was the first of many discursive shifts away from imaging prostitution as a "necessary evil" and toward thinking of it as a "social evil" that required eradication. In 1910 the Committee of Fifteen was reconstituted as the Committee of Fourteen, which published *The Social Evil in New York City*.[12] That same year, Congress passed the White Slave Traffic Act (also known as the Mann Act), which prohibited the transport of women across state lines for the purposes of sexual slavery. Chicago by then had formed its own vice commission, which reported in *The Social Evil in Chicago* (1911) that commercialized prostitution brought in $15 million a year (about $350 million in 2015). The size of the industry, the report argued, was also a measure of its harm to women: "The traffic in women in this city annually demands and destroys the lives and souls of 5,000 young girls."[13] The stakes thus seemed high. The fight was about saving lives—even souls.

Organizations like John D. Rockefeller Jr.'s Bureau of Social Hygiene and Anthony Comstock's New York Society for the Suppression of Vice devoted themselves to eradicating commercialized vice and what was increasingly theorized to be aberrant female sexuality. Such organizations waged ideological battle with more progressive groups such as the Sociological Fund of the Medical Review of Reviews or feminist organizations. Many of these clashes took place in the theatre and in the public press.

The staging of prostitution thus engendered what I call "brothel performativity," a matrix of cultural discourses and embodied practices that played out both on and off the stage. If we take the efficacy of speech acts seriously, then brothel dramas can be understood as vital producers of cultural meaning—as embodied practices that performed important cultural work. The theatre was a literal producer of ideology and epistemologies, at times reinforcing hegemonic notions of "proper" sexuality and at other times subverting them. Dramas about the sex trade were therefore part of an elaborate system for constructing and regulating sexuality and gender; but, on occasion, they were also vehicles for rupturing that policing. And it goes without saying that women's bodies and female sexuality, particularly heterosexual sexuality within the confines of marriage, were at the center of these discursive and representational battles. One of the ironies that brothel performativity unveils is that prostitution became the uncanny sacred ground for staging morality debates. Moreover, insofar as narrative order was restored after tramping through the dramaturgical underworld, the brothel drama paradoxically saved heterosexuality from its own perceived perversions. The theatre was thus an important mechanism in both the staging and the censoring of the prostitute figure in the larger project of staging sexuality.

Take, for example, the spectacular premiere of George Bernard Shaw's *Mrs Warren's Profession* in New York City in 1905. So many people crowded Times Square to see the play (10,000 by some counts) that traffic came to a standstill. Bernard Shaw's play forever changed America's understanding of prostitution: how selling sex for money needed to be contextualized within a larger framework of the politics of women's work and patriarchal constraints on women in general. A decade after that tumultuous premiere (and while Bernard Shaw's play was still banned in England), U.S. attitudes had shifted regarding sex plays. As the *New York Dramatic Mirror* reported, "Times have changed and we applaud that from which we shrunk in *Mrs. Warren's Profession* a few years ago."[14] Indeed, far from avoiding plays about prostitution, the New York theatre scene was obsessed with them. Reviews for brothel dramas often pointed out the connection between actual reports of female sexual slavery and the stage. Elizabeth Robins's *My Little Sister* (1913), for instance, was widely billed as based on a true story, just as Witter Bynner's *Tiger* (1913) drew upon sensational headlines. A one-act play about the abduction of a young girl, *Tiger* dramatized the well-publicized account of a politician who entered a brothel only to discover that the girl he intended to violate was his own daughter. Reginald Wright Kauffman's "vice play" (originally a novel), as it was often called, likewise claimed to be based on true stories. "Throughout this narrative," Kauffman explained in the introduction to his novel, "there is no incident that is not a daily commonplace in the life of the underworld of every large city. If proof were needed, the newspapers have, during the last twelvemonth, proved as much."[15] If "proof" lay in headlines, then it soon found its way to the stage.

By virtue of newspaper articles, pulp fiction, and the theatre, the topic of prostitution had infiltrated most U.S. homes during the 1910s. The most common and sensational narratives were about women being abducted as "white slaves." In 1913 *Life Magazine* reported that "what is called white slavery has now become a favorite topic of dinner table conversation in our best circles."[16] *Everybody's Magazine* concurred and faulted the "sex-tangled drama" for serving up unsavory portions: "White slavery has been too widely admitted into polite dinner-table conversation."[17] Not just in theatre, but also throughout all facets of U.S. culture, sex debates, sparked by prostitution reform, had intensified to a breaking point. One cultural commentator observed that "a wave of sex hysteria and sex discussion seems to have invaded this country," striking "sex o'clock" in America.[18]

Brothel dramas fundamentally reoriented public conceptions of social problems at the heart of U.S. culture as it transitioned into a modern era: women's rights and reform work (*Ourselves*, *My Little Sister*); sexual double standards (*Ourselves*, *The Web*); birth control and sex education (*Moondown*, *My Little Sister*); and expanding urbanism (*Cocaine*, *Moondown*). These plays also intervened in key U.S. political debates and legislative initiatives, such as those concerning immigration (the Chinese Exclusion Act of 1882 and the Immigration Act of 1924), sexually transmitted diseases (the Page Act of 1910), and trafficking in women (the Mann Act of 1910).[19] While anxieties regarding immigration often resulted in antipathy toward immigrants—especially the Chinese—some white slave plays such as "A Shanghai Cinderella" (1918, renamed *East Is West*) briefly articulated short-lived miscegenated desire before succumbing to racist stereotypes. Racial anxieties found ample expression not only in brothel drama plots, but also in performance practices, as in the problematic use of yellowface in *East Is West*. Brothel dramas also tapped into the latest social problems, showing drug dependency, for instance, in Pendleton King's aptly titled *Cocaine* (1916) or in O'Neill's *The Web* (1913). In other words, these brothel plays were not only reflections of cultural practice but also *producers* of it. Brothel dramas thus fundamentally constitute a cultural archive in which embodied practices otherwise banned, shunned, or regulated found expression. Insofar as brothel dramas were enacted on the stage, the phenomenology of the living and breathing body is key to understanding the urgency and popularity of the form.

• • •

Part 1 of the volume surveys work from the budding theatres in Greenwich Village where radical writers first gave brothel drama a place on the early twentieth-century stage. We begin with three one-act plays by two well-known writers (Eugene O'Neill and John Reed) and another lesser-known figure (Pendleton King) in order to demonstrate the importance of their artistic experimentation in the larger project of modern theatre. Though largely overlooked in scholarship, these one-act brothel dramas (*The Web*, *Moondown*, and *Cocaine*, respectively) ignited American sexuality debates and made the Village theatre scene an important site for such discussions. Easy to produce and well-suited for aesthetic experimentation, the one-act play was crucial to the rise of American literature, theatre, leftist politics, and sexual discourse.[20] Many one-acts either were published in periodicals devoted to chronicling the zeitgeist (such as the *Masses* or the *Nation*) or were staged by small experimental companies that constituted the emerging art theatre and Little Theatre movements. Two companies in particular, the Provincetown Players and Washington Square Players, helped develop the one-act play as a vital American genre. It is no surprise that prostitution would grace their stages. One-act plays in art theatres would soon be eclipsed by full-length treatments on Broadway, as producers poached and commercialized what the one-act was innovating. The irony of selling commercialized sex in the theatre should not escape us.

Part 2 focuses on full-length Broadway brothel dramas. By 1913 so many mainstream plays concerned white slavery—the abduction of white women for purposes of sexual slavery—that newspapers bemoaned that "red light plays" had overtaken Broadway.[21] With salacious titles like *The House of Bondage*, *Queen of the White Slaves*, and *Escaped from the Harem*, white slave dramas offered melodramatic thrills with titillating details from the underworld. These narratives followed a predictable formula. A young white woman is abducted by a surly (and often swarthy) man, known in the language of the day as a "cadet" or pimp, and tricked into entering a brothel, where she is drugged, beaten, and held against her will as a sexual slave. These cautionary tales warned young women against crossing proscribed boundaries to explore their sexuality, develop independence, or strike out to the city to find work.

Like Native American captivity narratives, which flourished in colonial America, white slave plays belied an intense investment in conserving middle-class whiteness as well as protecting sexual purity. As George Lipsitz has shown, "the possessive investment in whiteness has always been influenced by its origins in the racialized history of the United States," and the theatre was no exception.[22] White slave narratives focused almost exclusively on the capture of innocent, young *white* women and celebrated heroic male efforts to protect and save white womanhood. Ernest Bell's 1910 tract, *Fighting the Traffic in Young Girls*, made this racialized dynamic clear: "By the white slave trade is meant commerce in white women and girls for wicked purposes."[23] White slave plots were both lurid and prominent, often exaggerating tales of abduction for melodramatic effect. Rumors were rampant that women were being plucked off the streets, or drugged while innocently eating ice cream, and forced into houses of ill repute from which they would never return. On its surface, the white slave panic articulated fears that women were being abducted, drugged, and driven into sexual slavery. On a deeper level, however, white slave melodramas became vehicles to work through divisive debates regarding sexuality, women's work, immigration, urbanization, birth control, public housing, eugenics, and racial purity.

If white slave dramas portrayed victims as both racially and morally white, then, by contrast, as M. Joan McDermott and Sarah Blackstone have pointed out, the captors were almost always nonwhite immigrants (usually Jews, Italians, Asians, or Eastern Europeans).[24] Edwin Sims, the U.S. attorney general, articulated the racialized logic of white slave discourse in 1910: "On the one hand the victims [are] pure, innocent, unsuspecting, trusting young girls—and not a few of them mere children. On the other hand, "[m]any of these white slave traders are recruited from the scum of the criminal classes of Europe."[25] Like the proverbial maiden tied to the train tracks, the white slave heroine is barricaded in a brothel, desperate to be saved before she is sexually, and thus racially, sullied. In both contemporary and Progressive-Era white slave tales, the racial characterization of villains reflects current geopolitical concerns: whereas twenty-first-century bad guys are Slavs and Arabs, the turn-of-the-twentieth-century abductors were cast as ethnic immigrants.

Magazine stories ("My Little Sister"), pulp fiction (*The Horrors of the White Slave Trade*), silent films (*Traffic in Souls*), and newspaper articles (ninety-four white slavery pieces appeared in the *New York Times* in 1909 alone) all promulgated white slave tales that attracted prurient readers and audiences alike.[26] White slave tracts like *The Traffic in Girls: White Slavery as Now Practiced in America* (1912) sought to document the horrors of the underworld with "plain, hard facts, without exaggeration or rhetoric."[27] In spite of such efforts to resist exaggeration, however, many of these reports were inflated.

For example, in September 1913 the *New York Times* reported the somewhat dubious claim that "Over 50,000 Girls Disappear in This Country Yearly" and offered *My Little Sister* as verifying such "gruesome stor[ies]."[28] Ernst Bell's inflammatory tract *Fighting the Traffic in Young Girls* epitomized the panic-infused rhetoric employed by "white slave hunters" like himself: its cover featured a helpless white slave trapped behind bars, pleading, "For God's Sake, Do Something!" (see fig. 1).

By 1913 the white slave scare had reached its zenith, prompting censors to regulate Broadway. In September 1913 two red-light plays, *The Lure* and *The Fight*, were shut down by the New York police and became embroiled in high-profile obscenity cases.[29] Weeks of front-page headlines made these brothel dramas among the most well-known cultural artifacts of their day. New York's muckraking newspaper the *World* participated in "the crusade against the 'red light melodramas,'" calling them immoral, gross, and revolting.[30] Editorials in New York papers called for censorship of these plays, demanding: "How long is New York going to stand for the two bawdy-house plays which outrage public decency at prominent theatres?"[31] *Theatre Magazine* also attacked the genre of the "Red Light drama" for its lowbrow content, claiming that "the stage is not the place on which to fight such crusades."[32] Of course, the stage was *precisely* the place to fight crusades, for its apparently salacious content galvanized social action. Even the *New York Times* took a stand against both *The Lure* and *The Fight*: "There is no saving grace about these plays. They are cheap, disgusting, and hopelessly stupid. Their performances should be stopped."[33] Given such pressures, the producers "laundered" their productions by excising offensive material, and the grand jury dropped the obscenity charges. Yet the changes were so extensive—eliminating the brothel altogether in one case—that the plays no longer made sense.

Even though activists like Emma Goldman had cautioned that the traffic in women concerned "not merely white women, but yellow and black women as well," such analysis was ignored in the fervent portrayal of white, female victimhood.[34] The focus on white women is particularly telling, given that initial investigations into sexual servitude were focused on the abduction of immigrant women.[35] Whereas "yellow slavery was a historically verifiable condition," as Karen Keely has shown, "white slavery seems to have existed primarily in the realm of anxiety, fears of miscegenation, and anti-Chinese rhetoric."[36] Nowhere is this unease more palpable than in the construction of the white slave in the theatre. Plays like *The Queen of Chinatown* (1899), *King*

**"MY GOD! IF ONLY I COULD GET OUT OF HERE"**
The midnight shriek of a young girl in the vice district of a large city, heard by two worthy men, started a crusade which resulted in closing up the dens of shame in that city. (See page 450.)

FIGURE 1. Illustration from an unattributed artist in Ernest Bell's *Fighting the Traffic in Young Girls* (1910).

*of the Opium Ring (1900)*, *Dealers in White Women* (1904), *Slaves of the Opium Ring: The Opium Smugglers of 'Frisco (1908)*, and *The Slave Girl: 20 Minutes in Frisco's Chinatown* (1913) all portrayed white women ensnared in opium dens as sexual slaves.[37] These heroines were all racially white, young, chaste, heterosexual, and naïve. But the villains of these plays were characterized by blatantly racist imagery: as kings and queens of drug dynasties, bumbling idiots, warring gang members, dragon ladies, polygamists, sex addicts, dope fiends, greedy capitalists, and conniving plotters—all speaking in exaggerated, broken dialect. When not portrayed as thugs or addicts, Asian male characters from these dramas were sketched as ruthless businessmen, thus revealing anxiety that Chinese immigrants were threatening the nation in spite of immigration restrictions.

Anti-Chinese sentiments found expression in nineteenth-century dramas like the transparently titled *The Chinese Must Go* (1879). These concerns were particularly visible in white slave plays featuring the Chinese underworld and especially opium dens.[38] Clearly a register of rising anti-Chinese immigration sentiments in the United States—beginning with the Chinese Exclusion Act of 1882 and continuing through the restrictive Immigration Act of 1924—such plays articulated panic about the so-called yellow peril. Packaged as thrilling melodrama and recycling elements of nineteenth-century opium-war plays, these white slave plays featured an array of stereotypes about Asians in general, and the Chinese in particular.

In addition to the theatre, reports in the popular press and literary texts perpetuated stereotypes of Asians as drug-peddling sex slavers. For example, Frank Norris's short story "The Third Circle," set in parts of Chinatown that even "the guides don't show you," demonstrates what happens when an upper-class white woman decides to slum in Chinatown with her fiancé.[39] On a whim, Miss Ten Eyck gets a tattoo: once Chinese ink penetrates her skin, her doom is indelibly sealed. When her fiancé leaves her unattended for just a few minutes, she is abducted and disappears forever within the San Francisco Chinese underworld. Norris's story points to the popular practice of staging fake opium dens for tourists interested in slum voyeurism.[40] The theatre capitalized on these voyeuristic desires, confining them to the stage and adding melodramatic flourishes.

While most white slave plays featured Anglo-American sexual slaves, they sometimes included Asian women in the den as well. These "yellow slave plays" paved the way for Hollywood's portrayal of Asian slave girls being rescued by white men and falling in love with them—the subject of *East Is West* in 1922 and 1930, *A Shanghai Gesture* in 1941, and *Walk Like a Dragon* in 1960, to name a few films. China's transition to a republic in 1912 had something to do with U.S. citizens thinking more favorably of it. Sexual slavery was increasingly being understood in relation to the yellow slave traffic. As the white slave "hunter" Clifford Roe wrote, "Deplorable and disgraceful as is the white slave traffic in the Orient, the yellow slave traffic in our own country is infinitely more disgraceful."[41] In her book *Yellowface*, Krystyn Moon has expressed this shift regarding the Chinese as follows: "what was once unconditional hatred became a form of fascination."[42] On one level, these dramas featuring concubines in harems, lush opium interiors, and wicked villains demonstrated a dual fascination with and repulsion from the East that Edward Said has characterized as Orientalism. Yet, on another level, some of these yellow slave dramas offered subversive moments by opening up spaces to pursue interracial mixing.

Occasionally a melodrama focused on an exceptionally beautiful—that is, Westernized—"yellow slave," who elicits sympathy and desire from the hero. This yellow slave is so beautiful, and yet so innocent, that the American hero immediately falls in love and seeks to liberate her. Significantly, the racialized erotics never work in reverse, with white women falling in love with Asian men. The theme of white men desiring Asian women has a long history in Western performance, epitomized by the doomed interracial lovers in Giacomo Puccini's opera *Madama Butterfly* from 1904 (it was initially staged as a play by David Belasco in 1900). Given that interracial attractions were inevitably portrayed as tragic, miscegenation was circumvented in a variety of makeshift solutions (the hero needs to ship off, the Asian slave kills herself, or it is revealed—as in a Shakespearean comedy—that she is not who she thought she was). The last play in this volume, "A Shanghai Cinderella" (*East Is West*), demonstrates the lure of the demure Chinese sexual slave. The play ran for nearly two years on Broadway and was made into a film twice (including a stunning version with Lupe Vélez in yellowface).

...

Prostitutes, especially hookers with hearts of gold, have tugged at the heartstrings of audiences since the mid-nineteenth century. No other character epitomized the demise of the good-hearted prostitute better than Marguerite of *Camille*, a courtesan "rehabilitated" by love, expressing self-sacrifice for her lover Armand, even in her dying moments. An astonishing number of stage and film heroines have coughed their way through musty plot lines, seen most obviously in Nicole Kidman's consumptive demise as Satine in *Moulin Rouge!* (2001). But lest we write this off as a mere historical phenomenon, we need only look to Hollywood to see the tenacious hold of the brothel imaginary. Consider the insanely popular *Pretty Woman* (1990), the predictable *Night Shift* (1982), the indulgent *Leaving Las Vegas* (1995), and Baz Luhrmann's spectacularly campy (yet ultimately ideologically traditional) *Moulin Rouge!* A hundred years after the height of white slave dramas, Hollywood continues to take its cue directly from this body of work with its unimaginatively titled blockbusters *Taken* (2009) and *Taken 2* (2012). Clearly, the brothel still has allure for cinema. As a 1996 *New York Times* headline bluntly put it, "Play a Hooker and Win an Oscar."[43] Given this rich legacy, it seems that we cannot quite get out of the brothel. (For additional brothel dramas and related material on the staging of sex work in the Progressive Era, see brotheldrama.lib.miamioh.edu.)

*Sex for Sale* explores how we got *into* the brothel—over a hundred years ago. After a spate of nineteenth-century hookers with hearts of gold, twentieth-century American playwrights struggled again and again to capture a sense of the modern by way of the brothel.

# Part 1

## ONE-ACT PROSTITUTE PLAYS IN ART THEATRES

# *The Web* by Eugene O'Neill

IF EVER an American playwright invested intellectual (and also emotional) capital in vice and depravity, it was Eugene O'Neill. Among the greatest American playwrights of the twentieth century, O'Neill wrote somewhat compulsively about prostitutes. Fallen women and hookers appear in no less than fourteen of his plays.[1] One of his first dramas, *The Web*, emerged just as one-acts were gaining popularity in U.S. culture. *The Web* portrayed the ensnaring mesh of prostitution for an impoverished girl named Rose. Written in 1913 while O'Neill was convalescing from consumption and originally entitled *The Cough*, *The Web* sketches what would become central O'Neill motifs of betrayal, illness, and the impossibility of love.[2] O'Neill's remarkable talents are evident in this early work, which bears the traces of a young writer seeking to break away from melodrama and the "old" theatre of his father, the celebrated actor James O'Neill. While Eugene O'Neill hoped that *The Web* would be produced in New York, the play was never performed in his lifetime.

Instead of anchoring the story in the salacious brothel interior, as did subsequent brothel plays, O'Neill limited the action to a destitute prostitute's room in a flophouse (a plot device that John Reed and Frank Shay would soon borrow for their one-acts). O'Neill's empathy for the down-on-her-luck streetwalker distinguishes his perspective from the pseudo-scientific tracts of the day, like George Kneeland's *Commercialized Prostitution in New York City*, which was published the same year. While these studies concentrated on the surveillance, regulation, and punishment of prostitutes, O'Neill instead crafted a sympathetic portrayal of a young woman whose poverty and illness have sent her into a downward spiral. Sick with consumption, Rose tries to reason with her heartless pimp, Steve, who disregards her pleas and callously commands her out onto the rainy streets to turn some tricks. This portrait of Rose is significant in that it prefigures Anna from "*Anna Christie*" with her lower-class slang ("Gawd!") and tragic life of being used and abused by men.

O'Neill adds an interesting element in this short work that rarely appears in other dramas about prostitution: an illegitimate baby. Writing about unwanted pregnancy (a topic that O'Neill explored in another early one-act play, *Abortion*) was a bold choice in 1913. Birth control was still illegal in the United States, and writing about it, as Margaret Sanger would discover in 1914, could mean prosecution under the Comstock Act for obscenity.[3] While modern readers can appreciate the risk of pregnancy for prostitutes, the subject is strangely absent from plays from this era (another notable exception is Rachel Crothers's *Ourselves*). In *The Web*, the baby is not coddled, pampered, or kept offstage with someone watching it. On the contrary, the child is on the stage during the dramatic action, where it is treated as a nameless thing to dispose of. In fact, most of the male characters seek to tear the baby away from its mother. Rose's pimp, Steve, callously demands that the infant be put on the floor so he can use the bed. He also insists that Rose give the baby away soon so she can continue to prostitute herself. Even the policeman's final handling of the baby is grotesque. The violence directed at the newborn parallels Rose's violation and thus marshals sympathy for women of the streets who are tossed around by pimps and men of the law alike. Rose's devotion to her baby establishes her, moreover, as one of O'Neill's most compelling mother figures. Though terminally ill, she fights desperately to protect her child. But, as the title suggests, Rose is ensnared in a web of circumstances beyond her control. She is framed for murder, arrested, and sent to prison, where she will likely die of consumption, a clear recycling of the *Camille* plot.

The final lines of *The Web* demonstrate an unusual modern twist for writing this early in American drama. The stage directions describe Rose's exit with what will become O'Neill's signature penchant for detail: "*A moment later Rose's hollow cough echoes in the dark hallway. The child wakes up and cries fitfully. The First Plain Clothes Man goes over to the bed and cuddles her on his lap with elephantine playfulness.*" O'Neill's novelistic description turns chilling in what follows. The child screams feebly, "Maamaaaa!" to which the police detective replies, "Mama's gone. I'm your Mama now."[4] These unnerving lines foreshadow the modern theatre that O'Neill would shape in the coming decades. Not only is Rose the first of many failed mother figures for O'Neill, but, more importantly, she is a mother failed by society—in this case by an "elephantine" symbol of the law. The cop's eerie declaration "I'm your Mama now" both proclaims and denies the mother's identity. Such pronouncements of evacuated motherhood would subsequently haunt O'Neill plays, where ghosts of absent mothers carry dramaturgical force.

O'Neill's early one-act anticipated important characters and motifs in future modern drama. There are traces of Rose in the protagonist from "*Anna Christie*," the prostitute drama that netted O'Neill his second Pulitzer Prize in 1921 and in so doing conferred a strange kind of respectability on the prostitute figure.[5] O'Neill's early experiment in representing sex for sale would prove fertile for his later body of work as well as for the spate of American modern drama to follow in its wake.

• • •

*The Web* (1913) never had a New York City production during O'Neill's lifetime. It was first staged in 1997 by the Metropolitan Theatre as part of an evening of O'Neill's early one-acts. The production was directed by Mark Harborth and featured the following cast:

| | |
|---|---|
| Rose | Keri Setaro |
| Steve *(Pimp)* | Andrew Firda |
| Tim Morgan | David Patrick Ford |

# *The Web*

A PLAY IN ONE ACT

by Eugene O'Neill

CHARACTERS:
ROSE THOMAS
STEVE, a "*Cadet*"
TIM MORGAN, a *Yeggman*[6]
A POLICEMAN
TWO PLAIN CLOTHES MEN

SCENE: *A squalid bedroom on the top floor of a rooming house on the lower East Side, New York. The wall paper is dirty and torn in places showing the plaster beneath. There is an open window in back looking out on a fire escape on which a bottle of milk can be seen. On the right is a door leading to the hallway. On the left a wash-stand with a bowl and pitcher, and some meager articles of a woman's toilet-set scattered on it. Above the wash-stand a cracked mirror hangs from a nail in the wall. In the middle of the room stands a rickety table and a chair. In the left hand corner near the window is a bed in which a baby is lying asleep. A gas jet near the mirror furnishes the only light.*

*Rose Thomas, a dark-haired young woman looking thirty but really only twenty-two, is discovered sitting on the chair smoking a cheap Virginia cigarette. An empty beer bottle and a dirty glass stand on the table beside her. Her hat, a gaudy, cheap affair with a scraggy, imitation plume, is also on the table. Rose is dressed in the tawdry extreme of fashion. She has earrings in her ears, bracelets on both wrists, and a quantity of rings—none of them genuine. Her face is that of a person in an advanced stage of consumption—deathly pale with hollows in under the eyes, which are wild and feverish. Her attitude is one of the deepest dejection. When she glances over at the bed, however, her expression grows tenderly maternal. From time to time she coughs—a harsh, hacking cough that shakes her whole body. After these spells she raises her handkerchief to her lips, then glances at it fearfully.*

*The time is in the early hours of a rainy summer night. The monotonous sound of the rain falling on the flags of the court below is heard.*

ROSE: (*Listening to the rain—throws the cigarette wearily on the table*) Gawd! What a night! (*Laughing bitterly*) What a chance I got! (*She has a sudden fit of coughing; then gets up and goes over to the bed and bending down gently kisses the sleeping child on the forehead. She turns away with a sob and murmurs)* What a life! Poor kid! *(She goes over to the mirror and makes up her eyes and cheeks. The effect is ghastly. Her blackened eyes look enormous and the dabs of rouge on each cheek serve to heighten her aspect of feverish illness. Just as she has completed her toilet and is putting on her hat in front of the mirror, the door is flung open and Steve lurches in and bolts the door after him. He has very evidently been drinking. In appearance he is a typical "cadet," flashily dressed, rat-eyed, weak of mouth, undersized, and showing on his face the effects of drink and drugs.)*

ROSE: *(Hurriedly putting her hat down on the wash-stand—half frightened)* Hello, Steve.

STEVE: *(Looking her up and down with a sneer)* Yuh're a fine-lookin' mess! *(He walks over and sits down in the chair.)* Yuh look like a dead one. Put on some paint and cheer up! Yuh give me the willies standin' there like a ghost.

ROSE: *(Rushes over to mirror and plasters on more rouge—then turns around)* Look, Steve! Ain't that better?[7]

STEVE: Better? Naw, but it'll do. *(Seeing empty beer bottle)* Gimme a drink!

ROSE: Yuh know there ain't any. That's the bottle yuh brought up last night.

STEVE: *(With peevish anger)* Yuh lie! I'll bet yuh got some buried around here some place. Yuh're always holdin' out on me and yuh got to quit it, see?

ROSE: I never hold out on yuh and yuh know it. That's all the thanks I get. *(Angrily)* What'ud yuh do if I was like Bessie with your friend Jack? Then yuh might have some chance to kick. She's got enough salted to leave him any time she wants to—and he knows it and sticks to her like glue. Yuh don't notice him runnin' after every doll he sees like some guys I know. He's afraid of losin' her—while *you don't care.*

*STEVE: (Flattered—in a conciliating tone)* Aw, shut up! Yuh make me sick with dat line of bull. Who said I was chasin' any dolls? *(Then venomously)* I'm not so sure Jack is wise to Bessie holdin' out on him; but I'll tell him, and if he isn't wise to it, Bessie'll be in for a good beatin'.

ROSE: Aw, don't do that! What 'cha got against her? She ain't done nothin' to you, has she?

STEVE: Naw; but she oughta be learned a lesson dat's all. She oughta be on the level with him. Us guys has got to stand together. What'ud we do if all youse dolls got holdin' out on the side?

ROSE: *(Dejectedly)* Don't ask me. I dunno. It's a bum game all round. *(She has a fit of horrible coughing.)*

STEVE: *(His nerves shattered)* Dammit! Stop that barkin'. It goes right trou me. Git some medicine for it, why don't yuh?

ROSE: (*Wiping her lips with her handkerchief*) I did but it ain't no good.

STEVE: Then git somethin' else. I told yuh months ago to go and see a doctor. Did yuh?

ROSE: (*Nervously, after a pause*) No.

STEVE: Well den, yuh can't blame me. It's up to you.

ROSE: (*Speaking eagerly and beseechingly, almost in tears*) Listen, Steve! Let me stay in to-night and go to the Doc's. I'm sick. (*Pointing to breast*) I got pains here and it seems as if I was on fire inside. Sometimes I git dizzy and everythin' goes round and round. Anyway it's rainin' and my shoes are full of holes. There won't be no one out tonight, and even if there was they're all afraid of me on account of this cough. Gimme a couple of dollars and let me go to the Doc's and git some medicine. Please, Steve, for Gawd's sake! I'll make it up to yuh when I'm well. I'll be makin' lots of coin then and yuh kin have it all. (*Goes off into a paroxysm of coughing*) I'm so sick!

STEVE: (*In indignant amazement*) A couple of beans! What'd yuh think I am—the mint?

ROSE: But yuh had lots of coin this mornin'. Didn't I give yuh all I had?

STEVE: (*Sullenly*) Well, I ain't got it now, see? I got into a game at Tony's place and they cleaned me. I ain't got a nick. (*With sudden anger*) And I wouldn't give it to yuh if I had it. D'yuh think I'm a simp to be gittin' yuh protection and keepin' the bulls from runnin' yuh in when all yuh do is to stick at home and play dead? If yuh want any coin git out and make it. That's all I got to say.

ROSE: (*Furiously*) So that's all yuh got to say, is it? Well, I'll hand yuh a tip right here. I'm gittin' sick of givin' yuh my roll and gittin' nothin' but abuse in retoin. Yuh're half drunk now. And yuh been hittin' the pipe too; I kin tell by the way your eyes look. D'yuh think I'm goin' to stand for a guy that's always full of booze and hop? Not so yuh could notice it! There's too many others I kin get.

STEVE: (*His eyes narrow and his voice becomes loud and threatening.*) Can that chatter, d'yuh hear me? If yuh ever t'row me down—look out! I'll get yuh!

ROSE: (*In a frenzy*) Get me? Wha'd I care? D'yuh think I'm so stuck on this life I wanta go on livin'? Kill me! Wha'd I care?

STEVE: (*Jumps up from the table and raises his hand as if to strike her. He shouts*) Fur Chris' sake, shut up! (*The baby, awakened by the loud voices, commences to cry.*)

ROSE: (*Her anger gone in a flash*) Sssshhh! There, we woke her up. Keep still, Steve. I'll go out, yuh needn't worry. Jest don't make so much noise, that's all. (*She goes over to the bed and cuddles the child. It soon falls asleep again. She *begins to cough and rising to her feet walks away from the bed keeping her face turned away from the baby.*)

STEVE: (*Who has been watching her with a malignant sneer*) Yuh'll have to take that kid out of the bed. I gotta git some sleep.

ROSE: But, Steve, where'll I put her? There's no place else.

STEVE: On the floor—any place. Wha'd I care where yuh put it?

ROSE: (*Supplicatingly*) Aw please, Steve! Be a good guy! She won't bother yuh none. She's fast asleep. Yuh got three-quarters of the bed to lie on. Let her stay there.

STEVE: Nix! Yuh heard what I said, didn't yuh? Git busy, then. Git her out of there.

ROSE: (*With cold fury*) I won't do it.

STEVE: Yuh won't, eh? Den I will. (*He makes a move toward the bed.*)

ROSE: (*Standing between him and the bed in a resolute attitude, speaks slowly and threateningly*) I've stood about enough from you. Don't yuh dare touch her or I'll—

STEVE: (*Blusteringly, a bit shaken in his coward soul however*) What'll yuh do? Don't try and bluff me. And now we're talkin' about it I wanta tell yuh that kid has got to go. I've stood fur it as long as I kin with its ballin' and whinin'. Yuh gotta git rid of it, that's all. Give it to some orphan asylum. They'll take good care of it. I know what I'm talkin' about cause I was brung up in one myself. (*With a sneer*) What'd *you* want with a kid? (*Rose winces.*) A fine mother *you* are and dis is a swell dump to bring up a family in.

ROSE: Please, Steve, for the love of Gawd lemme keep her! She's all I got to live for. If yuh take her away I'll die. I'll kill myself.

STEVE: (*Contemptuously*) Dat's what they all say. But she's got to go. All yuh do now is fuss over dat kid, comin' home every ten minutes to see if it's hungry or somethin'! Dat's why we're broke all the time. I've stood fur it long enough.

ROSE: (*On her knees—weeping*) Please, Steve, for Gawd's sake lemme keep her!

STEVE: (*Coldly*) Stop dat blubberin'. It won't do no good. I give yuh a week. If yuh don't git dat brat outa here in a week den I will.

ROSE: Wha'd'yuh mean? What'll yuh do?

STEVE: I'll have yuh pinched and sent to the Island.[8] The kid'll be took away from yuh then.

ROSE: (*In anguish*) Yuh're jest tryin' to scare me, ain't yuh, Steve? They wouldn't do that, would they?

STEVE: Yuh'll soon know whether dey would or not.

ROSE: But yuh wouldn't have me pinched, would yuh, Steve? Yuh wouldn't do me dirt like that?

STEVE: I wouldn't, wouldn't I? Yuh jest wait and see!

ROSE: Aw, Steve, I always been good to *you.*

STEVE: Git dat kid outa here or I'll put yuh in the cooler as sure as hell!

ROSE: (*Maddened, rushing at him with outstretched hands*) Yuh dirty dog! (*There is a struggle during which the table is overturned. Finally Steve frees himself and hits her in the face with his fist, knocking her down. At the same instant the door from the hallway is forced open and Tim Moran pushes his way in. He is short and thick set, with a bullet head, close-cropped black hair, a bull neck, and small blue eyes set close together. Although distinctly a criminal type his face is in part redeemed by its look of manliness. He is dressed in dark ill-fitting clothes, and has an automatic revolver in his hand which he keeps pointed at Steve.*)

TIM: (*Pointing to the door, speaks to Steve with cold contempt*) Git outa here, yuh lousy skunk, and stay out! (*As Steve's hand goes to his hip*) Take yer hand away from that gat or I'll fill yuh full of holes. (*Steve is cowed and obeys.*) Now git out and don't come back. If yuh bother this goil again I'll fix yuh and fix yuh right. D'yuh get me?

STEVE: (*Snarling, and slinking toward door*) Yuh think yuh're some smart, dontcha, buttin' in dis way on a guy? It ain't none of your business. She's my goil.

TIM: D'yuh think I'm goin' to stand by and let yuh beat her up jest cause she wants to keep her kid? D'yuh think I'm as low as you are, yuh dirty mut? Git outa here before I croak yuh.

STEVE: (*Standing in the doorway and looking back*) Yuh got the drop on me now; but I'll get yuh, yuh wait and see! (*To Rose*) And *you too.* (*He goes out and can be heard descending the stairs. Rose hurries over to the door and tries to lock it, but the lock is shattered, so she puts the chair against it to keep it shut. She then goes over to the baby, who has been whimpering unnoticed during the quarrel, and soothes her to sleep again. Tim, looking embarrassed, puts the revolver back in his pocket and picking up the table sets it to rights again and sits on the edge of it. Rose looks up at him from the bed, half bewildered at seeing him still there. Then she breaks into convulsive sobbing.*)

TIM: (*Making a clumsy attempt at consolation*) There, there, Kid, cut the cryin'. He won't bother yuh no more. I know his kind. He's got a streak of yellow a yard wide, and beatin' up women is all he's game for. But he won't hurt *you no more—not if I know it.*

ROSE: Yuh don't know him. When he's full of booze and hop he's liable to do anythin'. I don't care what he does to me. I might as well be dead anyway. But there's the kid. I got to look after her. And (*Looking at him gratefully*) I don't want you to git in no mixups on account of me. I ain't worth it.

TIM: (*Quickly*) Nix on that stuff about your not bein' worth it!

ROSE: (*Smiling*) Thanks. And I'm mighty glad yuh came in when yuh did. Gawd knows what he'd'a done to the kid and me not able to stop him.

TIM: Don't yuh worry about my getting' into no mix-ups. I c'n take care of myself.

ROSE: How did yuh happen to blow in when yuh did? There usually ain't no one around in this dump at this time of the night.

TIM: I got the room next to yuh. I heard every word the both of yuh said—tonight and every other night since I come here a week ago. I know the way he's treated yuh. I'd'a butted in sooner only I didn't want to mix in other people's business. But tonight when he started in about the kid there I couldn't stand fur it no longer. I was jest wantin' to hand him a call and I let him have it. Why d'yuh stand fur him anyway? Why don't yuh take the kid and beat it away from him?

ROSE: (*Despondently*) It's easy to say: "Why don't I beat it?" I can't.

TIM: Wha'd'yuh mean? Why can't yuh?

ROSE: I never have enough coin to make a good break and git out of town. He takes it all away from me. And if I went to some other part of this burg he'd find me and kill me. Even if he didn't kill me he'd have me pinched and where'ud the kid be then? (*Grimly*) Oh, he's got me where he wants me all right, all right.

TIM: I don't get yuh? How could he have yuh pinched if yuh ain't done nothin'?

ROSE: Oh, he's got a drag somewhere. He squares it with the cops so they don't hold me up for walkin' the streets. Yuh ought to be wise enough to know all of his kind stand in. If he tipped them off to do it they'd pinch me before I'd gone a block. Then it'ud be the Island fur mine.

TIM: Then why don't yuh cut this life and be on the level? Why don't yuh git a job some place? He couldn't touch yuh then.

ROSE: (*Scornfully*) Oh, couldn't he? D'yuh suppose they'd keep me any place if they knew what I was? And d'yuh suppose he wouldn't tell them or have some one else tell them? Yuh don't know the game I'm up against. (*Bitterly*) I've tried that job thing. I've looked fur decent work and I've starved at it. A year after I first hit this town I quit and tried to be on the level. I got a job at housework—workin' twelve hours a day for twenty-five dollars a month. And I worked like a dog, too, and never left the house I was so scared of seein' some one who knew me. But what was the use? One night they have a guy to dinner who's seen me some place when I was on the town. He tells the lady—his duty he said it was—and she fires me right off the reel. I tried the same thing a lot of times. But there was always some one who'd drag me back. And then I quit tryin'. There didn't seem to be no use. They—all the good people—they got me where I am and they're goin' to keep me there. Reform? Take it from me it can't be done. They won't let yuh do it, and that's Gawd's truth.

TIM: Give it another trial any way. Yuh never know your luck. Yuh might be able to stick this time.

ROSE: (*Wearily*) Talk is cheap. Yuh don't know what yuh're talkin' about. What job c'n I git? What am I fit fur? Housework is the only thing I know about and I don't know much about that. Where else could I make enough to live on? That's the trouble with all us girls. Most all of us ud like to come back but we jest can't and that's all there's to it. We can't work out of this life because we don't know how to work. We was never taught how. (*She shakes with a horrible fit of coughing, wipes her lips, and smiles pitifully.*) Who d'yuh think would take a chance on hiring me the way I look and with this cough? Besides, there's the kid. (*Sarcastically*) Yuh may not know it but people ain't strong for hirin' girls with babies—especially when the girls ain't married.

TIM: But yuh could send the kid away some place.

ROSE: (*Fiercely*) No. She's all I got. I won't give her up. (*She coughs again.*)

TIM: (*Kindly*) That's a bad cough yuh got, Kid. I heard yuh tellin' him tonight yuh hadn't seen a doctor. (*Putting hand in his pocket*) I'll stake yuh and yuh c'n run around and see one now.

ROSE: Thanks jest the same but it ain't no use. I lied to Steve. I went to a doc about a month ago. He told me I had the "con" and had it bad.[9] (*With grim humor*) He said the only hope fur me was to git out in the country, sleep in the open air, and eat a lot of good food. He might jest as well 'uv told me to go to Heaven and I told him so. Then he said I could go out to some dump where yuh don't have to pay nothin', but he said I'd have to leave the kid behind. I told him I'd rather die than do that, and he said I'd have to be careful or the kid 'ud catch it from me. And I have been careful. (*She sobs.*) I don't even kiss her on the mouth no more.

TIM: Yuh sure are up against it, Kid. (*He appears deeply moved.*) Gee, I thought I was in bad, but yuh got me skinned to death.

ROSE: (*Interested*) You in bad? Yuh don't look it.

TIM: Listen! Yuh talk about tryin' to be good and not bein' able to—Well, I been up against the same thing. When I was a kid I was sent to the Reform school fur stealin'; and it wasn't my fault. I was mixed up with a gang older than me and wasn't wise to what I was doin'. They made me the goat; and in the Reform school they made a crook outa me. When I come out I tried to be straight and hold down a job, but as soon as any one got wise I'd been in a Reform school they canned me same as they did you. Then I stole again—to keep from starvin'. They got me and this time I went to the coop fur five years. Then I give up. I seen it was no use. When I got out again I got in with a gang of yeggmen and learned how to be a yegg—and I've been one ever since. I've spent most of my life in jail but I'm free now.

ROSE: What are yuh goin' to do?

TIM: (*Fiercely*) What am I goin' to do? They made a yegg outa me! Let 'em look out!

ROSE: When did yuh get out?

TIM: (*Suspiciously*) What's it to you? (*Then suddenly*) Nix, I didn't mean that. Yuh're a good kid and maybe yuh c'n help me.

ROSE: I'd sure like to.

TIM: Then listen! (*Looking at her fixedly*) Yuh swear yuh won't squeal on me?

ROSE: I won't, so help me Gawd!

TIM: Well, I'm Tim Moran. I jest broke out two weeks ago.

ROSE: (*Staring at him with a fascinated wonder*) You! Tim Moran! The guy that robbed that bank a week ago! The guy they're all lookin' fur!

TIM: Sssshhh! Yuh never c'n tell who's got an ear glued to the wall in a dump like this.

ROSE: (*Lowering her voice*) I read about yuh in the papers. (*She looks at him as if she were half afraid.*)

TIM: Yuh're not afraid of me, are yuh? I ain't the kind of crook Steve is, yuh know.

ROSE: (*Calmly*) No, I ain't afraid of yuh, Tim; but I'm afraid they may find yuh here and take yuh away again. (*Anxiously*) D'yuh think Steve knew yuh? He'd squeal sure if he did—to git the reward.

TIM: No, I could tell by his eyes he didn't know me.

ROSE: How long have yuh been here?

TIM: A week—ever since I cracked that safe. I wanted to give the noise time to blow over. I ain't left that room except when I had to git a bite to eat, and then I got enough fur a couple of days. But when I come in tonight I seen a guy on the corner give me a long look. He looked bad to me and I wanta git out of here before they git wise.

ROSE: Yuh think he was a cop?

TIM: Yes, I got a hunch. He looked bad to me.

ROSE: (*Wonderingly*) And yuh come in here tonight knowin' he was liable to spot yuh! Yuh took that chance fur me when yuh didn't even know me! (*Impulsively going over to him and taking his hand which he tries to hold back*) Gee, yuh're a regular guy, all right.

TIM: (*In great confusion*) Aw, that's nothin'. Any one would'a done it.

ROSE: No one would'a done it in your place. (*A slight noise is heard from the hallway. Rose looks around startled and speaks hurriedly almost in a whisper.*) Supposin' that guy was a cop? Supposin' he had a hunch who you was? How're yuh goin' to make a getaway? Can't I help yuh outa this? Can't I do somethin' fur yuh?

TIM: (*Points to window*) That's a fire escape, ain't it?

ROSE: Yes.

TIM: Where does it lead to?

ROSE: Down to the yard and up to the roof.

TIM: To hell with the yard. I'll try the roofs if it comes to a showdown. I'll stick in here with you so's if they come I c'n make a quick getaway. Yuh tell 'em yuh don't know anything about me, see? Give 'em a bum steer if you kin. Try and hold 'em so's I c'n get a good start.

ROSE: (*Resolutely*) I'll hold 'em as long as I c'n, don't worry. I'll tell 'em I seen yuh goin' down stairs an hour ago.

TIM: Good Kid! (*They are standing in the middle of the room with their backs to the window. Steve's face appears peering around the edge of the window-frame. He is crouched on the fire-escape outside. His eyes glare with hatred as he watches the two persons in the room. Rose starts to cough, is frightened by the noise she makes, and holds her handkerchief over her mouth to stifle the sound.*)

TIM: Ssssshhh! Poor Kid! (*He turns to her and speaks rapidly in low tones.*) Here, Kid. (*He takes a large roll of money out of his pocket and forces it into her hand—as she starts to remonstrate*) Shut up! I ain't got time to listen to your beefin'. Take it. It ain't much but it's all I got with me. I don't need it. There's plenty more waitin' fur me outside. This'll be enough to git you and the kid out of town away from that dirty coward. (*Steve's face is convulsed with fury.*)

Go some place out in the mountains and git rid of that cough.

ROSE: (*Sobbing*) I can't take it. Yuh been too good to me already. Yuh don't know how rotten I am.

TIM: (*Suddenly taking her in his arms and kissing her roughly*) That's how rotten I think yuh are. Yuh're the whitest kid I've ever met, see? (*They look into each other's eyes. All the hardness of Rose's expression has vanished. Her face is soft, transfigured by a new emotion. Steve moves his hand into the room. He holds a revolver which he tries to aim at Tim but he is afraid to fire.*)[10]

ROSE: (*Throwing her arms around his neck*) Tim, Tim, yuh been too good to me.

TIM: (*Kissing her again*) Lemme know where yuh are and when it's safe I'll come to yuh. (*Releases her and takes a small folded paper from pocket.*) This'll find me. (*She takes it, her eyes full of happy tears.*) Maybe after a time we c'n start over again—together! (*A sound like the creaking of a floor board is heard from the hallway.*) What's that? (*They both stand looking fixedly at the door. Steve noiselessly disappears from the window.*) Gee, Kid, I got a feelin' in my bones they're after me. It's only a hunch but it's never gone wrong yet. (*He pulls a cap out of his pocket and puts it on.*) I'm goin' to blow.

ROSE: (*Goes over to the door and listens*) Sounds as if somebody was sneakin' up the stairs. (*She tiptoes quickly over to him and kisses him.*) Go, go while yuh got a chance. Don't let 'em git yuh! I love yuh, Tim.

TIM: Good-bye, Kid. I'll come as soon as I c'n. (*He kisses her again and goes quickly to the window. Steve stretches his hand around the side of the window and fires, the muzzle of the gun almost on Tim's chest. There is a loud report and a little smoke. Tim staggers back and falls on the floor. Steve throws the gun into the room, then quietly pulls down the window and disappears. The child in the bed wakes up and cries feebly.*)

ROSE: (*Rushes to Tim and kneels beside him, holding his head on her breast.*) Tim! Tim! Speak to me, Tim! (*She kisses him frantically.*)

TIM: (*His eyes glazing*) Good Kid—mountains—git rid of that cough. (*He dies.*)

ROSE: (*Letting his head fall back on the floor sinks to a sitting position beside him. The money is still clutched in her right hand. She stares straight before her and repeats in tones of horrible monotony*) Dead. Oh Gawd, Gawd, Gawd! (*The sound of people running up the stairs in the hall is heard. A voice shouts: "Must be in here." The door is pushed open and three men enter. One is a policeman in uniform and the other two are evidently plain clothes men. The landlady and several roomers stand in the doorway looking in with frightened faces.*)

THE POLICEMAN: (*Goes to Rose and, taking her arm, hauls her to her feet.*)

Come, get up outa that! (*The two plain clothes men take one look at the dead man and both exclaim together*) Tim Moran!

FIRST PLAIN CLOTHES MAN: I told yuh it was him I seen comin' in here tonight. I never forget a face.

SECOND PLAIN CLOTHES MAN: (*Picking revolver off the floor and examining it*) I didn't think he'd be fool enough to stick around here. (*Turning suddenly to Rose*) What did yuh croak him for? (*Ironically*) A little love spat, eh? (*sees the roll of money in her hand and grabs her quickly by the wrist*) Pipe the roll! Little sister here attends to business, all right. Gave him a frisk before we had a chance to get here. (*To Rose in loud, rough tones*) Why did yuh kill him? It was for this coin, wasn't it? (*During the detective's remarks Rose gradually realizes the position she is in. Her expression becomes one of amazed pain as she sees they think she is guilty of the murder. She speaks brokenly, trying to hold herself in control.*)

ROSE: Honest to Gawd, I didn't do it. He gave me this money. Some one shot him from the window. (*Then quite simply as if that explained it all away*) Why, I loved him.

SECOND PLAIN CLOTHES MAN: Stop that noise! Wha'd'yuh take us for—boobs? The window ain't even open and the glass ain't broken. He gave yuh the money, eh? And then shot himself, I suppose? Aw say, Kid, wha'd'yuh take us for?

ROSE: (*Losing all control, frenziedly breaks from the Policeman's grasp and throws herself beside body*) Tim! Tim! For the love of Gawd speak to them. Tell 'em I didn't do it, Tim! Tell 'em yuh gave that money to me. Yuh know what yuh said—"Take the kid into the mountains and git rid of that cough." Tell 'em yuh said that, Tim! Speak to 'em! Tell 'em I loved yuh, Tim—that I wanted to help yuh git away. Tell 'em yuh kissed me. They think I shot yuh. They don't know I loved yuh. For the love of Gawd speak to 'em. (*Weeping and sobbing bitterly*) Oh Gawd, why don't yuh speak, why don't yuh speak?

FIRST PLAIN CLOTHES MAN: (*Sneeringly*) That's good stuff but it won't get yuh anything. (*Turning to his two companions*) Looks to me as if this doll was full of coke or something. You two better take her to the station and make a report. I'll stay here and keep cases on the room. I'm sick of listenin' to that sob stuff.

ROSE: (*The Policeman taps her on the shoulder and she rises to her feet with a spring, wildly protesting.*) But I tell yuh I didn't do it! It was from the window. Can't yuh believe me? I swear I—(*She stops appalled by the unbelieving sneers of the policemen, by the white faces in the doorway gazing at her with fascinated horror.*

*She reads her own guilt in every eye. She realizes the futility of all protest, the maddening hopelessness of it all. The child is still crying. She notices it for the first time and goes over to the bed to soothe it. The Policeman keeps a tight hold of one of her arms. She speaks words of tenderness to the child in dull, mechanical tones. It stops crying. All are looking at her in silence with a trace of compassionate pity on their faces. Rose seems in a trance. Her eyes are like the eyes of a blind woman. She seems to be aware of something in the room which none of the others can see—perhaps the personification of the ironic life force that has crushed her.*)

FIRST PLAIN CLOTHES MAN: Your kid?

ROSE: (*To the unseen presence in the room*) Yes. I suppose yuh'll take her too?

FIRST PLAIN CLOTHES MAN: (*Misunderstanding her, good naturedly*) I'll take care of her for the time bein'.

ROSE: (*To the air*) That's right. Make a good job of me. (*Suddenly she stretches both arms above her head and cries bitterly, mournfully, out of the depths of her desolation.*) Gawd! Gawd! Why d'yuh hate me so?

THE POLICEMAN: (*Shocked*) Here, here, no rough talk like that. Come along now! (*Rose leans against him weakly and he supports her to the door where the group of horrified lodgers silently make way for them. The Second Plain Clothes Man follows them. A moment later Rose's hollow cough echoes in the dark hallway. The child wakes up and cries fitfully. The First Plain Clothes Man goes over to the bed and cuddles her on his lap with elephantine playfulness.*)[11]

THE CHILD: (*Feebly*) Maamaaaa!

FIRST PLAIN CLOTHES MAN: Mama's gone. I'm your Mama now.

(*Curtain*)

# *Moondown* by John Reed

Like Eugene O'Neill, whose earliest pieces were one-act plays, fellow Provincetowner John (Jack) Reed also tried his hand at a short dramatic work with *Moondown*. Virtually ignored by scholars for decades, *Moondown* was first published in the radical magazine the *Masses* in September 1913. *Moondown* was one of Reed's last plays before turning to political writing full time, and as an important chronicle of American prostitution, it deserves scholarly treatment that has thus far eluded it.[1] This volume includes two endings of the play: the one published in the *Masses* in 1913 (reprinted in 1977 in a collection of Reed's writing) and a more hopeful version that Reed submitted to the Library of Congress for copyright, which has never appeared in print or been performed.[2]

More a dialogue than a true one-act, *Moondown* nonetheless provides a glimpse into Reed's leftist views on women's rights, sexual double standards, and the criminalization of prostitution. A portrait of two "working" girls (one who works off-duty as an escort and another on the cusp of doing so), *Moondown* dramatizes some of the issues that Reed canvassed in his essay "A Taste of Justice" that appeared in the *Masses* in April 1913. Reed's essay reported the unfair treatment of prostitutes that he observed in night court, and *Moondown* was his attempt to give justice to those unfairly judged. In a way Reed's play provided a dramaturgical counterpart to a sympathetic drawing by artist John Sloan. The lithographic crayon sketch *Before Her Makers and Her Judge* featured a prostitute in Night Court (also known as Women's Court) in front of an all-male jury, with their leering and judging eyes (it appeared in the *Masses* in March 1913; see fig. 2).[3] Proceeding from Sloan's sketch of a voiceless prostitute who appears before her "makers"—decidedly *not* a jury of her peers, as playwright Susan Glaspell would call it in her 1917 short story—Reed's one-act play sought to give voice to women enmeshed in patriarchal institutions that repeatedly fail them.[4] Just as Sloan's art documented the perilous fall from the working class to working the streets, so

Reed's drama explained why women sold their bodies when other options were exhausted.

Reed's early experimentation with the Provincetown Players is often unacknowledged, even though he was part of the original group of bohemian artists and helped shape the Players' core commitments: experimentation over classics, hubris over humility, fire over reason.[5] The 1921 edition of the *Provincetown Plays* bears tribute to Reed's early passing; while the anthology does not include *Moondown*, the editors list Reed as one of the founding members, characterizing him as a person with a "pure spirit, held completely by what his imagination saw."[6]

*Moondown* lacks O'Neill's dramaturgical finesse, but it nonetheless provides a fascinating snapshot of two women weighing the decision to sell themselves. Roommates in a run-down tenement house, Mame and Sylvia represent the opposite ends of the spectrum for fallen women: "one [is] a cynical disillusioned victim of circumstances," as the *New York Times* put it in 1915, whereas "the other cling[s] to the romance of youth."[7] The innocent Sylvia believes that a man she has met in the park will come to rescue her at an

FIGURE 2. John Sloan (1871–1951), "Before Her Makers and Her Judge, Illustration for 'The Masses,'" August 1913. Whitney Museum of American Art, New York; purchase 36.38. Digital Image © Whitney Museum of American Art. © 2014 Delaware Art Museum/Artists Rights Society (ARS), New York.

agreed time: when the moon goes down later that evening. But just as Rose from *The Web* is not saved from her tragic ending, so Sylvia's fate sinks with the moon. In fact, Reed takes great pains to fault the male romancer, a struggling poet, for using Sylvia as subject matter for his writing. Mame cautions Sylvia: "He'll never come. You're nothing to him but material for a poem. He'll sell you to a magazine for seven dollars."[8] Having been failed by the job market and now by her beau, Sylvia has nowhere to turn but to a job in a shop where girls moonlight as escorts. Reed suggests that writers and artists who use prostitutes for inspiration are no different from the johns who use them for sex. As Mame wryly says: "He's back in his dinky studio chewing off a lyric about you." Given that the poet's name in this play is Jack, Reed also seems to be implicating himself in this enterprise.

Another innovative facet of *Moondown* is its focus on women. Quite unusually, the play includes *only* female characters. With the exception of Rachel Crothers's *Ourselves*, most prostitute dramas hinged upon the relationship of prostitutes to various men: policemen (*The Web*), judges (Frank Shay's *The Machine*), lovers (*"Anna Christie," Cocaine*), or pimps ("A Shanghai Cinderella" [*East Is West*], *The Web*). In *Moondown*, however, it is the women who occupy the storyline. In giving space to women talking about their own problems, the young Reed heeds the feminist call for women to be active participants in sexuality debates.

*Moondown* hints at another facet of early twentieth-century U.S. urban culture: miscegenation and racially diverse contact zones. The script suggests that Sylvia's suitor, who proposes they live in Harlem, could be African American. While never explicitly referencing his race, Sylvia refers to him as "dark," with eyes like "coal fire." Regardless of whether her beau is black or not, the prospect of living in an African American neighborhood reveals the porous nature of racialized topographies. Although Sylvia is willing to give up her Bowery dive to join her admirer in Harlem, Reed resists portraying this union as a solution for a destitute white woman. Mame cautions Sylvia against a life "in a dirty little flat up on 126th street" with "puking little kids" who will "grow up into panhandlers." And given that the gentleman caller never comes, Reed shows that young women have nowhere to escape poverty's tenacious hold—not even Harlem.

If O'Neill wrote a better play than Reed, then Reed beat him to production with *Moondown*.[9] As Leona Egan makes clear, Reed was unique in getting his play produced outside of the Provincetown Players.[10] *Moondown* was performed in 1915 as part of the Washington Square Players evening of four one-acts and a pantomime. It was only their second bill of the season. While the play was staged very simply, it was "better still" than the previous bill, according to critic Walter Prichard Eaton, and the acting received positive notices.[11]

In spite of the synergies between *Moondown* and *The Web*, Reed's play is rarely discussed in relation to O'Neill's writing. Yet, as John Bak shows, a productive comparison can be made here.[12] After those blissful Provincetown summers, Reed became increasingly politicized as a writer and activist. He would abandon playwriting, devoting his life to political reporting, especially covering the Russian revolution. The two Provincetowners thus parted ways: Reed put his life on the line in order to deliver the message, whereas O'Neill devoted his life to the theatre.

• • •

*Moondown* was performed as part of the Washington Square Players bill of four one-acts and a pantomime on 26 March 1915 at the Bandbox Theatre. It was directed by Edward Goodman and featured the following cast:

| | |
|---|---|
| Mame | Josephine A. Meyer |
| Sylvia | Ethel Howard |

# *Moondown*

by John Reed

CHARACTERS:

MAME, *about twenty-three. Light.*

SYLVIA, *about eighteen. Dark.*

PLACE: New York

TIME: The Present[13]

SCENE: *A typical room in a typical New York boarding house on West Thirteenth Street. A double bed, bureau, and two chairs. A door left, and at the rear two windows opening on the street, of which one is ajar.*

*It is a warm spring night. Mame sits in her nightgown, with a violently colored kimono over it, reading what is called a "French Novel," and smoking a cigarette.*[14] *Her legs are crossed, and her feet bare, except for enormously high-heeled slippers. She wears an exaggerated quantity of puffs.*[15] *Enter Sylvia. She is dressed in a modest, careless, shabby blue suit and shirtwaist.*[16] *She takes off her coat and hat, and hangs them behind the door. Her hair is dark, and piled on her head in careless waves. She sinks into a chair, with an air at once weary and quietly joyous. Mame watches her stealthily over the edge of her novel.*

MAME: You're lookin' happy. Got a job?

SYLVIA: Nope.

MAME: How much money you got left?

SYLVIA: (*Producing them with a little laugh*) One dime and a subway ticket.[17]

MAME: I s'pose you'll want me to lend you another half-dollar in the morning.

SYLVIA: (*Independently*) No, thanks.

MAME: Well, I won't, so there. You was a fool to quit your job just because the manager wanted to give you a good time.

SYLVIA: But I hate him. He's like a big white worm. Ugh!

MAME: But he spends money like a cop off duty. I'd like to see him offer to buy *me* a hat. Would I fall? (*She shakes her head in mock disgust.*)

SYLVIA: I been beating the pavement all day long. Guess I must 'a been in fifty places. There don't seem to be no work for a girl.

MAME: Sure there is. For a good-looker like you. Ain't I got a steady job? And didn't I offer you one at my place? I got a pull with the floor-walker.

SYLVIA: No, thanks, Mame. I believe that a girl can keep straight and get work if she wants to.

MAME: Well, she can't. I know this town. *You're* a kid yet, and you've always been a little fool. I used to be that kind too; but I got over it. Take it from me, it's money that counts in little old Manhattan.

SYLVIA: No, it ain't. *It can't be.* (*With confidence*) I *know* it ain't.

MAME: Why, what's happened to you?

SYLVIA: I'm quit with this rotten game. I got somebody to look after me.

MAME: (*Surprised*) Who?

SYLVIA: Jack.

MAME: Jack who?

SYLVIA: I don't know his last name; I—

MAME: Steer clear of the boys that don't give their names.

SYLVIA: I only met him to-night—

MAME: (*Interested*) What is it, a flat for yous in the White-hot District,[18] or an apartment at the Plaza?

SYLVIA: He said we'd live up in Harlem until he—

MAME: Has he got money?

SYLVIA: No.

MAME: My God, you ain't goin' to get married and have a lot of dirty kids?

SYLVIA: (*Spiritedly*) They won't be dirty.

MAME: Say, you got me going. Only met him to-night,—don't know his last name,—going to get married—

SYLVIA: (*Swiftly*) I was comin' across Madison Square about six o'clock, and along came a fellow behind me. He says "Good evening." I thought he was one of them loafers that hunt girls down the side streets at night. They often speak to me. So I says, "Go along and mind your business." Then he says, very soft, "I'm not trying to insult you. Won't you speak to me?"

MAME: I know the kind. They ain't got a nickel in their pants.

SYLVIA: I turned around and looked at him. I guess he had the finest face I ever saw. Slim, and dark and young; and big eyes like a coal fire. He says very quiet, "Sit down" . . . We sat on a bench in the park.

MAME: Never sit down with a man. When a girl sits down with a man she's giving him something for nothing.

SYLVIA: Then he put his hand on my shoulder so gentle I didn't take it away, and he pointed up through the trees to the moon. He says, "The moon is a woman—a little woman with silver feet—"

MAME: (*Sarcastically*) O my God.

SYLVIA: O it was beautiful! Then he told me the most wonderful things about the stars. He told me about a wind that comes up from the sea at night and sweeps away the dust from the stars—

MAME: Say, what's a matter with you? That'd give me the willies.

SYLVIA: He asked me what I did and I told him. He's a poet—

MAME: A poet! They get a dollar seventy-five a week. Go on.

SYVLIA: Then he says, "You're the most beautiful of all the beautiful things of the night—"

MAME: Help! Help!

SYLVIA: And he says, "Will you marry me?" . . . And then he took me in his arms so tenderly, so tenderly, like my mother . . . a long time ago—

MAME: And then you got a taxicab and went up to the Fifth Avenue Baptist Church,[19] and they all lived happily ever after—

SYLVIA: No, I says, "I got to go to one place more," I says. And he says, "I'll try and wait for you here, dear. What's your name, dear?" "Sylvia," says I. "What's yours, dear?" "Jack," he says. Then he kissed me, and it seemed like all the stars was falling through the trees—

MAME: Go on, go on.

SYLVIA: He says, "If you're not back in half an hour, I'll go home and fix up for you. Where do you live?" I told him. "All right, dear," he says. "I'll call for you to-night when the moon goes down. You be sitting at the window—"

MAME: So you finished your business quick, and when you come back, he was gone.

SYLVIA: Why, yes. How did you know?

MAME: I know them fellows that talk about moons and make dates. Take it from me; your Pegasus is a kidder. He'll never come.

SYLVIA: (*Serenely*) O yes, he will . . . Is the moon going down? (*She crosses to the window, right.*) Hurry, moon, and go down. I feel like I am on fire. (*She stands looking out the window.*)

MAME: Well, *I'm* going to hit the hay. (*She grinds the cigarette under her heel, takes off her puffs and lays them on the bureau, kicks off her slippers, throws off her kimono, turns the gas low, and gets into bed.*)

SYLVIA: Where's the cigarettes?

MAME: On the bureau. One's all you get. You've smoked up a whole box since you lost your job.

SYLVIA: (*Takes cigarette and lights it. Laughing happily*) Never mind. I'll pay you back. Jack'll pay you back.

MAME: (*From the bed*) He'll never come. I know them charity boys. They live down on Washington Square.[20]

SYLVIA: I never saw the stars so beautiful as to-night. They look so calm way up there in the quiet sky . . . And the moon *is* like a woman, too. Funny, I never noticed it before . . . Like a woman with silver hair. It goes down so slow, the moon—

MAME: That "silver hair" you're talkin' about means rain to-morrow. Freddy promised to take me for an auto ride. You see what you're missing.

SYLVIA: You *don't know* what you're missing.

MAME: I'm old enough to know better. Now look a' here, Sylvia, you got to make up your mind. This Jack won't come—

SYLVIA: (*Serenely*) O yes, he will. When the moon goes down.

MAME: You're moony all right. Well, suppose he *does* come. You'll live in a dirty little flat up on 126th Street, scrubbing and cooking and washing.[21] You'll have some puking little kids, and they'll grow up into panhandlers and street-corner bums. Why, you might as well live in Jersey City as New York—

SYLVIA: It will be so wonderful to have a baby of my own—like my mother had me and your mother had you—

MAME: I don't want to have no children like me.

SYLVIA: O don't you see, Mame! It don't make no difference what they're goin' to be. Just to have 'em, to have 'em, to have 'em—

MAME: Well, you'd better be sensible and take that job in my place. I've got a pull. You'll have a good time. There's several nice gentlemen up at the store just looking for somebody to spend money on. You'll have nothing but lunches at Shanley's, and auto rides, and theatres, and good clothes, and champagne—I tell you that's *living*.[22] You don't know this town.

SYLVIA: I don't want to know it—like that. The moon's going down fast now. It's almost to the house-tops. (*The moon appears through the open window.*)

MAME: He'll never come. You're nothing to him but material for a poem. He'll sell you to a magazine for seven dollars. Come on now, Sylvia, do you want that job?

SYVLIA: (*Light-heartedly*) I'd take it if he didn't come. But he will—(*Silence. Sylvia sits in the window.*) I'll let down my hair, so he can see it when he comes up the street. He said my hair was beautiful . . . (*She lets it down out of the window.*) It *is* beautiful. It looks like the hair of the moon. (*She smokes.*) The old moon's nearly down. It's touching the roofs. He ought to be here soon.

MAME: Come to bed, Sylvia. Don't be such a little fool. You'll catch cold.

SYLVIA: (*Joyfully*) He's coming now! I hear footsteps! She leans out the window. (*Silence. Footsteps approach, pass, and die away.*)

SYLVIA: No, it's not him. (*A little frightened*) He ought to be here by now. The moon's almost half gone. (*She smokes.*)

MAME: (*Drowsily*) He'll never come.

SYVLIA: (*To herself*) O if he shouldn't come! (*She looks up the street.*) Nothing! I don't see him! (*Aloud*) Mame, Mame!

MAME: (*Drowsily*) What d'you want?

SYLVIA: Mame! If he shouldn't come—

MAME: Of course he won't come. He's back in his dinky studio chewing off a lyric about you.

SYLVIA: Mame! The moon is almost gone, and he hasn't come. There's nobody on the street—

MAME: Haven't I been telling you that he's too busy writing up his Romance to remember a date?

SYLVIA: There's only a little tip left! I'm afraid!

MAME: It'll go like this:

"When the moon was going down,
For she wears not Virtue's crown."

SYLVIA: Mame! If he doesn't come, will you lend me just a little more money? Only a quarter? I'll get a job, honest to God I will. I won't eat any lunch, I'll—

MAME: No. I told you once I wouldn't. It's for your own good. A girl's got to depend on herself in this burg. It's bad for you to begin borrowing. And you got to learn to be less stuck-up.

SYLVIA: O, *please*, Mame! I'll never ask you another thing as long as I live. If I don't get a job to-morrow I'll—

MAME: You'll do a high dive off Brooklyn Bridge with no charge for admission. I guess not. I ain't going to see you make a fool of yourself any more. Come on to bed.

SYLVIA: Mame! Have a little pity! I ask you like I was praying to God!

MAME: You'd get just about as much if you did, I guess. There ain't anything in this God business. I tell you a girl's got to stand on her own feet. And money's the only thing that counts.

(*Silence.*)

MAME: He'll never come. You'll take that job.

(*Silence.*)

MAME: How's your moon now?
SYLVIA: The moon's gone down. (*She bows her head upon her knees and sobs.*)

(*Curtain*)

## Second Ending of *Moondown*

Another version of *Moondown*, which was submitted for copyright on 25 July 1918, has a different ending. Jack comes in that version, and these lines are added:

> SYLVIA: The moon's gone down. MAME! Mame! He's come. Jack! Jack!!!
> MAME: Don't leave me, Sylvia. I don't mean what I said; everything I got I'll give you; plenty of money, wait until morning, you don't know nothing about this guy. SYLVIA! She's gone and I'm all alone.
>
> (*Curtain*)

This version was never performed, as far as I can tell. The first version, without Jack coming, is the one that the Washington Square Players performed.

# *Cocaine* by Pendleton King

IF ONE-ACT brothel dramas chronicled the struggle to define and contain prostitution, then the female prostitute was undoubtedly their central character. But *male* prostitution was not represented on the American stage until Pendleton King wrote his gripping one-act *Cocaine*. Staged in the 1916–1917 Provincetown Players season, *Cocaine* also addressed female prostitution, slum living, and pervasive drug use among the destitute.[1] While it had a limited run and was the only play by King that the Provincetown Players performed, it was a drama "for which they had much affection," as historian Jeffrey Kennedy has put it.[2] King came from money, something that he likely kept hidden from his struggling bohemian collaborators in Greenwich Village. His wealth makes his grasp of the desperation facing his characters even more remarkable. Unlike some of the early one-acts that resorted to melodramatic flourishes, the pressing circumstances of *Cocaine* ring true, demonstrating King's attentive ear for lower-class dialogue as well as his understanding of the interrelation of drugs, poverty, and prostitution.

Strikingly little has been written about King's play.[3] Frank Shay first published *Cocaine* in his fifth volume of *Provincetown Plays* in 1917, and George Cram Cook and Frank Shay incorporated it in their definitive ten-volume *The Provincetown Plays* in 1921.[4] But it has fallen into obscurity since then, as has King, whose untimely death at a young age prevented him from writing more. A well-written piece, *Cocaine* vividly and creatively captures the complexities of the underworld, making it an important cultural artifact. *Cocaine*'s appearance in this volume marks its first reprint in ninety years.

Written just three years after O'Neill's *The Web*, *Cocaine* is shorter, tighter, and stronger. King places his characters in an attic bedroom of a rundown flophouse in the Bowery, not unlike the setting in O'Neill's *The Web*, Reed's *Moondown*, and Belasco's staging of Eugene Walter's *The Easiest Way* (1909). Yet *Cocaine* differs in important respects. First, the characters depart radically from the expected prototypes of the brothel genre (and American drama in general). *Cocaine* features only two characters, Joe and Nora, destitute people bound together by love and addiction to cocaine. The play opens at four o'clock in the morning, with Nora coming in after an unsuccessful night walking the streets. The darkness and the early hour give the opening scene a haunting atmosphere. Nora lights a candle to reveal the set: the audience sees Joe, her lover, asleep in the dark in his undershirt and trousers. Neither hero nor villain, Joe is unusually introduced first as an object to be seen and second as speaking subject. Anticipating the muscular animality of Stanley Kowalski in *A Streetcar Named Desire*, Joe is presented as an eroticized object, a position normally assigned to female characters as recipients of the male gaze on the stage and in film.[5] In staging Joe's body as part of the opening mise-en-scène, King inaugurates a scopophilic gender reversal, presenting male bodies as something to be consumed—as bodies for sale.

While Nora at first seems to be the familiar hooker with a heart of gold, she is far from it. She is a drug addict, a "wistful looking girl of thirty" who is visibly marked by her trade and disease. Due to a fever blister on her lip, she is unable to find a john when out roaming the streets. This Nora is hardly the birdlike ingénue from Henrik Ibsen's *A Doll's House*. In yanking Nora from her bourgeois household and placing her in the drug-infested Bowery, King retools an icon of modern drama. Moreover, he gives an uncanny retort to the famous last line of *Hedda Gabler*, "People don't do such things!" "Yes, they do!" *Cocaine*'s entire plot suggests. Perhaps this is why in 1917 Constance D'Arcy Mackay called the play "powerful though repulsive" in her landmark study, *The Little Theatre in the United States*.[6]

While seen by some critics as repulsive, King's play was timely, given that stories about cocaine trafficking abounded in the headlines.[7] With the exception of *Lulu Belle* a decade later, few brothel dramas made addiction a central concern, though it was certainly a crucial problem linked to prostitution during the Progressive Era. As the title implies, cocaine is Joe and Nora's central fixation. In fact, it has been four days since Nora and Joe "finished up that last deck," as Joe puts it, and they are becoming increasingly desperate to score some cocaine.[8] Joe, a failed boxer with injuries that prevent him from competing, is less addicted than Nora. But even he realizes that their addiction is the basis of their romance: "Dope brings funny people together." As they brainstorm ways to score some "good old sniff" to forget their troubles, Joe presents a solution: the landlady could provide some dope. She would also forgive the couple's overdue rent, if he just showed her some affection.

And so *Cocaine* portrays not only male objectification, but also male prostitution. It was the first U.S. play to do so. Given their dire situation, Joe reasons that they have no other option. In a speech that echoes those of many a fallen woman, Joe reasons: "As long as you can bring in the money—all right. But you ain't having any luck, and I just got to do it, that's all." What makes *Cocaine* so extraordinary is not only that Joe contemplates selling his body for money and drugs, but also that he and Nora debate the differences between men and women turning tricks. When Nora objects to Joe hooking, he points out, "Well, I let you, don't I?" and reveals the faulty logic driving sexual double standards. In another reversal, King portrays Joe as the figure whose sexuality is safeguarded, something that usually typifies female characters. "It doesn't matter about me," Nora reasons. "You are the clean part of me. You are the part I live for. And you are sacred, do you understand? Clean." Such lines anticipate O'Neill's invocation of the fog to cleanse the sexual sins of his prostitute character Anna Christie.

If *Cocaine* inaugurates the representation of drug use and gender reversals in sex-for-sale, it also reworks another staple plot device by eliminating the prostitute's imminent death. King's plot culminates instead in an attempted double suicide. When Joe and Nora decide not to sell themselves, they turn on the gas to end it all. In this scene, which recalls Hurstwood's suicide in *Sister Carrie*, Nora blows out the candle, leaving the stage completely in the dark, another scenic innovation. The ensuing dialogue relays the couple's final words as they anticipate death. Soon, however, they realize that the gas has been turned off due to nonpayment. With relief, Joe opens the window, revealing the rising sun, a counterpoint, perhaps, to Reed's sinking of the moon. King gets to have it both ways: the suspense of impending suicide and the reversal of tragic formulas. Unlike the scores of prostitute characters who kill themselves or are killed, Joe and Nora have the chance to work things out. *Cocaine* does much work in a single act.

• • •

*Cocaine* was first produced under the direction of Margaret Wycherly by the Provincetown Players in the 1916–1917 season with the following cast:

Joe Eugene Lincoln
Nora Ida Rauh[9]

The scenery was designed and executed by Ira Remsen and Carroll Berry.

# *Cocaine*

A PLAY IN ONE ACT

by Pendleton King

CHARACTERS:

JOE
NORA

SETTING: *The action takes place in an attic bedroom on Grand Street, between Allen and the Bowery, in the late summer of 1916, and occupies the time between four o'clock a.m. and daylight.*[10] *The ceiling slopes down at the back to within a few feet of the floor. There is a dormer window in a recess at back. Door left centre, bed at right of window, table left, bureau down left, trunk down right, chair at foot of bed. The room is in terrible disorder and confusion, faintly seen in the glare from open window as curtain rises.*

(*Joe is discovered lying on the bed asleep, snoring gently, dressed in undershirt and trousers. He is good looking, powerfully built, twenty-four years old. Nora comes in and lights a candle on the bureau. She is a wistful looking girl of thirty.*)

JOE: Nora, 's 'at you?

NORA: I didn't mean to wake you up. Go on back to sleep.

JOE: I haven't been asleep. What time is it?

NORA: (*Takes off hat.*) About four o'clock.

JOE: You're pretty late.

NORA: (*Takes off jacket.*) Had to walk from uptown.

JOE: How far uptown?

NORA: O, way up town. I let a crowd shake me like a fool. (*Sits in chair at foot of bed and fans herself.*) And didn't have sense enough to get carfare. Whew! You don't realize how hot you are till you sit down.

JOE: Poor kid.

NORA: You must have had the gas lighted to make it as hot as this in here. Lord, I'm so glad to get home.

JOE: (*Gently.*) You didn't bring in—nothing?

NORA: Not a cent, Joe. (*Gets up and goes to bureau.*) I don't know what's the matter with me. (*Looks in glass.*) It's that darn fever blister. If I had only had sense enough to get some camphor that first day.[11]

JOE: But it's most well now. Can't hardly notice it any more.

NORA: Of course it's perfectly well. There won't be a trace of it tomorrow. I oughtn't to have tried to go out those two days the first of the week when it was so bad. Everybody was afraid of me and it made me feel like a leper. I lost my grip in some way and now I can't get it back. It all depends on yourself. (*Picks up candle.*) If you're sure of yourself you have luck; if you aren't, you don't. That's all there is to it. (*Crosses with candle, which she puts down on trunk.*) If I'd had a wee bit of a sniff tonight I'd have got some money out of that crowd. (*Sits on foot of the bed.*) But drinks don't brace me up somehow.

JOE: Hum. 'sright.

NORA: Poor old boy. Have you been lying here all night in this heat waiting for me? It's hard luck on you, Joe. O, I thought I'd go crazy tonight. My nerves are just all to pieces. I did think I was going to get some money this time.

JOE: Why don't you take your clothes off and come on to bed.

NORA: (*Gets up and takes a packet of cigarettes out of her jacket.*) I swiped these for you, anyway. Here. (*Throws him the box.*)

JOE: (*Catching it*) Gee! Ta![12]

NORA: Joe, I wish you wouldn't say "Ta." (*Goes up into recess.*) I don't know why I hate it so. (*She begins to undress.*)

JOE: All right, Missis. (*Gets up to light his cigarette with the candle.*) Common stuff, uhm?

NORA: (*Undressing*) No, it doesn't matter. I'm just nervous and irritable. Don't pay any attention to anything I say. If I don't get some money tomorrow I just don't know what I'll do. It's terrible to be so dependent on *anything* as that.

JOE: (*Lies down again.*) Four days.

NORA: No, tonight's Saturday.

JOE: Well, that's four days, ain't it? We finished up that last deck Tuesday night.

NORA: That's right. I wouldn't have believed I could go so long. I don't see how you stand it, Joe, all night like this, doing nothing.

JOE: I been out. Don't worry about me. I can git on widout de stuff—for awhile.

NORA: (*Comes down in kimono.*) I *can't*. (*Takes cigarette.*) But then I've been using it so much longer than you have. (*Lights cigarette at the candle.*)

JOE: I been goin' it some little time—a month or so before we took up together last summer.

NORA: To think. (*Sits on bed.*) Only a year. I wonder what would have become of you if I hadn't found you?

JOE: What becomes of all de other poor bastards who gets knocked out and can't get back in de ring? I don't know.

NORA: That's the trouble with you boys. You are brought up with only one idea, to fight, and if anything does happen to you, you're not fit to do anything else. You're only twenty-four, and you're done.

JOE: Be twenty-four in October, I guess.

NORA: Lord, it makes me feel so old. That's how you stand the strain the way you do. You are as firm and strong as you ever were, and look at me.

JOE: Well, if a fellow has to do as much trainin' as I used to, he more or less keeps in condition, I guess.

NORA: (*Lies down beside him.*) I feel so old, and tired, and discouraged, Joe. If I didn't have you I don't think I'd go on with it.

JOE: (*Tightens his arm about her.*) I'm stickin' to you, see.

NORA: I never thought of your leaving me. (*She puts her arm up about his head and strokes his hair.*) I love you too much, Joe. I love you more than anybody else will ever love you if you live to be a thousand years old.

JOE: I don't reckon anybody'd love me much if I was that old.

NORA: (*Laughs.*) I should. But you're only a baby now. A little old infant. (*She snuggles up to him and presses her cheek to his.*) Joe?

JOE: Um?

NORA: (*In a whisper*) My darling. (*He gathers her closer. Long pause.*)

JOE: Tired, kid?

NORA: No, not now. I get strength from you. You've got plenty of strength for both of us, haven't you? Um?

JOE: It's funny, ain't it, for a girl like you to take up wid a rough guy like me, dat ain't never knowd nothin' but how to get his heart put on the blink. Dope brings funny people together.

NORA: Not so funny.

JOE: You needn't tell me, kid. I may be nothing but a prizefighter, but I can tell a lady when I see one. And besides, you won't even own up to it. That's a sure sign.

NORA: (*Laughs.*) Not a very fine kind of a lady. I've told you all about myself. I did work on the *Evening Sun*, and before that I used to live on a farm in Kentucky. That's all there is.

JOE: Well, that's what you say. I don't want you to tell me nothing you don't want to. (*Moves his position slightly.*) Are you all right?

NORA: Yes.

JOE: I got something I want to talk to you about. We're up against it.

NORA: I know we are. And yet I can lie here like this and it doesn't seem possible that there is such a thing as trouble in the world. It is so serene to lie still, and just stroke your hair. I don't want ever to move again. I can feel your heart beating. Do you feel how much faster mine is going than yours?

JOE: Yeah.

(*The sound of Elevated is heard.*)[13]

NORA: The Elevated sounds like wind. Like a spirit that can't rest. The spirit of the city, that goes on and on day and night and never stops and never will stop, no matter what becomes of you and me. But when I am lying close to you like this, touching you—there's a sort of electric current that radiates from you all over because you're so alive. What was I going to say? What was I talking about?

JOE: You was talking about the El.

NORA: Yes. I was going to say while I am lying close to you like this it all seems so far away, doesn't it? It is like lying snug in bed and listening to the sea. There may be death and storms and shipwrecks and things out there, but they're far away. They can never touch us.

JOE: I wisht we could get a good old sniff, and forget our troubles right.[14]

NORA: Poor old Joe. (*Raises up and sits on the side of the bed again.*) I declare I thought I would go crazy tonight; I haven't got a nerve left in my body. I wanted to know what you were doing. I thought all sorts of fool things. I could picture you getting desperate and breaking in somewhere and getting locked up, and I don't know what.

JOE: I could have got some stuff tonight, at that.

NORA: What do you mean? How? Who?

JOE: The landlady. She was up here talking to me about it.

NORA: When she knows how broke we are? We owe her two weeks' rent.

JOE: No, I guess she would have give me some.

NORA: How do you mean, Joe?

JOE: You know.

NORA: Do you mean to tell me that woman has been up here after you again? (*Her eyes narrow.*) I knew something was the matter. Did you—What did you tell her?

JOE: Told her to get to hell out of here. What do you think I told her? I said I was off de stuff.

NORA: (*Buries her head in his shoulder.*) O, Joe.

JOE: Well,—I didn't want it so bad then. She come up here when she heard me come in, about twelve o'clock, and put it up to me.

NORA: (*Desperate*) If we had any other place on earth we could go, I would have got out of this house the night you told me she first came up here and bothered you. But we couldn't get another place. She'd hold our things until we paid her. And I haven't got a dollar to deposit on a room. I suppose she knows all that.

JOE: That's what I got to talk to you about. She's going to kick us out.

NORA: Kick us out?

JOE: That's what she says. Unless—

NORA: Unless what?

JOE: Well,—you know—I been thinking pretty hard and figurin' on puttin' it up to you, if you think it's worth while—just to keep the room on and have a place to sleep. You see—

NORA: What are you talking about?

JOE: Well,—I think the old lady's reasonable. She come up here and made a big fuss over me and said she was gone on me and all that stuff, and I was staying on in her house and not paying no rent and everything, and—if I was too good for her I'd have to get out of her house, that's all. That was after she offered me the dope.

NORA: Joe, am I mad or what are you talking about?

JOE: Well—

NORA: Never let me hear that again. Do you think I'd let you—

JOE: Well, I let you, don't I?

NORA: That's altogether a different matter. Don't ever let me hear that again, do you understand? I can't argue about it. (*Gets up and crosses to bureau.*) God, it's hot in here!

JOE: (*Swings his feet out and sits on the side of the bed. Kindly:*) Now look here, kid. (*Stands a moment and goes over to her.*) I got to live, ain't I? You are the swellest little girl any fellow ever had and all that, and I'm awful fond of you, but we got to live. We got to do something. We got to get some money some way. If we can't get on—the way we been gettin' on, then I got to shift for myself, see? (*Takes her by the shoulders.*) I'm puttin' it up to you square, because I'm goin' to be straight with you.

NORA: Of course we've got to do something. I'll do something. I'll get some money. You don't understand what you are saying. If it were the last night we'd ever spend under a roof it wouldn't alter the question.

JOE: (*Turns back to the bed.*) By God, it looks like it is the last night, with the luck you're having. (*He sits and leans his chin on his right hand, gazing at the candle.*) If I was able to do any kind of work it'd be different. But de stuff's got me I guess. I couldn't no more stick to any kind of a job than I could fly. You reckon if I was able to get back in the ring I'd have you working? But we're up against it, that's all. As long as you can bring in the money—all right. But you ain't having any luck, and I just got to do it, that's all. If I'm willing for you to go out every night, I don't see why you kick on one old measly landlady.

NORA: But Joe. You don't understand. (*Crosses to bed.*) Listen to me. (*Sits beside him.*) You don't love me the way I do you. It isn't your fault. It's the way you're made. I can—go out, as you call it— It's a sort of sacrifice to you, a sort of way of showing how much I love you. It doesn't matter about me. You are the clean part of me. You are the part I live for. And you are sacred, do you understand? Clean.

JOE: (*Still gazing at candle.*) Sure, I get you. (*Nora slips down on one knee and buries her face against his arm.*) And I've always been straight with you. I think a whole lot more of you than you think.

NORA: Go on. Say you love me. I love to hear you say it.

JOE: (*Puts his left arm about her.*) I love you all right. And I'll stick to you. But we got to live, ain't we? We got to get some money some way. And if you can't get it, I got to. That's if we're going to stick together.

NORA: No, you haven't, Joe. I'd rather be dead. (*Raises up.*) I'll starve to death before I'll see you do that, and let you starve to death. (*Gets up.*) The horrible old slut. I think I'll kill her. (*Goes up into alcove and looks out of window.*)

JOE: O, we can get out of here if you want to. It don't have to be her. There's more'n one way of pickin' up money round this town.

NORA: (*Turns toward him.*) What do you mean?

JOE: I guess you must know. It's the only way I see. I ain't got nothing but my looks.

NORA: (*Turns back to window.*) Joe, don't talk like that, *please.*

JOE: (*Kindly*) We got to, kid. We're up against it. I'm going to be fair with you, that thing you got on your mouth ain't going to get well so as you can't see it for two or three days yet. We get kicked out of here today. What the hell can we do? Sleep in the park? I guess not. Not while I got a way to make easy money. Why, kid, I wisht you'd see the number of 'em tries to speak to me every time I go out. It's easy, I tell you. And there's good money in it. I don't like to talk about it—'specially with you—but we got to—if we're going to stick together. We can get a nice room somewheres and keep a little stuff on hand all the time. I ain't going to leave you. But I gotta have de stuff, that's all. (*Lies down on the bed and turns toward the wall.*) I've gone without it four days now.

NORA: (*Comes down and crosses to trunk.*) You are a strange boy. (*Sits on end of trunk facing him.*) Can't you see that you are the only thing I've got left in the world?

JOE: But I ain't leaving you, I tell you.

NORA: Don't you understand that I found you when you were down and out, done for? That you belong to me? I saved you from this very thing, I suppose, a year ago. Don't you see, darling?

JOE: (*Turns on his back.*) But I'm not— Gees, Nora, can't you listen to me? I don't want to do it, kid, but we got to, to live.

NORA: But don't you understand that I wouldn't touch you with a ten foot pole afterwards? Don't you see that?

JOE: (*Turning back in a huff*) Of course, if you feel that way about it, we can bust up, 's far as that goes. If you don't think no more about me than that.

NORA: (*Stands up against the wall, Right.*) Don't, Joe.

JOE: (*Sits up in bed.*) I've always been straight with you. I've treated you right all the way, and I'm trying to stick by you. But of course, if that's the way you feel about it, all right. I got to live, ain't I?

NORA: No.

JOE: What do you mean, "no"?

NORA: I don't see any reason why we should live.

JOE: Well, I'm *going to live.*

NORA: (*Sits down on bed and tries to turn him towards her.*) Joe, my darling, listen to me. You've been a wonderful boy and I love you as very few people have ever been loved in this world. Because I had lost everything, you see, when I found you, everything. I had thrown everything away. And you've had to be the whole world for me since. The whole world, you see. There isn't anything else. When dope got me I just went down because I didn't care about anything. I gave up my job and just let myself slide. I intended to kill myself when my money gave out, and I didn't even care how much I had left. Then I found you that night at Mitchell's place.

JOE: (*Turns on his back.*) I remember.

NORA: (*Puts her head down on his chest.*) You can't remember much. I can't bear to think even now how you were beat up. But you were so full of it you didn't know your arm was broken.

JOE: That's right. I think it was broke about two days before that. I remember when it went.

NORA: And since then, Joe, we've had a wonderful time. Do you remember when we used to have to sleep under the Bridge? I love that old Bridge now because it's associated in my mind with you.

JOE: We had a good time, all right.

NORA: (*Straightens up.*)

"But now the white sails of our ship are furled,
"And spent the lading of our argosy."[15]

We've come to the end of our tether, Joe.

JOE: Um.

NORA: What do you say we don't go on with it?

JOE: What do you mean don't go on with it?

NORA: Turn on the gas.

JOE: (*Sits up.*) Nix! What are you gettin' at? (*Lies down.*) Not for mine.

NORA: Joe, we've had such a wonderful time. We've known everything there is to know in the world worth knowing. Don't let's go down hill. We've reached the top. Let's let this be the end. I can't keep you any longer and have got to let you go. I won't do it, that's all.

JOE: (*Sits up and props himself against the head of the bed incredulously.*) You must be kiddin'. Aw, come on.

NORA: (*Quietly*) I never was more serious in my life. I can't go on with it, and I won't leave you behind to live without me. It's you that I love, the little strange spirit that makes you you, and different to everybody else that ever lived. If you go on you are going to destroy that. Then you won't be you, and I won't love you any more. Think. This may be the last night we'll ever spend together—the last chance we'll have. Let's turn it on now. No telling (*She turns front*) what'll happen in the daylight tomorrow. I can't wait to face it.

JOE: I don't want to, kid. It ain't right to kill yourself.

NORA: Are you afraid to die?

JOE: Sure I'm not afraid to die.

NORA: What have you got to live for?

JOE: Well—a lot of things, I guess.

NORA: Joe, you've slipped. You've slipped away further than I thought. The stuff's got you sure enough. You've slipped further than I have.

JOE: I guess not. I'm not so bad off at that.

NORA: (*Slightly hysterical*) You're pretty bad off, Joe. Don't you see that your life is finished. You are nothing. You are less than nothing. What you really are is the lowest thing that can be on earth and here you talk calmly about—something even worse. There's no reason for you to go on living—except your fear of death.

JOE: I'm not afraid of dying, I tell you.

NORA: (*Rising*) Well, let me turn on the gas then. I'm not afraid. Look at me. Think of the trouble it takes to live. Think of the effort to keep yourself going on and on, like a rat in a trap. And when you lose me you'll just slip and slip. And you've got to die in the end anyhow. And when you're dead it won't make any difference to you how long you lived. It will be just as if you'd never been born.

JOE: (*Sits up and follows her with his eyes.*) I don't get you.

NORA: O, I just can't face the daylight again, Joe. I'm too tired. Aren't you tired? What will become of you without me to take care of you? (*She is edging towards the gas jet in the alcove.*)

JOE: I don't know.

NORA: Let's turn on the gas. Then we won't have to wake up in the morning and be bothered. And you can't tell—maybe— But I believe you're scared.

JOE: (*Lies down and turns face to the wall petulantly.*) Aw, turn on your god damned gas. I'll show you whether I'm scared.

NORA: (*In an excited whisper*) O, Joe.

(*She closes the window and hangs an old skirt over it, turns on the gas jet and the gas stove on the table, then comes down on tip toe, trembling, and blows out the candle on the trunk. The stage is completely dark.*)

JOE: Did you turn it on?

NORA: (*Gets back into the bed.*) Yes. The stove, too.

JOE: How long will it take?

NORA: Not long I think. I don't know. Don't let's talk about it. Joe, do you think I've got the right to take you with me?

JOE: With you? Where?

NORA: Now. Like this. But I couldn't bear for anybody else to have you, Joe.

JOE: Gee, you're tremblin'. I believe you're scared now.

NORA: I'm not scared. I'm just happy.

JOE: Happy?! . . . !

NORA: I thought I'd lose you, Joe.

JOE: Um. (*Very long pause.*) This is a tough thing to do, all right, kid. You reckon they'll put it in the papers?

NORA: I expect so.

JOE: Will they put in much? They'll be sure to find out who we was. You got letters and stuff in the trunk.

NORA: We weren't anybody much. I expect they've forgotten about us.

JOE: Aw. They got to put it in the papers.

NORA: They'll put in something. Please don't let's talk about it. Joe?

JOE: Um?

NORA: (*In a whisper*) My darling.

(*Long pause.*)

JOE: (*With a tremor in his voice*) I don't smell no gas.

NORA: It hasn't had time yet. Maybe we won't smell it.

JOE: Gee, we got to smell it. (*The bed creaks.*) I don't smell nothing way down here.

NORA: Just wait and you will. It's only been on a minute. O, Joe, come on back here. We've only got such a little while.

JOE: I'm going to see what's the matter. Gimme a match. (*The bed creaks as he gets out.*)

NORA: For heaven's sake! Don't strike a match! Might be an explosion!

JOE: It can't blow up if you can't smell it. (*He finds matches on the trunk and crosses to centre stage.*) I can smell it over here. (*Strikes a match to the gas burner, which lights in a feeble blue flame.*) Gees, the meter's run out on us.

NORA: (*Sits up in bed.*) The meter? But it can't have run out. (*A wave of terror comes over her.*) Have you been using the gas nights?

JOE: Not but very little.

NORA: But that's ridiculous. I haven't got a quarter to put in it. What can we do?

JOE: Nothin'—'less we had a quarter.

NORA: (*Laughs.*) But that's ridiculous. We've got to do something.

JOE: Naw, I guess not.

NORA: But, Joe—!!!

JOE: (*With a note of relief in his voice*) Naw, I guess it wasn't meant for us to kick out tonight, kid. (*Gently*) Let's get the window open. (*He takes down the old skirt and opens the window. The dawn has come up outside.*) Gee, it's daylight.

(*Curtain*)

# Part 2

## BROADWAY BROTHEL PLAYS

# *Ourselves* by Rachel Crothers

DURING the censorship battles of the 1913 white slave season, theatregoers felt that Rachel Crothers's *Ourselves* would determine the future of the "bawdy-house" plays.[1] Astonishingly, *Ourselves* escaped censorship. Even more strangely, in spite of positive reviews, the Drama League refused to endorse it. The show closed after just twenty-nine performances.[2] Yet the box-office failure of *Ourselves* belies its artistic merit, for it is far better written and more thoughtfully composed than other brothel dramas. Why, then, did it fail?

Most critics of the period suggested that *Ourselves* simply opened at the wrong time. "If *Ourselves* had been produced last season or even in September," wrote Norman Hapgood in the December 1913 *Harper's*, "it would have attracted much more attention."[3] *Everybody's Magazine* concurred: "It is too bad it did not come early in the season, before the public's stomach turned against the whole sex morality as a play problem."[4] Although "the public had tired of the 'ugly, but vital' stories" of prostitution, this alone cannot explain the failure of *Ourselves*, for the tug of the brothel would remain powerful in American popular culture for many years.[5] One newspaper article even argued that the white slave play was still an asset to the theatre in 1913.[6]

From its very inception, *Ourselves* was written with feminist insights into prostitution and the social problems associated with it. And as such it brings a new perspective to the predictable dramaturgy of representing prostitution on the New York stage. Crothers, according to Brenda Murphy, was "the most significant woman playwright the United States produced in the early twentieth century."[7] Up until this point, no female playwright had written about white slavery.[8] While its timing may have been bad, *Ourselves* challenged prevailing red-light dramas in focusing not on the obvious site of the brothel, but rather on the thorny problem of reform.[9] *Ourselves* circumvented established routes to Broadway largely dominated by male writers, producers, directors, and artists. Whereas other playwrights capitalized on the brothel drama's popularity and churned out their plays rather quickly (George Scarborough claimed that he produced *The Lure* in just eight days), Crothers took nearly a year to research, revise, and write *Ourselves*. Even though *Ourselves* premiered after the popular swell in 1913 of white slave plays—all of which were written by men—Crothers had begun her play long before them. She also co-directed the play with J. C. Huffman once it hit Broadway and was perhaps the only female writer/producer of her day.[10]

Crothers's cultivation of the script was likewise remarkable. She rejected sensational stories from the headlines and instead interviewed prostitutes incarcerated in the Bedford State Reformatory for Women under the direction of Dr. Katherine Davis, a primary figure in Progressive reforms. As Timothy Gilfoyle has shown, Davis "wrote some of the first studies of female sexual behavior in the early twentieth century," rejecting "behavioral models that assumed the existence of a criminal female personality."[11] Similarly, Crothers rejected prevailing theories of female delinquency or the criminalization of prostitution that found their most explicit articulation in George Kneeland's *Commercialized Prostitution in New York City* (1913), which included interviews with prostitutes on Blackwell's Island Prison. Crothers's yearlong partnership with Davis resulted in a uniquely feminist artistic project that anticipated what we now call community-based and prison theatre. Of all the playwrights who consulted source materials in writing their prostitute plays, Crothers was the first who extensively used a girls' reformatory. Moreover, in privileging prostitutes' own testimonies about sexuality, economics, and possibilities for reform, as opposed to the usual statements about the so-called sexual fall or white slave captivity, she shifted the focus away from sensational portraits of the sexual underworld to a practical reform agenda. This change in perspective caused one reviewer to complain: "Rachel Crothers, social worker has rather obtruded on Rachel Crothers, dramatist."[12]

Crothers's unprecedented focus on women's relationships is established in the first act, which is set in a girls' reformatory and features *only* women. Run by the efficient and liberally minded Miss Carew, the home allows the young women to be themselves without "masculine society present," as one reviewer put it.[13] Beatrice Barrington, an upper-class woman interested in volunteering, visits the reform house, eager for a project in salvation. Crothers is careful to critique women engaged in reform activities who have little knowledge of them.[14] Miss Carew cautions: "We have a lot of dabblers who do more harm than good, you know." Crothers was skeptical about reformers who knew little about the people whom they wished to help. Given "barriers of class, race, and ethnic prejudice, along with political and economic naiveté," the relationship between "the lady and the prostitute," as Ruth Rosen puts it, was often problematic.[15] *Ourselves* stresses such problems with complexity, "with all the terse vividness with which it might be described by a good police reporter and all the deeper understanding which would be supplied from the experience of a Miss Maude Miner or a Jane Addams."[16] Beatrice chooses one of the girls, Molly, to work in her home to see how she might live an "honest" life. But it is precisely the so-called proper bourgeois home that becomes dangerous for Molly, who is seduced and deceived by Beatrice's married brother. Though Beatrice's learning curve is steep, she ultimately understands how sexual double standards ruin women of all classes and supports Molly when all others condemn her (see fig. 3).

FIGURE 3. Mattie Keene as Miss Carew and Grace Elliston as Molly in Rachel Crothers's *Ourselves* (1913). Photo by White Studio © Billy Rose Theatre Division, The New York Public Library for the Performing Arts.

With its focus on women leaving prostitution, *Ourselves* was, in a sense, an anti–white slave play. By taking the prostitute out of the brothel, Crothers short-circuited the voyeuristic interest in the sexual underworld that defined the season. One review noted Crothers's reworking of the red-light drama formula: "the white slave is shown once removed from the stage brothel, which was her accepted rendezvous of the early season."[17] Switching from the expected site of sexual encounter to reform, *Ourselves* featured a female-centered space, focusing not on the problem, but rather on the solution. In comparing Crothers's approach with *The Lure* and *The Fight*, a reporter from the *Morning Sun* noted the omission of the brothel: "There was no parlor. But there was the sitting room of a 'reform home' for girls."[18] This change in focus allowed Crothers to circumvent melodramatic formulas and focus instead on the challenges for women to get off the street—told from a woman's perspective.

*Ourselves* offered another innovative solution. It portrayed daycare as a way of addressing the inevitable problem of pregnancy within prostitution. While O'Neill broke ground by featuring a baby in *The Web*, the poor child cannot be properly cared for by its sick mother: we can only surmise that tragedy will befall it. By contrast, *Ourselves* depicts a solution to the problem of unwed motherhood. When Beatrice asks whether the girl holding the baby is his mother, Miss Carew replies, "No—we've got work for the mother now. She isn't here—but we keep the baby for her in the day time. The girls love it." These lines caught the attention of the *Woman's Journal* for showing "women grappling as a group for the first time with an age-old problem which they had hitherto avoided as something too dreadful for discussion."[19] Crothers's inclusion of a female-operated daycare center is radical and visionary, if not utopian.

*Ourselves* not only privileged a female perspective regarding solutions to prostitution; it also advocated feminist ideas about sexual responsibility. "What's the use shutting up a few hundred girls a year, while the men are running around loose looking for more?" Miss Carew asks. "Once we take to locking up man—we'll get somewhere, not before." In scrutinizing cultural constructions of sexuality, Crothers did not lay the blame solely at men's feet, even though some critics believed otherwise. Rather, the play argued that women should take responsibility for sexual double standards and become informed. As Beatrice pleads in act two, "So long as we *accept* immorality in men, do you suppose they're going to change?" While other playwrights had previously tackled this issue in limited ways, Crothers gives her female characters more agency in this discussion. This is one reason she was derided for her "female" point of view, as the press called it. The *New York Herald* lamented that "when the final curtain dropped the voting half of the species had all the worst of it" and argued that the title *The Woman's Point of View* might better have fitted the text.[20] Male audiences were not used to being critiqued by female playwrights. "It is a woman's show," declared the reviewer of the *Telegram*: "One had only to watch the part of the audience which voiced its white gloved approval to decide the theme would not be a popular one with the men folk."[21] The reviewer continued: "Any man who takes his wife to that play will never again be able to convince her he is on the square."[22] It seems that Crothers's play, originally titled *When It Strikes Home*, raised uncomfortable questions about the ways in which the brothel can strike the sanctity of the family.

Much of the press criticized Crothers's "peculiarly feminine play," as one review put it.[23] But the *New York City Tribune* defended the play, calling it a "work of unusual distinction; red hot with conviction."[24] The *New York City Review* pointed out that the criticisms of *Ourselves* were "amusingly transparent," claiming that "[t]here isn't a reason in the world why the woman's standpoint should not be propounded as well as the man's . . . Heaven knows the man's standpoint is idiotic enough standing alone."[25] And the *Baltimore News* brought the point home: "If Rachel Crothers had produced her latest play, *Ourselves*, under a man's name or even anonymously, it would have had very different treatment at the hands of the critics, and might have proved a success."[26] In spite of Crothers's other successes, it seems clear that "More Underworld Put on the Stage," to quote one headline, could only go so far in the hands of a woman, given prevailing masculinist double standards about sexuality, authorship, directing, and production of theatre.

If *Ourselves* failed in Broadway venues, it succeeded beyond expectations in alternative performance spaces. Much in the spirit of community-based theatre, Crothers continued to cultivate her relationship with the Bedford Reformatory for over a year and brought the play back there for a performance. According to Crothers, the Bedford production was "a very daring experiment" because it was the first time a play had been performed behind bars in the reformatory.[27] Crothers recalled that this production meant more to her "than any approval from the outside world possibly could."[28] The Bedford performance was the highlight of her career, "the most impressive thing I have ever seen."[29] Grace Elliston, the actress who asked Crothers to write the part of Molly for her, responded to the "tears and tornadoes of applause" at the Bedford performance by saying, "If I could get this response on Broadway I'd be the greatest actress in the world."[30] While Crothers and the cast never made it back to Bedford for another performance, they did present *Ourselves* as a fundraiser for women's rescue work.[31] The play's triumph in these two venues is not unrelated to its failure at the Lyric, for prostitution discourse and performances were distinctly gendered. Women's prostitution plays, as we shall see with Elizabeth Robins, were far more difficult to produce than men's in the Progressive Era.

• • •

*Ourselves* premiered on 13 November 1913 at the Lyric Theatre with the following cast, co-directed by Rachel Crothers and J. C. Huffman:

| | |
|---|---|
| Miss Carew | Mattie Keene |
| Beatrice Barrington | Jobyna Howland |
| Molly | Grace Elliston |
| Irene Barrington | Selene Johnson |
| Wilson | Gertrude Le Brant |
| Leever | Geoffrey Stein |
| Collin Ford | Stanley Dark |
| Bob Barrington | Thurlow Bergen |

It ran for twenty-nine performances.

# *Ourselves*

by Rachel Crothers

CHARACTERS:
BOB BARRINGTON
COLLIN FORD
LEEVER
JOSEPH, *a Butler*
BEATRICE BARRINGTON
IRENE BARRINGTON
MISS CAREW
WILSON
MOLLY
GIRLS IN THE HOME (Harriette, Florence, Mary, Rose, Clara, Sadie, Stella, Lena, Delia, Mabel, Kitty, and Lettie)

## Act I

SCENE: *The sitting room in a reform home for girls in New York. It is the conventional oblong room of a New York house with two windows at left, opening on to street—double doors at center back, showing the hall and stairway and double glass doors at right opening into another sitting room and office. The wallpaper and woodwork show the house to have been once fairly good but now somewhat going down hill. The furniture is covered with dull chintz. The curtains at the windows are the same over white muslin ones. Between the windows on a low table is a large oblong glass case holding gold fish. In front of the lower window, an upholstered armchair. Against the wall at left of center doors is an old-fashioned grand piano with a turning stool before it. The piano is littered with books and sheet music. At upper left center, another armchair. Against wall at back to right of center doors are open bookshelves built in and filled with nondescript books, novels, etc. A long, heavy, old-fashioned walnut table is at right center with chairs below and at left of it. A cabinet filled with a few plates and ornaments stand below doors at right. Before this cabinet, an armchair. The room is neat, comfortable and unhomelike, with rather a forlorn air.*
TIME: *Noon—a day in February.*
(*At curtain, Florence and Harriette hurry in from hall and cross to windows at left.*)

FLORENCE: (*Looking out the window, kneeling on armchair*) Pipe the machine. It's as big as a house. Look at the chauffeur. Some guy. (*Waving her hand*) Hello, kid.

HARRIETTE: (*Standing beside Florence*) Stop that. Somebody'll see you.

FLORENCE: Look at him smile. Say, he's alright. Gee, wouldn't I like to hop in and take a spin.

HARRIETTE: Listen! The lady's upstairs with Miss Carew. Come on—everybody's half through dinner. Come on, beat it. If she catches us up here she'll— (*Moves as if to run.*)

FLORENCE: You ain't got no nerve at all lately. What's the matter with you? Bye-bye, cutie. (*Waving her hand out the window*)

HARRIETTE: Come on. Come *on.*[32] They're coming down. I hear 'em. (*They hurry out center and to right as Miss Carew and Beatrice Barrington come down the stairs.*)

(*Miss Carew is a dignified and very good-looking woman of about 40—rather brusque, practical and kind—wears a plain dark cloth gown. Beatrice Barrington is a tall, distinguished woman of 35—very smartly and simply dressed in street clothes, with furs, etc.*)

MISS CAREW: Why aren't you down stairs eating your dinner, girls?

FLORENCE and HARRIETTE: We're goin', Miss Carew. (*They exit to right.*)

MISS CAREW: (*Coming into the room*) They've probably been looking out the window at your chauffeur. (*Going towards window*) Yes, I can tell it by the way he's looking in.

BEATRICE: (*Goes to center.*) Really?

MISS CAREW: (*Left of her*) Something's doing every minute.

BEATRICE: Tell me, Miss Carew, how do you get your girls? Where do they come from?

MISS CAREW: (*Coming to center*) Most of them have been arrested. If the Judge thinks one ought not to be sent to the workhouse or State Reformatory, he commits her to one of the smaller homes like this—here in New York.

BEATRICE: Aren't they glad to be put in such a decent comfortable place?

MISS CAREW: Glad? No, of course they're not. Nobody likes to be shut up. You see, Miss Barrington, when a girl's been on the loose in any way, she's free—and when you take away her liberty and her old associates—the excitement, the companionship—everything she's used to—and shut her up and try to teach her something else, of course she's bored to death—*bored*. Why shouldn't she be?

(*Beatrice goes right and takes off furs, sits right of table up right. Enter Mary and Rose.*)

MISS CAREW: Mary, are they almost through with dinner? Finish the piano now. (*To Rose*) Rose, go on with the books.

BEATRICE: And you have classes for them—in different things?

MISS CAREW: Oh, yes, sewing, cooking, housekeeping. We try to get them ready for work so they can take care of themselves. Work is splendid, of course, but they have to have fun too—fun, and anything we can offer them is pretty tame stuff after the way they've lived. They're bored—(*Girls interested.*)—that's the hardest thing we have to fight— Rub it hard, Mary— I give them as much liberty as I dare—more than they can in the big reformatories, but you have to keep an awfully firm hand on them.

BEATRICE: It's the most wonderful thing in the world—to take a girl, no matter how low she may have fallen, and make her over into a good woman.

MISS CAREW: Um—we don't do that with all of them by any manner of means. You can't expect miracles. (*Sits left of table up right.*) Rosie—the windowsills— The life vitiates them, my dear Miss Barrington, through and through. Mind, body, soul, willpower—all weakened. It's a long, slow hard tussle re-generating a girl, I can tell you. It takes a tremendous personal experience of some kind to make her want to be good for the good's sake. And until that *comes*, you haven't got her at all. (*Enter Clara.*) This is your day to keep this room in order—look at it now—look out for the finger marks.

(*Clara picks up things in chair down right and puts things in order. Crash of piano by Mary.*)

BEATRICE: Well, Miss Carew, as I said, I've made up my mind to go into this work, seriously—with my whole heart. It seems to me about the biggest, most worthwhile thing a woman can do.

MISS CAREW: Yes, that's the way you feel about it—once it gets hold of you.

BEATRICE: And by way of a beginning, what can I do right here—that's practical?

MISS CAREW: We have a lot of dabblers who do more harm than good, you know.

BEATRICE: I suppose so.

MISS CAREW: But if you want to *stick*, I advise you to interest yourself in *one* girl—at first. Keep close to her—get her a job—get fond of her—understand her. It will open your eyes—educate you more quickly than anything else.

BEATRICE: I'd like that. May I see some of the girls?

MISS CAREW: Certainly. I allow them to be free absolutely for a little while after dinner. We'll leave them alone a few minutes so they won't be self-conscious. They're up from dinner now. You can watch them from my room.

(*Voices of girls are heard laughing and talking in the hall outside. Mary exits center. Miss Carew and Beatrice go into room at right. Sadie and Stella enter from the hall. Sadie is 18 and very pretty. She wears a shabby blue serge dress with a wide white collar.*[33] *Stella is 30—tall, angular and wears glasses—dressed in a shabby black skirt and colored shirtwaist. Sadie is singing a ragtime popular song and goes to the piano to pound out a crude accompaniment.*)

STELLA: Oh, have a heart—lay off that. You can't play.

SADIE: Shut your mouth. Who are you?

(*Stella takes some knitting from the table and sitting down right, knits on a washcloth, mumbling to herself. Enter Lena.*)

LENA: (*Coming on from hall and beginning to dance alone. Goes down left, sits.*) We got a visitor.

SADIE: What?

LENA: We got a visitor. Pipe the swell big machine outside. Gee—I wish I had it.

STELLA: You'll never get that kind of a wagon.

SADIE: Aw. Maybe she will. But I'm right here to tell you, my friend, *you'll* never have one. You don't look it.

(*Lena and Sadie laugh boisterously. Delia, Florence, Mabel and Kitty come into the doorway with their arms around each other. They are girls from 14 to 25. Some of them are pretty, some of them are dull and heavy. Some are wearing skirts and shirtwaists—some print dresses and sweaters. Kitty up by table, Mabel on settee left of door. Delia and Florence come down center.*)

DELIA: That was a swell dinner Mary cooked to-day, all right— Gee, them cakes— Why didn't you sneak some out, Flossie?

FLORENCE: Oh, can that boarding school stuff. After snaggin' bank notes all me life, do you want me to start in snippin' cake?

SADIE: (*Getting up from piano*) Where's Cutie? Get her to pound the piano.

FLORENCE: She's washing the dishes—her and Rosie.

SADIE: Hit 'er up, Mabel. (*Knocks paper out of Mabel's hand.*)

(*Mabel goes to piano and plays. Harriette enters singing ragtime in a loud way with a great deal of swing and spirit. The girls all dance with the exception of Stella, who *knits. Molly comes into the room. She leans against right side of hall-door—watching the dancers. She is the prettiest of the girls and wears a striped cotton frock, cut a little low at the neck, with a white collar. Four more girls come in talking—two of them begin dancing—the other two take work from the table. One knits, the other is putting a band on a baby skirt. They all sing as they dance.*)

LENA: (*Calling out*) Dance, Molly. Come and dance.

FLORENCE: Cut 'er loose, kid.

THE OTHERS: Come on—dance, Molly. Get busy.

MOLLY: Don't want to.

FLORENCE: (*Going to her and pulling her away from the door*) Come on. Wake up and do something for a living.

MOLLY: Go chase yourself—I don't feel like it. I et too much. Take a slant at this. (*She picks up the furs which Beatrice has left on the chair left of table and throwing the boa about her neck, puts her hands in the muff and goes to look at herself in the glass.*)

KITTY: Holy gee! Don't she look swell?

SADIE: Who wouldn't with junk like that on?

MOLLY: *You* wouldn't. (*The girls laugh.*) Wonder how much they cost?

FLORENCE: Fifty plunks, I bet.

MOLLY: Go on—you boob, you ain't seen no class—500, you mean.

ALL THE GIRLS: Aw—go on.

MOLLY: What's the matter with you? Don't I know the real thing when I see it? This ain't no *near* nor *next*—it's *it*. Who is she? Who sports these?

KITTY: The dame with the big machine outside.

MOLLY: (*Going to Kitty*) I should worry! A reformer? Has she come to give us a heart to heart talk this afternoon? She needn't shoot any o' that dope off at me. (*She throws the muff at Kitty. Kitty to someone else—they all reach for it, throwing it back and forth while Molly swings the boa over her head as the other girls laugh boisterously. The muff falls and one girl, Sadie, kicks it.*)

MOLLY: Stop that! Ain't you got sense? (*Picks up muff.*) You never had no furs—you don't know how to treat 'em.

SADIE: You've had so many yourself.

MOLLY: You bet I have and I'll have plenty more. The nearest you'll ever come to furs is a box of moth halls.

(*Molly puts furs on table and begins to dance a few steps. The girls gradually stop to listen. Singing a common song with a great deal of talent, Molly throws herself into the dance with abandon. Miss Carew and Beatrice come into the doorway at right to watch. When Molly finishes, the girls applaud, and she goes to the case of gold fish at left.*) Go on, Mabel, play something. Hit her up. (*Mabel plays and Molly sings and dances. Sadie starts to dance alone.*)

FLORENCE: Go on, Sadie—you're grand.

KITTY: She ain't as good as Molly.

SADIE: I don't want to be. (*Mabel stops playing—Sadie stops dancing.*) I ain't never speeled in cheap dumps fer money.

MOLLY: (*Turning*) Good reason why. You couldn't hold the job ten minutes. They'd throw you out. Look at her feet. If I had feet like them, I'd get a shape like a phonograph and lose my record. (*Molly laughs.*)

SADIE: (*Flying at Molly*) What you laughing at? Not at me! (*She strikes Molly.*)

MOLLY: (*Taking her by the arm and throwing her away*) Aw, you make me sick.

SADIE: You think you're something because your fella is a singer, don't you? I know 'im. He's a low down, dirty—

MISS CAREW: (*Going between the girls*) Girls! I'm ashamed of you. I thought I'd let you have a little fun. Pull yourselves together. Sadie—go down and scrub the kitchen floor.

SADIE: (*Quickly*) I will not.

MISS CAREW: You will—and you will do it now. And you'll keep on doing it every time you give way to your temper like this.

SADIE: What are you going to do with her? (*Glaring at Molly. Business of Molly advancing. Miss Carew rushes toward Molly.*)

MISS CAREW: I'll see to that. (*There is a pause. Sadie, hesitating, turns sullenly and goes into hall and to right.*) Molly, go into my room and close the doors. (*Molly goes slowly into the room at right and closes the doors.*)

MISS CAREW: Harriette, you and Kitty are going to the matinee. It's time for you to get ready. I'll give you the tickets when you come down.

HARRIETTE: Yes, ma'am. (*She goes out and up the stairs.*)

KITTY: (*Going to Miss Carew*) Miss Carew, couldn't Molly go with me instead of Harriette?

MISS CAREW: Certainly not. I promised Harriette she could go this afternoon. It's her turn.

KITTY: I don't want to go with her.

MISS CAREW: Very well. You can stay at home if you want to—some one else can go in your place.

KITTY: (*Sullenly*) Oh, I'll go. (*She goes out through hall.*)

FLORENCE: Leave me go, Miss Carew. She don't want to.

(*Beatrice comes down right corner.*)

MISS CAREW: Oh, I think she does.

(*As Kitty goes into hall, Mary enters—a large blonde girl about 22. She carries a six-months old baby in her arms, wrapped in a pink blanket. Miss Carew goes before chair left of table. Beatrice comes down right.*)

MARY: She's got a tooth, girls. So help me God, she's got a tooth. (*The girls all crowd around Mary and the baby—laughing and talking.*)

BEATRICE: (*To Miss Carew*) Is that the baby's mother?

MISS CAREW: No—we've got work for the mother now. She isn't here—but we keep the baby for her in the day time. The girls love it.

LETTIE: (*Taking the baby skirt to Miss Carew*) I don't know how to put this here band onto the skirt, Miss Carew.

MISS CAREW: It goes—

BEATRICE: (*Advancing and sitting left center*) Let me help you. (*She takes off her gloves and going down left, sits and takes the skirt.*) Are you sure this is large enough?

LETTIE: I don't know.

BEATRICE: Couldn't I measure the baby?

LETTIE: Sure. Mary, bring the kid here—the lady wants to measure it.

(*The girls fall aside and Mary takes the baby to Beatrice and kneeling before her, holds the baby up to her.*)

BEATRICE: How pretty it is! Dear, dear little thing!

MARY: She's a peach—ain't she?

BEATRICE: (*Beatrice measures the band about the baby.*) There you are; that's about right.

MARY: (*Rising with the baby*) You're going to have a new skirt. You need it—don't you, kid? (*Goes to Miss Carew, right center.*)

BEATRICE: (*To Lettie*) And you turn that over—like this.

MISS CAREW: You put too much shortening in your pie crust yesterday.

MARY: I guess I used too much butter.

MISS CAREW: Don't let it happen again—we have to cut down expenses.

LETTIE: (*Taking the skirt from Beatrice*) Yes, ma'am—thank you. Come on, some of you, and take the baby.

STELLA: (*Rising and going to Mary to take the baby*) I'll take her. Come on, baby. (*She goes out and up the stairs.*)

MARY: I'm goin' to make a puddin' fer supper, Miss Carew. Can Mabel come and seed the raisins fer me?

MABEL: Sure I will.

MISS CAREW: Yes—but wait till the other girls are through in the kitchen.

MARY and MABEL: All right. (*They go out through hall and to right. The rest of the girls follow, talking—some turn to right, some go up the stairs.*)

MISS CAREW: Well, what do you think?

BEATRICE: (*Still seated left center. After a pause.*) It's the saddest, awfullest thing I ever saw. They're so young.

MISS CAREW: Yes—they're so young and so ignorant. So *terribly* ignorant. Why, they haven't any more realization of what they've done—of what it *really means*—than that chair. (*Florence crosses the hall to go upstairs.*) Florence, tell Lena to come down here to me, please.

FLORENCE: All right, Miss Carew. (*She goes upstairs.*)

BEATRICE: Is it poverty that drives them into this life? What do *you* think after all your years of experience?

MISS CAREW: Well, you know, Miss Barrington, there are plenty of women, respectably married who are bad at heart—so you can't put it all on poverty. But in a broad sense— yes, of course, that's it. That is—a girl born on Fifth Avenue has a better chance of keeping straight than the one on Avenue A, because she has everything to protect her—and the other everything to pull her down. Wretched homes—ignorant parents—all *that* enters into it—but *the* reason, back of it all, is that the sex attraction is the strongest thing in the world and if people aren't taught what to do with it they'll go *wrong*. That's as certain as that water runs down hill. Why, these girls aren't all naturally bad by any means. But they want to *live*. They've got to love *somebody*—and if they don't get it the right way they will the other. That's all. Records show that almost every first fall comes because a girl's been fooled and deceived—then she drifts and then she keeps on—because it's too hard to get out—once they're in it.

BEATRICE: Who's the one who danced? The one you sent in there?

MISS CAREW: That's Molly.

BEATRICE: I like her.

MISS CAREW: Yes. Everybody likes Molly. That's her trouble. She's a difficult case because she's got so much good in her. She doesn't drink nor steal—hasn't the drug habit—and has the biggest heart in the world—but she's hard to get hold of. One minute you think you've got her and the next you know you haven't touched her. (*Sees Lena.*) Come in, Lena. This is Miss Barrington. She wants to talk to you a few minutes. (*She goes to right, closing the door.*)

BEATRICE: (*After a pause*) Won't you sit down?

(*Lena speaks with a slight and very pretty German accent. She crosses and sits down right of table slowly—watching Beatrice curiously. There is a painful pause. Beatrice clears her throat. Lena lowers her eyes.*)

BEATRICE: It's awfully cold to-day, isn't it?

LENA: Yes, ma'am. (*Another pause.*)

BEATRICE: I scarcely know how to begin. I—I'm interested in you girls—and I—I came to see if I couldn't help Miss Carew in some way. Get you positions—or something— (*A pause. Lena looks at Beatrice without speaking.*) What would you like to do when you—you—leave here?

LENA: (*Quite glibly and cheerfully*) Manicuring.

BEATRICE: Oh—do you think that would be a good thing for you to do?

LENA: Sure. It ain't such hard work and you can dress nice.

BEATRICE: But wouldn't you rather be in a good home where you'd be protected and do house work?

LENA: Oh, I couldn't do no house-work. It's too lonely. You god shut up all day.

BEATRICE: I—you—aren't you glad to be here—in this nice place, now?

LENA: Sure.

BEATRICE: Miss Carew is a wonderful woman.

LENA: Sure; she's fine.

BEATRICE: She's giving you this chance to begin all over again—and—and to—

LENA: Sure—she's awful kind but der ain't nothin' to do here. You get tired.

BEATRICE: Would you mind telling me something about yourself? Where were you born?

LENA: Well—I was born in Sweden and I came over here when I was fifteen.

BEATRICE: How old are you now?

LENA: Twenty. I come over here alone and I was goin' to my cousin in Philadelphia an' a man on de train say he give me a good job. I couldn't speak no English, and I go wid him and he shut me up in a place. (*She swings her foot, talking glibly.*)

BEATRICE: Good heavens! Why didn't you run away?

LENA: How could I? I fight at first—but what's the use—and you get drugs.

BEATRICE: But didn't you keep on trying to get out?

LENA: You can't. Dey take your clothes away. Where would I go? After while a man took me out and marry me. Den he made me go on de street.

BEATRICE: How could he make you—if you didn't want to?

LENA: Oh, he say if I try to get away he kill me—and he shoot me in de shoulder to show me.

BEATRICE: What?

LENA: Sure—I can show you de marks.

BEATRICE: But why didn't you have him arrested then—for that? That was your chance. You could have had him sent to prison.

LENA: I didn't know. He say he kill me. I tell a policeman one day and he laugh at me and say "You better stick to your man." De cops don' do nothin' for a girl.

BEATRICE: Surely some of them do. They can't be all bad.

LENA: I don't know. Dere men. Unless a girl pay—or go wid him—she gets pinched. Dat's all I know.

BEATRICE: (*After a helpless sigh*) At least you're here now—in a good place. You don't want to go back to that life, do you?

LENA: I don't know if Miss Carew can get me a good job. I got to live.

BEATRICE: Oh, but my dear girl—

(*Enter Miss Carew right crossing to center, left of door.*)

MISS CAREW: Have Harriette and Kitty come down yet?

LENA: No, ma'am.

MISS CAREW: Go up and tell them to hurry please, Lena. (*Beatrice rises.*)

LENA: Sure. (*Rises and goes up center.*)

BEATRICE: (*Advancing a few steps*) I hope I'll see you again. Good-bye.

LENA: Good-bye. (*She goes out and up the stairs slowly.*)

MISS CAREW: Well—what do you think?

BEATRICE: It makes me ill. The despair of it. She reels it off as if it were the most ordinary thing in the world. Oh, why don't we do something? Why don't we stop it? (*Crosses left center.*)

MISS CAREW: Um! That's what we all say.

BEATRICE: Some of them are saved, aren't they? (*Sits left center.*)

MISS CAREW: Yes—a good many are made over absolutely.

BEATRICE: Then it is worthwhile.

MISS CAREW: (*Standing center*) Oh yes—it's worthwhile. Dear lady, we spend an awful lot of time and money—millions—millions—you know—saving a few girls—and it's like dipping the water out of the ocean with a spoon so far as getting at the bottom of the thing is concerned.

BEATRICE: Why?

MISS CAREW: What's the use shutting up a few hundred girls a year, while the men are running around loose looking for more? Once we take to locking up man—we'll get somewhere, not before. You may talk to Molly now. (*Calling*) Molly! Molly! (*Molly enters right.*) Come and entertain Miss

Barrington for a few minutes while I get the girls started. (*Miss Carew goes up the stairs center and Molly comes in from right.*)

MOLLY: Hello.

BEATRICE: You seem to like to sing. Have you ever had any lessons?

MOLLY: (*Goes right center.*) No.

BEATRICE: Would you like to have some?

MOLLY: Oh, I don't know.

BEATRICE: Why not?

MOLLY: What's the use?

BEATRICE: There's some use in everything that's good. You have a voice. Why not do something with it?

MOLLY: Go in the chorus you mean.

BEATRICE: No, I didn't mean that. To really study so you can sing nicely.

MOLLY: Oh, I like to sing—but I wouldn't like to study.

BEATRICE: What would you like to do? Come and sit down and tell me. (*Molly sits.*) If you could do the thing you most want in all the world—(*Slight pause.*) What would it be?

MOLLY: Get married. (*Beatrice leans back, smiling.*) I'm going to be. I got a friend. (*Begins to speak with a mingling of shyness, defiance and natural sweetness.*)

BEATRICE: Do you love him?

MOLLY: He is my ideal.

BEATRICE: Was he good to you? (*Molly shrugs her shoulders.*) Are most of the men kind to the girls who work for them?

MOLLY: Oh—you get used to it.

BEATRICE: Why don't the girls live for themselves and save their own money?

MOLLY: Oh, you want somebody of your own—somebody to go home to.

BEATRICE: Do they have any fun—any real pleasure?

MOLLY: Sure we do. (*Whirls half around on stool.*) We have dance halls and restaurants like anybody.[34] Sure we have fun. And you get better clothes. I was a swell dresser. He always let me keep enough to look swell.

BEATRICE: Did you give him all you made?

MOLLY: Sure. You gotta.

BEATRICE: Now listen. A girl as clever as you are can't be fool enough to go back to a man who put you on the streets. For goodness sake, let me help you. Let me show you what life can be. What fun you can have in a decent way. You know what the end of the other will be. Don't you?

MOLLY: I'll be all right. I'm goin' to marry my friend. He's goin' to get work.

BEATRICE: But he isn't fit for you to marry. If he were, he wouldn't have—Listen—wouldn't you like to feel again as you did when you were an honest girl—when you weren't ashamed of anything?

MOLLY: Oh, I didn't feel so good then. I didn't have any fun. My mother wasn't straight—she fooled me. The man she was livin' with wasn't my father at all. This man'll marry me and I'm going to do it. 'Tain't every man that'll marry a girl off the streets. Do you s'pose I'm goin' to give him up? Not on your life. Miss Carew got me to write a letter and tell him I won't see him for a month and give him that time to get work—but that's all I'll do.

BEATRICE: Well, isn't that a good idea.

MOLLY: Oh—I don't know. You're a fool to leave a man layin' around loose for a month. I don't see what right they got to put me here. They want me to give up the only human being that really cares whether I live or die. Ain't you goin' to marry somebody?

BEATRICE: Yes.

MOLLY: You bet your life you are. Nobody wants to die an old maid. I got a man that wants me—wouldn't I be a nice one to throw him down? Ain't I got a right to him?

BEATRICE: (*Rises.*) Yes—yes, you have. If he's worth such love he'll work for it. Oh Molly—I want to help you. Listen. How would you like to come to my house for a little while?

MOLLY: Un?

BEATRICE: I can give you some work and you can make some money.

MOLLY: Oh, I—

BEATRICE: I'll ask Miss Carew if she'll let you go.

MOLLY: Oh—I don't know if I want to.

(*Miss Carew comes down the stairs with Kitty and Harriette.*)

MISS CAREW: Come in, girls, I'll get the tickets. (*She crosses to right and goes off right.*)

BEATRICE: (*To Kitty and Harriette*) It's awfully nice for you to go to the play, isn't it? (*Molly sits at table.*)

KITTY: Yes ma'am. There's a stock company round the corner. The leadin' man's a peach. Me and Harriette's the only ones allowed out alone. We been here the longest. She can trust us.

BEATRICE: I see. You surely wouldn't want to run away from a place as nice as this? Would you?

MOLLY: Ha!

KITTY: (*Winking at Harriette*) Some might.

HARRIETTE: A girl run away last month in the middle of the night. She'd only been here a day.

KITTY: You can run away enough if you want to—but you get the worst of it if you do. If you get pinched again you get *longer* time in a *worse* place.

HARRIETTE: You bet your life. It don't pay.

(*Miss Carew enters right. Gives tickets to Molly.*)

MISS CAREW: (*To Beatrice*) Will you come in now?

BEATRICE: (*Crosses before them to door right.*) Good-bye, girls. I hope you enjoy the play.

KITTY and HARRIETTE: Thank you.

BEATRICE: Good-bye.

KITTY and HARRIETTE: Good-bye.

(*Beatrice goes in. The manner of the girls at once changes from restraint to freedom.*)

KITTY: (*As they watch Beatrice out*) She's some swell, ain't she?

MOLLY: You should worry. She's no cheap skate.

HARRIETTE: Give us the tickets. We'll be late.

MOLLY: You think you're damned smart don't you—walking out like two little maids from school?

HARRIETTE: Come on, Kitty.

KITTY: Well, chase yourself if you're in such a push. (*To Molly. Harriette goes out.*) I wish I had something better than this cheap pin to wear.

MOLLY: (*Unfastening her own pin*) Here, take mine.

KITTY: Oh—no.

MOLLY: Sure thing. Why wouldn't you? A dandy guy give me that. He was a good spender. Don't you let it get away from you!

KITTY: Much obliged. I'll freeze to it. Say—I wish you was goin' instead of Harriette.

MOLLY: Oh, that's all right, kid. I'm glad you can go. She won't leave me poke my nose outside—without her. (*Jerking her head towards room at right*)

KITTY: Are you going to stick?

MOLLY: I will till Leever gets a job and then I'll beat it quick. So quick you can't see me going.

KITTY: You know what you'll have to do if he don't work.

MOLLY: Oh, Leever can make swell money all right. We're going to be buckled up. Do you think I'd shake him for a little wise talk? Hear me laugh. What do you think I am? A lily blossom?

HARRIETTE: (*Coming back excitedly*) Molly, Molly! Leever's outside. Down the block. He give me this. What'll I say to 'im? (*She gives Molly a small note.*)

MOLLY: (*Snatching it and reading it*) God! He's waitin' round the corner with a taxi. Tell him to wait—I'll be there.

KITTY: How can you slip it?

MOLLY: (*Glancing at Miss Carew*) I'll beat it now. (*Starts to go up center. Stops suddenly at voice of Miss Carew. Enter Miss Carew and Beatrice, right.*)

MISS CAREW: (*Coming in—followed by Beatrice. Molly stops and goes to piano.*) Girls—why on earth don't you go?

KITTY: I started and I came back for my handkerchief. Come on, Harriette.

HARRIETTE: We got'a hurry. (*They rush out.*)

MISS CAREW: (*Looking at Molly suspiciously. Molly trying to appear unconcerned. After a pause in which she looks searchingly at Molly.*) Molly, Miss Barrington has just offered to take you in her house—what do you say?

MOLLY: When does she want me to go?

BEATRICE: Right now—with me.

MOLLY: Oh—I—it'll take me quite a while to get ready. I'll go to-morrow.

MISS CAREW: Nonsense! It won't take you but a few minutes to put your things in your suitcase.

BEATRICE: I'll wait for you.

(*Miss Carew turns to face Beatrice. Molly looks at note in hand. There is a pause. Molly turns slowly on her heel and goes up the stairs.*)

MISS CAREW: I don't know whether she'll go or not. Mind you, I think you're doing a splendid thing and I appreciate it, but at the same time it's rash and if you don't mind my saying so, I think you're rather emotional. She's going to be a handful. Suppose you think it over a day or two till you cool off?

BEATRICE: My dear woman, I'm not a child. Here's a girl in a crisis. I can put her in new surroundings—divert her mind—help her to forget the man. I know it will be hard, but I expect that.

MISS CAREW: But you don't know how hard. She'll fool you in spite of yourself. (*Miss Carew and Beatrice exit right, talking.*)

(*After a moment, Molly sneaks down the stairs, wearing a long grey coat and small close hat. She hesitates a moment at door of stairs, then dashes to left in hall as Sadie comes in sight of hall. Goes to window, looks out, turns—sees Molly coming downstairs, sneaks to center door. Gets right of it, rushes out, grabs Molly by wrist and swings her in room.*)

SADIE: (*Dragging Molly back into the doorway, holding her by the back of the *arms—they speak in low tones.*) You will—will you? Going to beat it, was you? (*Molly gives a quick turn and gets loose. Calling*) Miss Carew! Miss Carew!

MISS CAREW: (*Miss Carew and Beatrice hurry in from the right.*) What is the matter?

SADIE: (*Hanging on to Molly*) She's trying to beat it—I caught her.

MISS CAREW: (*The girls begin to struggle. She separates the girls. After a pause.*) Go into my room, Sadie. (*Sadie goes out center upstairs. Beatrice comes down left center.*) Were you going to run away, Molly? (*Molly doesn't answer.*) Answer me. What were you going to do?

MOLLY: That's my business.

MISS CAREW: Be careful. Do you want to go with this lady or not?

MOLLY: I don't want no charity. I can get out and get a job of my own. I'm sick of this.

BEATRICE: Oh, let me speak to her just a moment, please.

MISS CAREW: Molly, Molly—this is the chance of your whole life—surely you've got sense enough to see that. (*She turns to go in right closing the door.*)

BEATRICE: Did you hate going with me so that you were running away?

MOLLY: Oh, that ain't it.

BEATRICE: What is it, then? Something's the matter. What made you do it? Tell me quickly—before she comes back. Perhaps I can do something for you. (*Molly shuts her mouth firmly and turns away.*) Is it the man? Were you going to him? (*Molly looks at her quickly.*) Do you want him so much? Tell me—so I can see what to do. They'll watch you now, more than ever, and you won't be able to get away.

MOLLY: (*After looking at Beatrice keenly.*) You won't squeal?

BEATRICE: You *know* I won't.

MOLLY: My fella's waitin' for me round the corner with a taxi. He's all I've got. I'm much obliged to you, but I got to. He's waitin'—I can't throw him down. I can't; I won't!

BEATRICE: You needn't. If he loves you he'll work for you. You've told him you'd give him a month. Come to me while you're waiting for him. You'll like it better than here. You're caught. Come and try it. What else can you do?

MOLLY: That's it. What can I do?

BEATRICE: You haven't had a fair chance so far, Molly—but you've got it now.

MOLLY: Aw—chance! That's easy enough for you to say. What do you know about it?

BEATRICE: I want to help you.

MOLLY: Then let me go. Oh, please, lady. I can't stand this. I want him and I'm goin' to have 'im. I tell you I ain't goin' to give 'im up.

BEATRICE: But I don't ask you to. Only that little while with me and then you'll make up your own mind.

MOLLY: Come on then—I'll go.

BEATRICE: You mean you'll run when we get out the door?

MOLLY: No— honest I won't.

BEATRICE: Oh yes you will. Why shouldn't you?

MOLLY: Un?

BEATRICE: You'd run because you don't know what I am talking about. It hasn't sunk into you. (*Molly looks at her deeply and turns away.*) You've been down all your life—but you didn't put yourself there. I want to let you see the other side. Then, if you want to go back, you're free to choose. But it's not fair for you never to see the other side.

MOLLY: Come on, then.

BEATRICE: If you run when you get down the steps, I'll scream and raise a crowd. You couldn't get away. Here's Miss Carew. Will you come?

MISS CAREW: (*Coming in from right*) Well, Molly, what are you going to do?

MOLLY: (*Relaxing indifferently*) I'm going into society.

(*Molly and Beatrice start toward the door. Miss Carew follows them as*)

(*Curtain falls*)

## Act 2

SCENE: *The living room in the Barrington New York house.*

*The left side of the room runs obliquely. In the lower half is set a large and handsome fireplace of dark wood, with a leather seat before it. In the side of room are double doors opening into the music room, part of which is seen. Two-thirds of wall at left taken by a stretch of windows handsomely draped with a window seat. The third of the back wall at left is formed by a jog which comes into the room about six feet then forms a right angle with a straight wall going on to the hall doors which are wide and set in one at right upstage. Below hall doors is a small high table holding handsome vase. Below jog a long narrow couch with high back—an odd and beautiful piece. Below window at left a long desk table with a chair above and below it. Below window at right, a very large arm chair with high back. Before the fire and well out into the room, a handsome davenport luxuriously upholstered and well filled with pillows. Above this davenport a round table holding a very beautiful lamp—books, magazines, etc. Before the couch a low tea table. Above the fireplace a low simple chair. Down stage, a little to left, a long low slender seat back or arms.*

*The whole has the effect of luxury and good taste with homelike comfort.*

TIME: *Afternoon—one month later.*

(*At Curtain, Beatrice and Irene are on at rise seated. Irene Barrington has cup of tea in hand. Beatrice is pouring for herself as curtain rises. Irene is an ultra-fashionable society woman, good-looking and very smart. She wears an afternoon gown with a hat. One of her gloves has fallen on floor near her chair.*)

BEATRICE: She's been here a month to-day, and in all that time she hasn't mentioned the man's name to me *once*.

IRENE: You don't think for a minute you've changed her any? That she's really going to give him up?

BEATRICE: She *is* changed.

IRENE: Oh—outside—a little naturally, with all the time and trouble you've spent on her. But not *in*side—the real girl . . .

BEATRICE: Why do you say that, Irene? Why are you so hard and unfair to her?

IRENE: I'm not—only sensible. Two maids have left now because of her. You'll upset the whole house before you get through.

BEATRICE: Wilson says it wasn't Molly's fault they left.[35]

IRENE: And what if you *should* pull her through—save her—as you say? What of it? There are millions more like her and they *have* to be.

BEATRICE: Irene, it's just such talk as that from women like you and me that makes half the trouble.

IRENE: Oh come—

BEATRICE: Of course it is. So long as we *accept* immorality in men, do you suppose they're going to change?

IRENE: Oh bosh! You're getting dotty on the subject. Men are more animal than women and they *will* live differently, so what are you going to do about it?

BEATRICE: That's an awful bromide, Irene. It's a worn out argument. They're only more so than women because from the beginning of time they've over-emphasized and exaggerated that side of their nature. It doesn't *have* to be.

IRENE: Well—even if that's so—I loathe a goody goody man. So do you. All women do. They haven't a grain of magnetism. They aren't the vital men who make world go round. Let me tell you, dear girl—so long as a man is decent about his affairs a woman can't complain.

BEATRICE: (*Handing Irene her cup*) That's a high standard to live by.

IRENE: It's the one we've *got* to live by, by Jove! (*Drinks.*)

BEATRICE: Well, now, for instance, what would you do if you knew that Bob—

IRENE: Well—

BEATRICE: What would you do—divorce him—or wink at it?

IRENE: I've never pried into my husband's life and never will. Of course I know Bob likes women, and they run after him. I almost never drop into the studio without finding a pretty girl there. What of it? I've never even asked about one of his *models*. Of course an artist has all kinds of girls posing. I don't give it a thought.

BEATRICE: What if you had to? What if it were forced upon you as it is on many women? (*Takes cigarette from mantel—lights it.*)

IRENE: But it never will be. I know Bob. He'll never do anything common or scandalous.

BEATRICE: We think that because he's your husband and my brother—but according to your code—so long as he doesn't offend you with an open and flagrant affair—it's all right.

IRENE: I don't say it's all right. I say it's the way things *are*. So why eat your heart out about it? (*Sits left again.*)

BEATRICE: I never used to think about it at all—but now—that I understand the horrors of what we call the social evil—I know that good women are *terribly* to blame for it all—because of their indifference towards the whole thing. It's we—*we ourselves* who are responsible for conditions—*ourselves*. If we don't care—if we don't *demand* the highest morality in our own men how are we going to get it? Or do anything for anybody else?

IRENE: Ye gods! You're going to marry Collin Ford. Do you think for a minute he's been a saint all his life? (*Rises, goes center to bench, picks up muff and goes above table.*)

BEATRICE: No—I don't suppose he has—but I believe now his life is just as decent as mine is. I wouldn't marry him if I didn't.

IRENE: (*Molly appears at center door with a book.*) Be careful; here's Molly.

BEATRICE: Don't smoke before her, please.

IRENE: (*Putting down her cigarette on tray or mantel.*) It's rather amusing—changing one's habits for her.

BEATRICE: And it's rather absurd asking her not to smoke if we do it ourselves. (*Molly enters from center.*) Come in, Molly. I'm ready to finish those cards now. The new list is there.

MOLLY: (*Sits left of table right.*) Yes, Miss Barrington. (*Molly wears a very plain dark blue dress with soft white collars and cuffs. Her hair is smoother than in Act I and her manner more quiet.*)

IRENE: I don't know whether Bob's coming home to dinner or not tonight. I'm dining with the Brices, and then to the opera with them after.

BEATRICE: Are you?

IRENE: Why don't you come with me now to see those pictures? Bob says they're awfully good.

BEATRICE: Can't. Collin's coming at five.

IRENE: (*Going to door center*) Sorry. Oh hello, Collin—Bee's in here. (*Beatrice rises.*)

COLLIN: (*Coming in center*) How are you today, Mrs. Bob?

IRENE: Fine. I'm trying to get Bee to come and see some pictures Bob's crazy about. Why don't you both come?

COLLIN: Just as you say, Bee. How are you?

BEATRICE: Hello, dearest. You're early. (*Beatrice kneels on one knee on settee facing Collin.*)

COLLIN: Am I? My car's here. Do you want to go?

BEATRICE: I can't—but you take Irene and—

COLLIN: Oh—getting rid of me, are you?

IRENE: Yes, she is. Come with me, Collin.

COLLIN: (*To Beatrice*) Why don't we drop Irene then and go for a little—

BEATRICE: I can't really. I have some cards to get off for a lecture.

IRENE: Oh nonsense. Molly can surely do that without you.

BEATRICE: (*Shaking her head at Irene and glancing at Molly whose back is turned*) No—I have something I—especially want to do—just *now*. (*Nodding towards Molly*) But I won't be long. Come back in just a little while—please Collin—there's a dear.

COLLIN: You're neglecting me lately, you know. I won't stand it. Come then, Irene. I'm turned out. (*He goes out center.*)

BEATRICE: Don't be long.

COLLIN: (*Calling back*) I don't know whether I'll come back or not.

(*Irene follows him up out of double doors—stops—returns. Beatrice sits on sofa, sips tea.*)

IRENE: Oh, where's my other glove? There it is. My glove, Molly, my glove!

(*Molly looks at her but doesn't move. Irene stares at her—raising her eyebrows.*)

BEATRICE: Molly, give Mrs. Barrington her glove, please! (*After a slight pause, Molly rises reluctantly and crosses slowly to get gloves—taking them to Irene.*)

IRENE: (*Taking the gloves*) And pray why shouldn't you move when I ask you to? You're extremely impertinent. Don't let that happen again. I won't have it. (*Molly is about to speak, but closes her lips sullenly. Irene goes out. Beatrice goes to table, sits.*)

BEATRICE: (*Having watched this anxiously*) Will you finish those envelopes now? I want to get all those announcements off for the lecture to-day. (*Beatrice sits at right of desk—Molly at left.*)

MOLLY: I don't mind pickin' up her gloves if she'd ask me decent—but I'm not a servant and she needn't think it. (*Sits right of table.*)

BEATRICE: Oh—Mrs. Barrington didn't mean that, Molly. Why shouldn't you pick up her gloves? That's only polite.

MOLLY: Every time I get to feeling fine somebody comes along and gives me a biff.

BEATRICE: Are these all addressed? (*Indicating letters back of desk*)

MOLLY: Yes—all of 'em.

BEATRICE: You addressed the others so well. You're improving every day. This is such good practice for you.

MOLLY: It's a good way to get paralysis too. I thought I couldn't straighten out my fingers yesterday.

BEATRICE: Don't hold your pen so tight. Like this—see? (*Beatrice shows her.*) Now, when you're finished with these, study your spelling lesson and do the shorthand exercises—that's the practical thing for you rather than the music.

MOLLY: Oh, I can't waste time doin' things like that singin' teacher wants me to. (*She laughs.*) Now honest, Miss Barrington, I ask you—ain't that silly? (*Rising*) Look. She said I must do this to strengthen my diaphragm—Ah—ah—ah. She did—I'm not stringin' you. Diaphragm! I'd die away doin' that.

BEATRICE: But you'd like it if you'd really work.

MOLLY: I'd like it if I could sing a song right out the way I feel it inside me, and not waste time makin' a noise like a sheep. If I could just let go and make it sound like I feel it—

BEATRICE: How?

MOLLY: (*Wistfully*) Oh, sweeter than anything—so it makes you forget and just feel happy. Sweet, you know—like somethin' you've kind a dreamed about—but never seen.

BEATRICE: That's the sweetness and goodness in your heart that wants to come out. But you have to help it—you have to work for it.

MOLLY: (*Puts book on table left.*) What's the good a' workin' so hard fer anythin'? We're a long time dead. I think we ought to get things awful *quick* while we're here.

BEATRICE: You're a funny little girl, Molly—with the biggest heart in the world. Do you want to do something for me?

MOLLY: Of course. What?

BEATRICE: I wish you'd wear your hair some other way.

MOLLY: Why—what's the matter with it?

BEATRICE: Nothing—only it isn't simple enough.

MOLLY: Oh, I know you want me to look like a peeled onion. That's just the trouble with you, Miss Barrington—you dress too awful plain. Honest you do. If I had your money I'd look like something.

BEATRICE: (*Laughing*) Would you?

MOLLY: Well, I guess yes. Why look at you—not a bit o' jewelry on now. What's the use of havin' pearls and diamonds if you don't flash 'em? Look at Mrs. Bob. She don't mind puttin' on a little paint and lightin' up a little. Why don't you? I think you're awful pretty, Miss Barrington. I didn't at first, but I do now. You kinda grow on a person. It's sort of little things. You ain't flashy but you certainly count when you come in. I'm catchin' on to that. No wonder Mr. Ford's crazy about you.

BEATRICE: You funny child! You've been here a month to-day. Do you know it?

MOLLY: You bet I know it.

BEATRICE: (*Rises—taking gold purse from desk.*) I'm going to give you your salary now.

MOLLY: Oh, never mind that.

BEATRICE: Come get it. (*Giving her three bills*) There! You've earned it honestly. Doesn't that feel great?

MOLLY: (*Putting the bills in her stocking*) It's a shame to take the money.

(*Beatrice goes to table, and pauses. Molly moves to left center, putting away money in her belt or sleeves.*)

BEATRICE: Have you been happy here, Molly?

MOLLY: It's a nice place.

BEATRICE: And this is the day we promised you could write to Leever. What are you going to say to him?

MOLLY: I wrote to him yesterday.

BEATRICE: Oh—Molly!

MOLLY: Sure I did. Why not? Only one day ahead. I wanted him to get it to-day on the date.

BEATRICE: (*Goes to Molly.*) And—what did you say to him?

MOLLY: I told him I'd meet him tomorrow and talk it over.

BEATRICE: (*Quickly*) You didn't tell him where you are?

MOLLY: Yes I did. He wouldn't believe *anything* if I didn't. I told him where I'd meet him.

BEATRICE: But you don't care for him any more, do you? That's all over isn't it?

MOLLY: You promised me I could see him and talk it over.

BEATRICE: (*Crosses before Molly.*) Yes I did. Now listen. I have a great scheme for us. For you and me—and I'll tell you now so you can think it over before you see Leever tomorrow.

MOLLY: (*Suspiciously*) Uh?

BEATRICE: Next year I'm going to have a home for girls—in the country. A pretty home—with gardens and a little farm—and there'll be a matron in charge—like Miss Carew—but—this is the important thing. *You* will be next to the matron—the special friend and confidant of the girls.

MOLLY: Un? (*Correcting herself*) Yes, Miss Barrington.

BEATRICE: I mean you'll make them understand that we want to help them—and show them how to wipe out the bad part of their lives and begin all over.

MOLLY: Oh, I wouldn't have the nerve—they'd give me the laugh too quick.

BEATRICE: A girl would believe you if you told her she could make her life neat and pure—because she'd know you'd gone all through it. I might talk forever and it wouldn't have the slightest effect.

MOLLY: That's no lie.

BEATRICE: The finest, biggest thing you can do with your life shall be to help other girls because of the lessons you've learned yourself. Isn't that so? (*Molly kneels on floor at side of Beatrice, looking up at her.*)

MOLLY: And what will I be doin' all the rest of my days? Don't you expect me to ever see any kind of a man?

BEATRICE: Of course.

MOLLY: Don't you expect me to marry one?

BEATRICE: Of course—a good one—and have a home of your own and children that you'll make into good men and women.

MOLLY: That's takin' awful long chances—waitin' for a *good* man. I got Leever. I'm goin' to marry him.

BEATRICE: Oh, Molly—you couldn't go back to him now?

MOLLY: Why couldn't I?

BEATRICE: He couldn't make you happy. You've grown. He isn't your kind; you've changed so.

MOLLY: Oh, I don't how as I have. I promised to wait for him. (*Beatrice raising body*) *You* got a man. You wouldn't give Mr. Ford up would you? (*Kneels.*) Don't you love him fit to die? I've seen you look at him. *I* know. When you kiss him could *anything* make you stop *caring*? (*Inspired*) That's how I feel. Every woman's got to have a man. What else is there? (*Molly rises on feet.*) Leever may not be what *you* call right—but he's mine. I'm so crazy to see him I can hardly wait. (*Beatrice looks at Molly.*) But I'll tell you one thing, Miss Barrington—I won't go back to the old life.

BEATRICE: Do you mean that, Molly?

MOLLY: So help me God. I mean it! I'll marry him and stick to him, but that's *all.* Don't think I ain't much obliged fer all you've done fer me—I tell you I just love my little room here. It feels awful good to go in at night and turn the key, to open my eyes in the mornin' feelin' fine, and know you're goin' to say "Good mornin', Molly" like I was somebody. Oh—I'm on to that end of it all right. I've learned a lot here. This house is grand but it ain't mine and I don't belong in it. I'd rather have two rooms of my *own* with him. I won't go back on him. I'm going to meet him tomorrow.

BEATRICE: But, Molly!

WILSON: (*The housekeeper—a dignified, middle-aged woman, comes in from center.*) Miss Barrington—there's a man here—wants to see Molly.

BEATRICE: Who?

WILSON: He says his name's Leever.

BEATRICE: What?

MOLLY: Leever!

WILSON: What shall I do?

MOLLY: I'll go out to him.

BEATRICE: Wait! (*A pause.*) Wilson, bring him in here.

MOLLY: Oh!

BEATRICE: (*To Wilson*) In here. I'm glad he came. You've got to see him somewhere—I promised you and I'd much rather it were in here than anywhere else. It's all in your own hands now, Molly, and remember it isn't what I say that makes right or wrong. It is your own soul you have to reckon with. You know that. (*Exit center and right.*)

WILSON: (*After a moment, entering*) She's in here.

(*Enter Leever. Exit Wilson.*)

MOLLY: (*Advancing to Leever—throwing arms around him*) Leever![36]

LEEVER: Pretty glad to see me, ain't you?

MOLLY: Yes. Are you workin'? (*Beginning to look at him doubtfully*)

LEEVER: You bet I am.

MOLLY: What you doin'?

LEEVER: I got a fine turn in a show. I was on last week and they're goin' to give me good time. Kiss me agin', kid. (*Molly kisses him.*) I'll make swell money now. You'll be the best dresser on Broadway.[37] You're the only skirt for me. I ain't had no other. Anybody'll tell you that. All the girls and fellas askin' about you. I seen Kitty last night.

MOLLY: Kitty? Where?

LEEVER: At Kelly's.

MOLLY: Did she go back?

LEEVER: Certainly she did. They didn't kid *her* with the reform business. (*Molly glances away.*) She was dancin' to beat the band last night—lookin' fine too—swell clothes. She come over to me and she says "Say, Leever—where's Molly?" and I said "Oh, I guess she's shook *us*" and she says "If you see 'er—tell 'er to take it from me. She'd better come back to the gay life and hit 'er up while she can.[38] There ain't nothin' in the other." That's what *she* said—and Kit's no fool, is she?

MOLLY: I—wonder what made her—go back? (*Turning to face him*) Did you—did anybody else ask about me?

LEEVER: They was all askin' about you. (*Getting her hands*) You come down to-night and have a look-in—to see your old friends. They'll give you a great send off. Come on.

MOLLY: Oh, I couldn't.

LEEVER: Why not? (*Pause.*)

MOLLY: I'll tell you— Listen, Leever—you save your money, and I'll keep on workin' and we can get married in about six months.

LEEVER: Six months? (*Throws her hands away.*) What are you givin' me?

MOLLY: That ain't so long—if you really want me—right, Leever. We must wait till we can have a little place—maybe a little flat—with a kitchen. I been learnin' how to keep house—Honest I have—so we can have a real home.

LEEVER: (*Swings left arm to strike her—says fiercely.*) Don't get funny.

MOLLY: (*With a great sweetness and tenderness*) Don't you know what I mean? Why shouldn't we live decent—like other people? We may have kids of our own some day and we don't want 'em to be ashamed of us. We can live straight as well as anybody. You *can*, Leever. We can wipe it all out and begin again. Honest we can. They all tell you that. It feels great, it does.

LEEVER: (*Swings her down in seat center—stands above her still holding her by wrists*) Oh—dry up! You make me sick. Don't hand me any of that. You're mine—you'll do as I say.

MOLLY: But, Leever, if you'd just try it once, you'd know what I mean. To hold up your head and not be sneakin' like a dog afraid of the cops. Kind of be *somebody*—get steady work and—

LEEVER: Don't talk so much about work—you.

MOLLY: I only mean I know you could be so different.

LEEVER: You want me different, do you?

MOLLY: Don't get mad. I want you honest. A girl likes to be *proud* of her fella—

LEEVER: What's the matter with me? Un?[39]

MOLLY: Leever—something *comes* to you. You see it—after a while—all you used to think was talk is *true*. I don't know what gets into you, but—you get to hating yourself so you can't stand it. You just *got* to be straight—after you *know*. That's what I want you to see.

LEEVER: Can that. That's enough—you loonie! Have they been dopin' you with this? What do you think I am? Ain't I waited a month fer you? Do you think you're worth it? Couldn't I get plenty more fer askin'? I've stuck to you and now you try to throw me. Have you got another man? Is that it?[40]

MOLLY: No—no!

LEEVER: You have too—I know you.

MOLLY: No! I ain't seen a man. I'm makin' something; I got my own money.

LEEVER: Hand it over then. (*She takes the money from her belt or sleeve and gives it to him.*) Is that all?

MOLLY: Yes—it is.

LEEVER: Who is he? A swell?

MOLLY: (*Fiercely*) You shut up. I tell you there ain't no—

LEEVER: (*Putting his hand heavily over her mouth and half pushing her from him and then snatching her back by the arm*) Oh ain't there? Where'd you get this then?

MOLLY: I earned it. I'm workin'.

LEEVER: (*Laughing in a brutal way*) *Yes, you did*. I know how *you* work.

MOLLY: Oh— (*Trying to get away*)

LEEVER: Listen—don't think you can come any funny business on me. You know me better than that. You've got more. Cough up.

MOLLY: I hope to die if I have.

LEEVER: He must be a cheap skate.

MOLLY: I tell you there ain't a man. Don't you say that again.

LEEVER: Do you think you'd throw *me* if there wasn't?

MOLLY: Oh—don't say that to me. I'm trying to be good, Leever.

LEEVER: You'll get out of this now pretty quick.

MOLLY: (*Determined—sits left of table.*) No—I'm going to stay.

LEEVER: (*Left of Molly*) I'll put you back where you belong.

MOLLY: I belong here. She trusts me. She's been good to me.

LEEVER: If you don't meet me at Kelley's tonight, I'll kill you.

MOLLY: No, you won't! I ain't afraid of you now. Get out of here. If you ever come near me again—I—

WILSON: (*Enter Wilson center, suddenly pushing open double door.*) What are you doing?

MOLLY: Put him out! Put him out!

(*Wilson rings bell. Leever looks at Molly, then slinks out. Molly sinks into chair, agitated.*)

WILSON: Well—you've seen him. Do you want him back? (*Molly shudders and covers face with hands on table.*) You're all right, Molly. It's the best thing that could have happened to you. You've had a taste of something decent and you've done with other. Stay here and be a good girl and—

MOLLY: (*Throwing out her arms in desperation*) Good! Hell! I can't stay shut up here forever. Holy gee! She don't know how I'm hangin' on to myself. I got a' have some fun. I can't stand this.

WILSON: But think what a fine place this is—

MOLLY: Oh, I know, I know. It's a big house and she's an angel. But what's going to become of me? I'd a' run away long ago if it hadn't been for you, Mrs. Wilson. She is good—but you're *human*. You kinda know.

WILSON: Know? I ain't worked with my bare hands since ten years old, without *knowin'*.

MOLLY: I never told her half of it; I got *some* pride. I never told her there was nine of us living in three rooms; I never told her we had a boarder, an Italian, and my mother tried to throw me in with his board. They thought I would stand for that because I was a kid, but I got wise and got out—found a job—but you can't live on three dollars a week. What was there fer me to do—will you tell me—but what I *did* do? I'm bad, am I? Well, it's kinda funny that's all. I ain't got much education to see there was something *wrong*. The men are runnin' after us and we get pinched. I was caught. Here I am. I give up my fella. I don't want him, but I want somebody. What am I goin' to do? What am I goin' to do? Stay here and dry up in this straight-jacket of a dress watchin' the *good* people dancin' and makin' love for the rest of my life? What am I goin' to do? I'm lonely. Christ! I'm lonely. I want somebody o' my own. (*She breaks for the first time, and as Wilson touches her Molly throws her arms about her neck and sobs.*)

BEATRICE: (*Coming in from center*) Well! (*Molly goes quickly to the desk and begins straightening letters—Wilson goes to left above door and touches the button which turns on the lights. Molly keeps her head down.*)

WILSON: Tell Miss Barrington about it, Molly.

MOLLY: You tell 'er.

WILSON: No, no, child—tell her yourself. (*Wilson goes up center, but does not close door.*)

BEATRICE: (*Sitting on the low seat center, her back to audience*) What is it, Molly? Come here.

MOLLY: (*She goes slowly down to stand before Beatrice.*) I'm going to give him up.

BEATRICE: What?

MOLLY: I'm done with Leever. That's all.

BEATRICE: (*Reaching for one of Molly's hands*) Oh Molly! My dear girl! I—I can't tell you how glad I am. You've taken your first big step—and you did it yourself? (*Molly stares before her with a half wistful, half sullen face.*) *Yourself*! That's what counts. Oh Molly, I'm so glad—I'm *proud* of you— (*She takes Molly's hand and turns her toward her.*) Proud of you.

MOLLY: There's a hair pin comin' out. (*Molly puts it in.*)

BEATRICE: Thank you. Aren't you *happy*, Molly?

MOLLY: (*Smiling bravely*) I guess so.

BEATRICE: Don't you feel like a new girl?

MOLLY: I s'pose I do.

BEATRICE: Wouldn't you and Wilson like to go to the theatre tonight and see something funny?

MOLLY: Whatever you say.

BEATRICE: Couldn't you and she have a jolly time?

MOLLY: I expect I'd laugh myself to death if I went with Wilson—she's such a cut up. If anybody was to ask me who I'd keep on going' with for the rest of my life of course I'd say Wilson. (*Runs out center.*)

BEATRICE: (*Beatrice sits, staring before her thoughtfully. Collin comes down to her side, slightly startles her.*) Oh, Collin. I have something wonderful to tell you.

COLLIN: About your hobby? I'm getting jealous of it. You don't think of anything else now.

BEATRICE: (*Hands on his arm*) Nonsense! Don't you expect me to ever think about anything on earth but you?

COLLIN: No!

BEATRICE: Don't be silly. Now listen, dear, seriously. Will you?

COLLIN: I suppose I must.

BEATRICE: I don't want you just to be tolerant and good natured about my work. I want you to *believe* in it. Use your influence and power. To strike at the thing which destroys more people and happiness than anything else in the world.

COLLIN: (*Reaches across playfully, tips her left arm with his right hand.*) Oh my dear, I want you to use your power and influence. (*She crosses down to left.*) All we can do is to openly and honestly acknowledge certain necessities and make conditions as clean and decent as possible. But that has nothing to do with the moral end of it that you are trying to take hold of. And it isn't a woman's job. It only makes you unhappy finding out disagreeable things. I can't bear to have you touch it.

BEATRICE: Nonsense! (*Advancing to him, placing hands on his arm*) It's good for me. I care more for humanity—feel more—love *you* more—understand life as I never did until I began to know the truth.

COLLIN: Why should you see anything but the beauty of life?

BEATRICE: Listen, please. (*Sits on low stool.*) When I saw Molly trying to find love—hanging on in her loyal ignorant way to what she had—when I saw how she could cling to that awful creature because he was hers—I wanted to teach her the right way—I couldn't wait to snatch her up and bring her here.

COLLIN: What?

BEATRICE: Yes. I thought of this huge house and the few people in it.

COLLIN: (*Rising*) She's not—you didn't—

BEATRICE: (*Rises.*) Yes she is, and yes I did. And she was worth it. She's proven it to-day.

COLLIN: You didn't get her there—one *of those*?

BEATRICE: I did.

COLLIN: Bee—are you out of your senses?

BEATRICE: (*The next two lines by Collin and Beatrice are spoken together.*) Not at all. What did you say?

COLLIN: You are. Why, I never dreamed—I beg your pardon.

BEATRICE: (*Going center*) I did it. It's done and it worked.

COLLIN: You can't—

BEATRICE: I can. To-day she gave up her man—herself—voluntarily—because in one month—in decent surroundings— (*Collin and Beatrice speaking together.*)

COLLIN: (*Goes to Beatrice*) But this is impossible. It's dangerous having her here—

BEATRICE: Why? Why is it?

COLLIN: You don't how *what* she might do. You mustn't keep her.

BEATRICE: I wouldn't send her away now for the world. If something new hasn't come into her soul today then I don't know anything—and it's my business to protect her—to keep everything away from her that might hurt her or drag her back.

IRENE: (*Coming in from center in time to hear Beatrice's last words. Collin leaves bench center and strolls down to left corner.*) Well, still at it, I see. Positively Beatrice has only one topic of conversation nowadays. What do you think of her protégé, Collin? (*Back of settee left*)

COLLIN: Oh, I think the whole thing is so removed from good women that it's horrible for them to go looking for it.

IRENE: Just what I say. Why drag it under our noses when it isn't necessary? (*Beatrice sits at table right.*) Why go out of our way to dig up tragedies? (*Goes to center.*)

COLLIN: Oh Bee, dear, you'll—well, I think the best way for you to get over this is to get your fill of it—and once you do, you'll settle back into the sensible way of looking at things.

IRENE: (*Coming to Collin down left*) What time is it, Collin? (*Irene sits on settee.*)

COLLIN: (*Looking at his watch*) Just six.

BOB: (*After a moment, Bob Barrington comes in center.*) Hello, everybody. (*Bob Barrington is 37, good looking, with a light and charming manner and altogether likeable personality. He comes down back of sofa and shakes hands with Irene playfully.*)

COLLIN: How are you, Bob?

BOB: How are you, Ford? Hello, wifie. (*Leaning over couch to kiss Irene's cheek.*) What's the matter, Bee? Anybody have a row?

BEATRICE: Oh—no. (*Rises, crosses off left. Goes in left, and playing a few bars begins a very beautiful love song, singing with great feeling.*)

IRENE: I went in to see the pictures, Bob.

BOB: Oh! What did you think of them?

IRENE: Pretty good.

BOB: Pretty good? They're corking. (*Irene rises and prims.*) Wish I had half his go. He's a young fella, Ford—needs a boost. There are one or two things you'd like.

COLLIN: Yes, I know.

(*Irene rises from settee.*)

COLLIN: Irene, you ought to be painted in that gown. You're looking particularly stunning to-day.

IRENE: You're a nice man. (*Collin goes off left.*)

IRENE: (*Going center*) Are you dining at home, Bob?

BOB: Why?

IRENE: I'm going to the Brices and to the opera with them. Will you come in later?

BOB: Um—perhaps I will. I think I'll get Susan Hoyt to go to dinner with me. You must meet her, Irene. She's a peach!

IRENE: Oh, you're always mad about somebody, Bob. I must fly. (*Exit Irene.*)

(*Enter Joseph, the Butler, who goes down for tray and up to table up center, looks at letters; turns out lights.*)

BOB: Bye-bye—hope you have a good time. (*He whistles what Beatrice is singing and goes in right.*)

(*After a moment Molly comes into through the room at back and down to desk, switches on lights. Begins to straighten papers. The music attracts her and she is gradually affected by it. Leaving the desk—she listens—beginning to hum and dance a little. She goes on with more abandon. Bob comes in from right, starts across the room, stopping to look at Molly as she dances. She suddenly faces him and stops.*)

BOB: Do you like to dance, Molly?

MOLLY: I used to.

BOB: You haven't stopped dancing forever have you?

MOLLY: Looks kind a' like it.

BOB: What do you do all day here?

MOLLY: Well—I address a good many envelopes.

BOB: That's important.

MOLLY: Yes—there's so many things your sister has to let people know about.

BOB: (*Laughing*) For instance? What's that?

MOLLY: (*Reading invitation*) This is to tell that Dr. Von Flexner is going to talk about the moral responsibility of the individual toward society.[41]

BOB: (*Laughing*) What do you think is the most important thing in the world?

MOLLY: Oh—just to be happy.

BOB: Poor little girl. You're too damned pretty to be shut up here. (*He catches her in his arms. Molly, amazed, struggles to get away. He kisses her and strolls out carelessly, leaving Molly horrified as the curtain falls.*)[42]

## Act 3

TIME: A month later. April.

SCENE: Same as Act 2.

*The furniture is covered with pale chintz covers. The fireplace has growing plants and ferns. A tall, tropical plant stands on the hearth. There are flowers and blooming plants on the tables. The heavy curtains at window are replaced by light ones. The windows are open and the curtains blow lightly. Stage empty at rise.*

(*Molly is just coming in from room at left, carrying a tray with coffee service. Her hair is more simply and becomingly dressed. There is a new sweetness and softens in her face and manner. Bob and Collin enter up right center. Bob enters first—half smiles at Molly who is at side of table down left, standing with her back to audience. Collin then enters. Collin gets cup of coffee and moves up toward door left. Molly has moved toward Bob who is lighting a cigarette. Bob shakes head annoyed. Collin has turned at door and sees this—then exits left. Business of glances between Bob and Molly.*)

MOLLY: The ladies are having their coffee in there! (*In front of table*)

COLLIN: (*Coming down to table*) Give me a cup, please.

MOLLY: (*Holds tray as Collin pours the coffee.*) Will you have some, Mr. Barrington?

BOB: (*Turning to window*) No, thank you. (*Lights cigarette.*)

(*Collin goes to door right and turns—seeing that Bob and Molly have exchanged glances. Molly stops guiltily. Collin looks suspiciously from one to the other, goes in slowly—closing the door. After Collin looks back, Molly comes down to right front of desk.*)

BOB: Be careful. Don't look at me when anybody's in the room. (*She stands close to him, lifting her face—he kisses her quickly.*) Stand over there! (*Molly moves to other side of table.*) Listen. You have to leave here.

MOLLY: Oh—

BOB: Right away.

MOLLY: What do you—

BOB: Be at the studio to-night and I'll—I'll see what to do—where you can go. I can't have you here. (*Picks up newspaper.*)

MOLLY: Why not?

BOB: I don't like it. It's too messy.

MOLLY: You mean it's wrong.

BOB: Get away to-morrow.

MOLLY: How can I?

BOB: Make some excuse!

MOLLY: But she'll—what can I say to your sister?

BOB: There's a dear girl! Do it as soon as you can. Be at the studio to-night. Will you come?

MOLLY: Why—yes—if you think it's wrong for me to be here. I—I'd ought to have gone away in the first place.

BOB: Sure?

MOLLY: Yes. You know I will if I promise you. You—you're not getting rid of me?

BOB: Can't you understand?

MOLLY: (*Springing to him*) If you do, I'll kill myself. (*She clutches him.*)

BOB: For heaven's sake—be careful. Get away to-morrow. I won't have you living here in this house. It can't be. Don't you understand? It's impossible. (*He takes up a newspaper and sits. Takes the coffee.*) Don't stay in this room. (*Molly crosses to tray and is at side of table.*)

IRENE: (*Coming in from left wearing a very beautiful evening gown, which is extremely smart and modish. She stops suddenly, looking at Molly, who is just taking the tray from the table.*) Why haven't you taken that away?

MOLLY: (*Nervously*) I—I stopped to fix the lamp. (*Molly exits right. Bob rises and advances to Irene center reading a paper. Irene stands center thoughtfully.*)

BOB: (*After a pause*) Will you have a cigarette?

IRENE: (*Looking after her*) I loathe that girl. I can't breathe when she's in the room.

BOB: What difference does she make to you? I say, will you have a cigarette? (*Going to her with the case open*)

IRENE: No. (*Goes to chair and sits.*)

BOB: (*Trying to be natural*) Why not?

IRENE: There's a subtle—insidious something that—that—sort of fills the air when she's about. It's as strong—as real as— (*She stops, still looking at him.*)

BOB: (*Turning his newspaper*) Why do you let a servant get on your nerves like that?

IRENE: Oh, it isn't my nerves—I assure you. Something much more definite than that.

BOB: (*Offering open case*) Are you going to have a cigarette or not?

IRENE: I am not. I've taken a peculiar dislike to your cigarettes.

BOB: (*Crosses to left corner of desk right and picks up newspaper.*) Quite peculiar, I should say. Since when?

IRENE: Yesterday I thought I smelled smoke in the upper hall. I followed the scent and it took me into the side hall—down to the end—growing stronger—to that girl's door. I went in. She was smoking one of yours, with a box on the table.

BOB: Um—I s'pose all the servants pick them up—more or less. (*Goes right of desk.*) What of it?

IRENE: Nothing—It's only one of a hundred little things that have made me—(*Bob yawns.*) You do look rather fagged.[43] You might have come in a little more quietly last night—this morning, rather. Five—it was. I don't complain of the hour—only the way you shut the door.

BOB: I'm so sorry. That was a slip. I didn't mean to be noisy.

IRENE: I'm sure you didn't.

BOB: You're in a pleasant mood. I'm going up.

IRENE: Bob!

BOB: Well? (*She puts her hands over her eyes. Checking a sob.*) What's the matter?

IRENE: I—I—don't know. Yes, I do.

BOB: What is it?

IRENE: I want to tell you something.

BOB: Well? (*Going back to her. A pause.*) Go on. What on earth is the matter with you, Irene? I never saw you act like this.

IRENE: (*Trying to control herself*) No, you never did.

BOB: Are you ill?

IRENE: Oh, Bob, be kind to me. I didn't—I—you won't understand just—all it means. It frightens me a little—but I'm glad.

BOB: What do you mean?

IRENE: I've always said I didn't want a baby but I do now. It's the most wonderful thing in the world.

BOB: (*After a pause*) My—dear—girl.[44]

IRENE: Don't—wait! You've always said I was—so—sensible and broad minded about—about men. And I've tried to be. But lately I—I've wanted to say something to you.

BOB: (*Lays his hand in hers—she clings to him.*) What difference does all that make? You *are* the most sensible woman—but now you're the most precious. You—you've made me—if you're happy about it—I'm the happiest man on earth.

IRENE: Are you?

BOB: Of course. Of course I am. You needn't ask me that. It's great![45]

IRENE: It's all more wonderful—and more terrible than I thought. Everything in the world is more so—now.

BOB: Yes, dear.

IRENE: More important. Oh Bob, I want to be fit for it—and—equal to all it means. I've been so thoughtless and—wrong about what marriage ought to be.

BOB: You're tired, dear. You're tired. Don't say these things.

IRENE: (*Suddenly clinging to him*) Oh Bob—you're so different to me now. You mean something more to me than you ever—I want to know that you are to me—what—I've been to you. I never used to care—but—

BOB: Irene—why do you say all these foolish things? You know—

IRENE: It—makes a difference to me now—what *you* are.

BOB: I know—I know, dear—my dear.[46]

IRENE: (*Suddenly putting her hands on his arms, looking into his face*) I want to trust you. I want to—

BOB: Why shouldn't you?

IRENE: (*Rising*) Can I?

BOB: Irene, why on earth do you ask me that?

IRENE: I've let you alone. I've tried to believe that everything was all right for man—to look at it from a man's standpoint. But now my ideas have changed. Bob, I can't bear it unless I have faith in you. I want the father of my baby to be—

BOB: Well dear—

IRENE: Oh my husband! (*Suddenly leaning against him weakly*) I love you in a new way. Bob—do you love me? (*She hides her face in his arm, sobbing.*)

BOB: Why, of course. Of course I do. You know that—you foolish girl. Put all that—if you've got any silly ideas in your head about me—get them out. Do you hear? You're my wife—the only woman in the world to me.

Dear girl, you've made me awfully happy. (*He kisses her hair tenderly, then her face.*)[47]

(*Collin and Beatrice are heard speaking as they open the door at right.*)

BEATRICE: (*Off scene*) That will do, Collin dear.

IRENE: I'm going up. (*She kisses Bob quickly and goes out center.*)

(*Beatrice comes in from left center followed by Collin from right up left. She wears a white evening gown—very beautiful and simple.*)

BEATRICE: What's the matter with Irene? (*Bob crosses to right staring before him, doesn't hear, crosses to window right of desk.*) Bob, was Irene crying? (*Beatrice goes to Bob, down right and puts hand on his shoulder.*)

BOB: Um? Oh no—no—I don't think—no, she wasn't!

COLLIN: (*At fireplace laughing*) Wake up—what's the matter with you?

BEATRICE: Headache? Headache? (*Goes up and around table, crosses down to Bob.*)

BOB: No—no I'm all right. What are you talking about? Like a little Scotch, Collin?

COLLIN: (*Sits.*) I could stand it.

BEATRICE: Such an easy way to drown your troubles, isn't it?

COLLIN: I wish it were. (*Comes to stool in front of table right and sits facing Bob.*)

BEATRICE: Well, it is—for men. You throw most anything off after you've—

COLLIN: If you don't stop taking things so seriously you'll think all men are knaves. Since you've been trying to reform the world, you are—

BEATRICE: Laugh all you want—you can't shake me now. I've got Molly as a living example that it's all worthwhile. (*Beatrice puts hand on Bob's arm.*)

COLLIN: Have you noticed this wonderful change in Molly, Bob?

BOB: Uh?

COLLIN: (*Watching Bob*) The goodness that's radiating from her presence?

BEATRICE: You can laugh, but it's true. Bob probably hasn't realized it because he scarcely sees her. But it's there. Why, it's like a miracle. (*Beatrice goes center.*) From the very day she gave up the man she's been a different girl. *From that very day.*

(*Bob goes to the window and lights another cigarette.*)

COLLIN: I'd like to believe it.

BEATRICE: (*Comes back to chair left of it and sits.*) You have to believe it. It's true. It would break your heart to see how well she works. But Bob, the most pitiful thing is to see her try to study. Bob— (*Goes near chair left of table.*) Are you listening?

BOB: Yes. Come on, Collin. Do you want that drink?

BEATRICE: Wait till I finish. And she pegs away at her spelling as if her life depends upon it. Reads, reads—just stuffing it in.

COLLIN: I'll be there in a minute. (*Collin lapses into thought.*)

BEATRICE: What's the matter?

COLLIN: Nothing.

BEATRICE: Yes there is. What are you thinking?

COLLIN: Nothing. Only—

BEATRICE: Only what?

COLLIN: (*Rises and goes to Beatrice.*) How long are you going to keep this girl here?

BEATRICE: Indefinitely.

(*Enter Wilson.*)

COLLIN: Bee, I tell you, you're making a mistake.

BEATRICE: Now, Collin.

WILSON: (*Excitedly*) May I speak to you a minute, Miss Barrington? I must.

BEATRICE: Right now?

WILSON: Yes, please.

(*Beatrice excuses herself to Collin. Collin goes out. Beatrice sits left of table.*)

BEATRICE: What is it?

WILSON: Molly! She's getting ready to go!

BEATRICE: Go where?

WILSON: She's packin' her things and says she's goin' to-night—she says she can't stand it here another minute.

BEATRICE: Has there been any more trouble with the maids? I'll go and speak to her—

WILSON: Oh, that isn't it—That's just an excuse.

BEATRICE: What?

WILSON: That isn't the real trouble!

BEATRICE: What then?

WILSON: I'm afraid it's the man.

BEATRICE: The man?

WILSON: Leever—yes—the one she gave up—or we thought she did. I'm afraid she's gone back to him.

BEATRICE: Oh no—no—no! Don't tell me that. I couldn't bear it. How do you know?

WILSON: Well—I caught her about two weeks ago, comin' in awful late one night, and I told her I wouldn't tell you if she never did it again—and twice since I caught her sneakin' in towards mornin'. I talked to her like anything—

BEATRICE: Oh, why didn't you tell me? Why didn't—

WILSON: She cried and promised if I wouldn't—

BEATRICE: Oh, horrible! Molly—Oh, I can't believe it. It can't be true—it can't!

WILSON: I'm afraid she'll get away now if you don't—

BEATRICE: (*Rises and starts.*) I'll go right up—

WILSON: Just a minute—don't let her know I told you—she's shut up like a clam and you won't get any—

BEATRICE: How can I help it?

WILSON: Let on you saw her yourself comin' in this morning.

BEATRICE: Oh no, I couldn't lie to her—

WILSON: Make out you know the whole business—that you know it's the man—and just where she goes—and the whole thing. Then she'll give it all up. It's the only way you can get the truth out of her.

BEATRICE: I don't like to do it that way!

WILSON: I know her better than you do, Miss Barrington and I advise you!

MOLLY: I beg your pardon, Miss Barrington—can I speak to you a minute?

BEATRICE: (*Motions Wilson to go.*) Yes, Molly. (*There is a slight pause. Wilson goes out center, closing the door.*)

MOLLY: I—

BEATRICE: (*Right center*) Well—

MOLLY: I don't want you to think I ain't—I'm not grateful for all you've done for me. I never could thank you enough if I talked forever. It isn't that—but—I—I—I can't stay any longer.

BEATRICE: What?

MOLLY: I'll get a job some place else, but you mustn't think—

BEATRICE: What is the trouble? Why are you—

MOLLY: It ain't you, Miss Barrington— It ain't you. You've been the—

BEATRICE: What is it then?

MOLLY: It's—another maid's going to leave on my account—and I'm going to get out first.

BEATRICE: (*Sternly*) Where are you going?

MOLLY: (*Looking at her quickly*) I—I—I'll go back to the home till I—just for tonight till I get a place. Miss Carew said I could always come back. (*Molly drops her face. Beatrice takes her by arms and leads her down a step.*)

BEATRICE: (*Coming close to her*) Molly—you're lying. I know just why you're going and just where you're going.

MOLLY: (*Shrinking back*) Wilson's been taking to you. I hope you don't believe anything—it ain't so—it ain't—

BEATRICE: Oh, don't make it any worse. Don't lie any more.

MOLLY: If she told you any—

BEATRICE: I know. I know about the whole thing. Who the man is and all about it.

MOLLY: What man?

BEATRICE: *The* man. I know everything. Oh don't deny it. (*Molly starts to speak.*) I know every bit of the horrible truth.

MOLLY: Does—he—know—you—know?

BEATRICE: He—will—now.

MOLLY: Oh, don't tell him you know. Don't tell him. Let me git away. I'll get away and never see his face again—so help me God I will. Don't tell him you know. What good would it do? It would be awful. I'll go where nobody'll ever—don't say nothin'—don't let nobody know— For God's sake don't tell his wife— Don't tell Mrs. Bob. What good would it do? Let me get away. (*She falls on her knees clasping Beatrice's knees.*)

BEATRICE: *Molly*! (*With a cry of horror*)

MOLLY: (*Clinging to Beatrice*) It—won't do no harm. Leave me go and don't tell it. He's—he's been so good to me. I'll do anything to make it right. (*Beatrice scarcely able to breathe, stands staring at Molly, who clings to her knees.*) He ain't like the others. I—I—I couldn't help it, Miss Barrington—on my soul I couldn't—He's made me a good girl—I ain't bad. I love him. I love him, I tell you—I love him. I couldn't help it.

BEATRICE: *Don't*! (*Beatrice pushes Molly so violently that Molly falls forward, her hands on the floor, and putting her face on her hands, gives up to her sobs. After a tense moment, Beatrice goes quickly to center door and locks it. Then walks about rapidly for a moment, digging her nails into her palms—at last she speaks in low harsh tone.*)

BEATRICE: Be quiet! Be quiet!

MOLLY: (*Raising herself up*) What are you goin' to do?

BEATRICE: Do? Do? What am I going to do?

MOLLY: Don't blame him. He—he said I must go. That it wasn't right for me to be here.

BEATRICE: What?

MOLLY: Yes, he did. He—don't blame him. He's fine. It ain't hurt nobody. A man can't help it. Oh honest, Miss Barrington, I wouldn't have done it but I love him. He's so different from the others.

BEATRICE: Don't say that again!

MOLLY: You ain't going to let him know—you know—are you? What good would that do? Keep quiet and let me get away. His wife will never know if you don't tell.

BEATRICE: Oh, don't! You—you miserable—what have I done? Don't you *know* what you've done? Don't you know *anything*? What are you made of?

MOLLY: (*Sitting on floor*) Oh, I'm made of flesh and blood. He grabbed me—he kissed me—first—right here in this room, and I love him.

BEATRICE: It isn't true. It isn't true.[48]

IRENE: (*Enter Irene center*) Beatrice! What's the matter?

BEATRICE: Nothing.

IRENE: What has she done?

BEATRICE: Nothing.

IRENE: (*To Molly*) What have you done that has made my sister like this? Tell me because I'm going to know. (*Molly rises.*)

BEATRICE: Molly, I forbid you to speak.

IRENE: She will speak.

BEATRICE: Molly, I forbid it.

IRENE: She *will* speak. Molly go on.

MOLLY: Oh, I'll speak all right. I ain't afraid to tell you. (*Going closer to Irene*) I done just what you expected me to. I went *back* to my fella. (*Pause. Irene goes to seat and sits. Beatrice closes her eyes in relief. Irene sinks into the nearest chair.*) She watched me and caught me. That's all. She caught me sneakin' in this morning.

IRENE: (*Turns her head quickly.*) This morning? (*She rises going to Beatrice—who stares at her in terror.*) Is she telling me the truth? (*Beatrice tries to speak.*)

MOLLY: Of course I am. Do you think she'd lie to you? Uh?— (*She goes above the two women.*) Why should she want to lie to you about me?

IRENE: Yes—in God's name, why should you? (*Rises over left to Beatrice.*) Why should you lie to me about her? (*Taking hold of Beatrice.*) Look at me. Swear to me that she's telling the truth.

BEATRICE: Yes—

MOLLY: Of course it's the truth!

IRENE: (*To Molly, holding Beatrice fiercely*) I don't believe you. There's something—It's not true—you can't look at me—oh! What's the matter with you? Why do you act like this? (*Shaking Beatrice*)

BEATRICE: Oh, you don't understand!

IRENE: (*Backing away*) I know, I know. It's Bob.

BEATRICE: No—

IRENE: I've known it. I've known it. I don't know how—but I—There's something in her eyes. (*Goes to Beatrice.*) You brought her into this house. I'll never forgive you, Bee—never—never!

BEATRICE: Irene—Irene!

IRENE: Send her away! Send her away! She's bad from head to foot.

BEATRICE: Irene, have a little pity.

IRENE: You brought her here and this is what she's done.

BEATRICE: (*Puts arm around Irene.*) She doesn't even know what she's done.

BOB: (*In door center*) What's the matter?

IRENE: It doesn't seem to matter to you that your wife and your mistress are in the same house—but it does to me.

BOB: (*Scarcely able to speak.*) What?

IRENE: Will you send her away or shall I go?

BOB: I don't know what you—

IRENE: Oh yes you do. What are you going to do?

BOB: (*Speaking to Molly and going to right of door*) Go! (*Molly goes up to door center.*)

BEATRICE: Oh—

MOLLY: I'm goin' fast enough. I didn't ask to come. Lord knows I didn't want to. I don't know what you call good and bad—the way you see it—all I want is to get out. You happen to find out one little thing and act like this when it's too late? Are you blind as bats? Don't you live in this world? Don't you know what's goin' on? If you feel like this about it, why don't you stop it? If this is the worst thing your men can do why do you let 'em? Why do you stand fer it and—and there wouldn't *be* any of us.

(*Curtain*)

## Act 4

TIME: An hour later.

SCENE: Bob Barrington's Studio

*The stage is in darkness, with the exception of the electric light from the street, which comes faintly in from the large studio window at right. A clock strikes seven. After a moment, a key is heard turning in the door at center back and Molly cautiously opens the door and enters. She wears a small black hat and long grey coat over a shabby dress.*

*She wears no gloves and carries her suitcase of Act 1. She presses the button at left of door, and the lights are turned on. Throwing the suitcase on the couch at the left of door, she walks to window in a tired broken way and drags the curtains across the window. Then goes slowly across to room at right and throwing the door open, goes back to couch and sitting, unstraps her suit-case. She does all this laboriously with an occasional long trembling sigh and half sob. When the suit-case is open she folds and repacks a few pitiful articles of clothing, sometimes stopping to stare before her, lost in thought. After some moments, she goes into room at left and returns with a bright silk Japanese kimona, which she folds and puts into the suit-case. Staring back into the room she turns to look at the clock and goes to the hall-door to listen. Then starts to room again as Bob unlocks and opens the hall door. Molly stops left center.*

BOB: (*Opening the hall door and stopping as he sees Molly*) What are you doing here?

MOLLY: Getting my things.

BOB: (*Closes curtain and comes to her.*) Well, be quick now and— (*Switches on light and goes down right of table and taking off overcoat and throws it on table.*)

MOLLY: Oh, you're mad at me because you think I give it away. I didn't mean to. That's what I come here to tell you. I'm sorry. I'm so sorry I could die. I don't blame you fer bein' mad—but I couldn't help it.

BOB: Oh, Molly. I'm not blaming you for anything. It doesn't matter, now—

MOLLY: Oh yes it does matter. I'd a had my tongue pulled out by the roots before I'd a done it on purpose.

BOB: (*Walks up and down right.*) Never mind. Don't talk about it.

MOLLY: Of course I know you couldn't stand up for me before the women. But I don't see why you act like this now. I—tell you I'm sorry—

BOB: Good heavens! Can't you understand? Oh no, of course you couldn't. I don't expect you to. Take this money and get away. (*Takes purse from table and puts it in on table.*)

MOLLY: (*Looking as if he had struck her*) You mean you're done with me?

BOB: Oh, Molly, don't look like that. The whole thing's my fault, not yours. I've been a fool. For heaven's sake, don't make a fuss. Be sensible—be sensible and say goodbye. That will take care of you for a long time. *(Pointing to the money)*

MOLLY: Do you think I'd ever come here fer money—when your sister was— Do you think I'd a' come to this studio if I hadn't loved you more than anything on earth?

BOB: Oh no, you didn't love me, Molly. You'll forget me in a week.

MOLLY: That ain't so—and you know it. You got me because you made me think you loved me. Didn't you care a little bit—Mr. Bob—just a little?

BOB: Oh Molly, you're too wise a girl to act this way.

MOLLY: Yes—I guess I'm getting' wise, all right! (*Looking about the room*) Un! When I think of the things you've said to me here. Didn't you even care a little bit? Do you mean I was just a common—wasn't you even stuck on me?

BOB: I've been pretty good to you, haven't I?

MOLLY: And you're payin' me off. Is that it?

BOB: That's it.

MOLLY: God! How easy you say it. At first I thought I couldn't have nothin' to do with you. That it wouldn't be right—then when you said it was, I thought well, what's the use? It must be, if he says so. An' I began to think it was somethin' different. It's the same old thing—now that you're through with me.

BOB: Oh Molly, can't you see?

MOLLY: You say *you've* been a fool. What about me? What did I do to your sister when she was trustin' me? I wish now she'd never took me in. I wish I'd never seen nothing decent or never knew what it was like.

BOB: No, no, Molly—please don't take it this way.

MOLLY: Un! What difference does it make how I take it *now*? What difference does anything make—anyway? I thought I got hold of something kind-a' to go *on*. When you said you loved me, I couldn't a' looked at nobody else then no more than— (*Her voice rises hysterically.*)

COLLIN: (*Knocking at the door without*) Are you there, Bob? It's Ford.

(*After Molly sits, Bob goes up to open door. Bob looks at Molly—she goes into the room at left, closing the door. Bob opens the hall door.*)

BOB: Go in that room—go on. (*Molly exits.*)

COLLIN: (*Coming in*) The women are coming. I dashed on ahead. Irene's bound to see you. I wanted to get at you first. You've got a desperate woman to deal with, Bob. Unless you make nice a clean breast of it—throw yourself in her mercy—you'll lose her—just as sure as you're standing there. Tell her the truth—fight for her forgiveness.

BOB: Of course I'll fight for her forgiveness—but I couldn't tell her the truth.

COLLIN: Why not?

BOB: She couldn't stand it. Women put too much importance on the whole thing. The girl's only been here a few times. I'm not proud of it, you know—but good heavens—I'm no saint and don't pretend to be. Irene knows that.

COLLIN: *I've* been saying just that kind of thing to Irene for the last hour—but the more I talked, the worse damned rot it seemed. Tell her you *know* it's an infernal, low-down thing you've done—that you're ashamed of it and will give the rest of your life to atone for it.

BOB: Don't preach.

COLLIN: I *could* preach for the first time in my life. It's because it's *you*, Bob, that it knocks me. It's because it's come home to *this* family that it seems a different thing altogether. Irene's suffering as I didn't know a woman could. It's all wrong, I tell you—our end of it.

BOB: Do you expect me to be a sniveling hypocrite? I won't tell her stuff I don't believe.

COLLIN: Then *believe* it, man. It's the truth, by God it is. We can excuse ourselves forever with the same old men's excuses—but down at bottom we know the whole game's crooked. (*Goes left center.*)

BOB: This—*is* new—from you.

COLLIN: We go on bluffing about the rights of nature. Nature be damned, I say. It's up to us to us to *control* it. Nothing else gets ahead of us. We don't stop at anything else we want to do—however gigantic it may be. The only thing on earth we give up to and say we can't help is the brute in us—and by heaven we pay a greater price for that—(*Pause—changes tone.*)—It wrecks more ruin than anything else in creation. (*Turns his back on Bob.*) You're getting yours now.

BOB: (*Slight pause.*) Well, I'll take it. You've said enough, Ford.

COLLIN: (*Goes to Bob and places hand on shoulder.*) Forgive me, old man. Don't lose her, Bob. Tell her the whole truth.

BOB: She'll get the truth all right—as I see it. As I *believe* it—as it *is.* (*Collin goes up right center. He throws open the door at left.*) Come here! (*Molly comes out.*)

COLLIN: Good God! (*A pause.*) Get her away. They'll be here any minute. (*He starts for hall door.*)

BOB: Hold on. She'll stay here.

COLLIN: Are you off your head?

MOLLY: Let me go! (*Starts to go.*)

BOB: You'll stay right here, I say.

COLLIN: What the devil do you mean? Do you *want* Irene to find her here?

BOB: Now you keep out of this. I'll see this through in my own way.

COLLIN: You can't do a thing like that!

MOLLY: Oh, let me go, please! (*There is a knock at the hall door.*)

BOB: Open that door! (*Collin hesitates.*) Open it! (*Collin opens the door. Irene enters, followed by Beatrice. Irene stands as if turned to stone. Beatrice stifles a cry. Molly slinks away below window at left. Collin closes the door. A pause.*) Go in there—you two. I want to speak to Irene! (*Beatrice goes in left followed by Collin who closes the door.*)

MOLLY: It ain't what you think.

BOB: Be quiet. And stay there. I found her here and kept her when Collin came. I—I'm going to try—it's hard for men and women to talk to each other honestly about this thing.

IRENE: Oh—let's be honest. Don't be afraid.

BOB: Look at that girl. Look at her. If it were someone I could be in love with I could understand your caring. But she—and what she represents means nothing personal to a man—

IRENE: Go on.

BOB: This girl hasn't anything more to do with you and me than the wind that blows.

IRENE: Oh! If *this* has nothing to do with you and me—then what has? What are we supposed to be to each other? Just what *should* I expect *of you*? Tell me. I want to know.

BOB: You're my wife—that sets you aside from every other woman on earth. I love you. I'm more sorry and ashamed of this than I can ever tell you, but oh, dear girl—it—there's nothing personal in it. If—if you could only *see* it that way—you—you wouldn't care—so much. It takes nothing from *you*—doesn't mean disloyalty. It doesn't *exist* so far as you and I are concerned. (*Molly gradually moves down and sits on stool, crushed.*) Don't think I don't know all that—and just how it seems to you. But Irene, dear—I—my God I—love you. I'm sorry. It only *happened*. It's over. Try to forgive me.

IRENE: Is that all?

BOB: Oh—it all comes down to the same old thing—men are men and women are women. Be a little—don't be too hard on me, Irene—try to understand. Oh, my dear girl,—we're not the same, I tell you—and we're not to blame for the way we're made. You stand there, a cold-blooded saint and condemn me—because you don't understand.

IRENE: That's not so.

BOB: (*Goes to Irene.*) Oh yes it is. Do you think for a minute if you had the same amount of animal passion in your make-up that I have—you'd blame me so—for this? You don't know. Your pulses beat evenly and slowly. You don't know what a man resists. You don't understand but you ought to *try* to. You're good because you don't want to be anything else—you couldn't if you tried. (*Goes down right.*)

IRENE: Don't be so mistaken. Don't count so much on the slow, even pulses of a woman—don't be so sure of the cool blood in her veins. I've kept myself for you—because I married you. I've *made* you the one man—not because no one else has ever stirred me—not because I'm not just as strong and healthy an animal as you are—but because of *you—you.* If you and I had begun the same—as boy and girl—if I'd taken the same liberties with my life that you've taken with yours, I'd be just as you are now. If you had lived as I have with the same ideals and control, the same dreams of what you might be to one woman—of what your children would be— (*Bob moans*) you'd be just as I am now. I've stifled and choked and hidden my fears about you. I've cackled the same stuff about a man's nature that most women do—but I know now they're all lies. They've come home to me—They're beating me in the face. They're lies. You're unclean—as *I* would be if I had done what you have. You've defiled yourself. You've been a beast not because it was not necessary, but because you let yourself. You're not my husband. I should despise myself if I ever called you that again. (*Bob turns to face her.*)

BOB: Irene! Irene!

IRENE: Don't touch me! I loathe you. Don't come near me!

BOB: Irene—Irene, forgive me.

IRENE: No—no—no! I can't.

BOB: Irene, I love you.

IRENE: We can't go on.

BOB: Above anything else on earth.

IRENE: It would always be the same.

BOB: Try to forgive me?

IRENE: I can't, I can't, I can't. (*Beatrice and Collin enter from left center.*)

BEATRICE: Irene. Irene.

MOLLY: Oh wait! I didn't know what I was doing. I didn't mean to hurt you. I didn't know what I done was as bad as this. Don't let two people like you break your hearts for a thing like me.

(*Beatrice motions to Collin, who advances and takes Irene out. He closes the door.*)

COLLIN: (*Following Irene*) Come home to her, Bob. (*He goes out, closing the door.*)

BOB: (*To Beatrice, who is looking at Molly.*) This is what you've done with your confounded ideas.

BEATRICE: There's only *one* thing to blame me for and that's for driving that girl out of the house for not defending her before you all and telling her *then* that I *did not* hold her responsible for all that's happened—but *you* entirely.

MOLLY: Do you mean that, Miss Barrington?

BEATRICE: I do. (*Placing her arms about Molly's shoulder*)

MOLLY: That means more than all you ever said to me put together. I never thought I was a real human being to you before. I always thought you was just experimenting on me. Do you think that don't put something new into me?

BEATRICE: Come with me now, Molly! I'm going to take you back to Miss Carew for tonight.

MOLLY: Only fer tonight then, Miss Barrington. I can't stay shut up no more. I want to stand on my own feet. I want to be alone and feel safe. I want to true to *myself*. Do you know what I mean?

BEATRICE: Yes, Molly.

MOLLY: If I can't go straight by myself now—*you* never can make me. You said I ought to have something to say to other girls—well, I guess I've got it now all right. I'd like to tell every girl on earth what I know now. (*She takes up the suit-case and opening the door goes out.*)[49]

(*Curtain*)

# *My Little Sister* by Elizabeth Robins

BEFORE *Ourselves* opened on Broadway, Elizabeth Robins—actress, activist, and author—was penning her own narrative about white slavery. Widely billed as based on a true story and known in the United States as *My Little Sister*, the novel portrayed two innocent young Englishwomen who are tricked by a madam posing as their aunt and lured to a brothel.[1] An abbreviated version of the novel was first serialized as a short story in *McClure's Magazine* in two installments: in December 1912 and January 1913 (see fig. 4). It then appeared as *Where Are You Going To . . . ?* in Britain.[2] Hugely popular, *My Little Sister* entered its fourth edition in just one month and was promoted as "the most widely discussed novel in New York."[3] Given the success of the novel, Robins had great hopes that a dramatic version would be staged in New York and London. Yet *My Little Sister* never made it to production for reasons that have never been explained in print. As the version of the play in this volume clearly demonstrates, the problem was not the quality of the script. Rather, the play became embroiled in a tangle of powerful social, legal, and obscenity controversies about the "proper" representation of prostitution and sexuality, culminating in its rejection by a major U.S. theatre producer and the Lord Chamberlain (the official theatrical licenser) in the United Kingdom. That this narrative never made it to the stage, after achieving astonishing popularity as a novel, is a testament to the power of the theatre as a vehicle for political and social debate, showing why it was so carefully guarded. The story of Robins's struggle to mount her drama—which is told below for the first time—reveals much about the powerful forces that affected representations of sexuality in the early twentieth century and shows why her still unstaged drama is an essential cultural artifact of Progressive-Era U.S. culture.

The novel version of *My Little Sister* became known in the United States as "The Story You Can't Forget," charging citizens to hear "the wail of our little sisters—thousands and thousands of them, every year, in every land, beaten, duped, drugged and held for ever in vilest bondage til death releases."[4] One

FIGURE 4. Illustration of the white slave abduction scene by William Berger from the serialization of "My Little Sister" in *McClure's Magazine* (December 1912).

article in the *New York Times* noted: "There is a great deal of discussion in progress concerning white slavery, statistics are published, papers are read, resolutions taken. . . . But how many of us are really vitally touched or interested?" Robins's novel provided a vivid and emotionally compelling portrayal of a problem that had been primarily depicted in relatively detached newspaper articles. "No one who reads Elizabeth Robins's *My Little Sister*," the article continued, "will thereafter consider the white slave traffic with the mind alone."[5] The novel's pathos was tied to the well-publicized fact that it was based on a true story. In one letter to a fellow suffragette, Harriet Burton Laidlaw, Robins wrote: "Of all the official people I consulted, not one of these experts doubted my story, and *all had known similar cases.* . . . If you will consult the findings of your own commissions you will see that in America 'no girl of any class is safe.'" Public discourse was often motivated by the apparent "Danger! Danger! Danger!" of white slavery.[6] Yet this danger was primarily represented as a threat to upper-class white women. Unlike the girls in *Ourselves*, who are largely lower class and slide into prostitution out of desperation, Robins's central characters are innocent middle-class girls who are abducted into white slavery. Class had everything to do with each narrative's success or failure.

In developing the story, Robins went undercover in London, wearing a Salvation Army uniform while walking the streets of Piccadilly, where she hoped to speak with prostitutes.[7] While this experience gave her material for her story, it also revealed the limits of her experiment. A Scottish prostitute whom Robins encountered on the street and whom she implored to visit her the next day never showed. Robins's diaries, as Sue Thomas has revealed, express not only her profound disappointment, but also her inability to comprehend "the reluctance of prostitutes to become the objects of cross-class female chivalry."[8] Interviewing prostitutes as part of performance research is not without precedent among American actresses: Mrs. Leslie Carter did it to prepare for her role in *Zaza* in 1898; Minnie Maddern Fiske roamed the streets before starring in *Salvation Nell* in 1908; and Pauline Lord did the same while in preparation for "*Anna Christie*" in 1921.

As the white slave season heated up on Broadway in 1913, and just before the Fifth International Congress for the Suppression of the White Slave Traffic was held in London in 1913, Robins turned to adapting her novel for the stage.[9] Several factors conspired to doom production of the play, in spite of the novel's intense success. The first had to do with the struggle over a dramatic adaptation. In fact, Robins's adaptation was not entirely her own.

According to biographer Angela V. John, Robins collaborated with John Masefield in 1912 in her earliest writing about white slavery (both as drama and as novel).[10] When Robins became too ill to work on her own dramatization in 1913, she asked Cecily Hamilton to adapt her novel for the stage. As much as the two women admired each other's work, however, Robins was dissatisfied with Hamilton's dramatization. In her edits of Hamilton's draft, Robins repeatedly called it "abominable."[11] Robins was not alone in this critical assessment. In a letter to Robins mysteriously signed "W" (most likely from theatre critic William Archer), the writer remarks, "I am rather surprised that C.H's [Cicely Hamilton's] work is not better—it is not really skillful at any point. Even if (by miracle) you and she were to accept my scenario, I don't think you could trust her to write the dialogue without careful and full revision."[12] If "W" is indeed William Archer, then he may have been a third, though anonymous, collaborator on the script. While it is uncertain whether his dramatic suggestions were adopted, it is clear that he advised Robins on this project for over a year. Ample evidence suggests that other collaborators may have helped shape the script as well.[13]

While the adaptation was taken on by Hamilton, Robins's first focus was getting produced in New York. She tried to negotiate a contract with Charles Frohman, a powerful theatre producer of the Syndicate, but failed to lock down a deal.[14] The failure is puzzling: Frohman's manager, Alf Hayman, announced in a prominent *New York Times* piece upon his return from England that he had piles of manuscripts in his bag, including Robins's drama.[15] This announcement was well covered in magazines such as *Munsey's*, *Theatre Magazine*, and *Field Illustrated*.[16] The *New York Dramatic Mirror* reported not only that Frohman had secured the rights to Robins's play, but also that "in its dramatized form, the play will be presented in England and America."[17]

Given such advance marketing and the popularity of white slave dramas in general, why did Frohman pass on *My Little Sister*? It would have been a fine addition to the eighteen shows that he produced in 1913. Was Frohman afraid that *My Little Sister* might be censored, like other white slave plays?

I suspect that Frohman—like the Lord Chamberlain a few months later—rejected Robins's play because of its radical full-length brothel scene (a point to which I will return) and its indictment of upper-class men and police for being complicit with prostitution. Robins felt that Frohman would not have rejected Hamilton's version of the script had it been rendered more skillfully.[18] So she began shopping around her own script and eventually approached the Women's Theatre in London, under the direction of the Actresses Franchise League. Although Robins claimed that Hamilton had given her permission to rewrite the dramatization, a battle involving herself, Hamilton, and the Women's Theatre would soon ensue, thereby burying the project forever.

The biggest difference between Hamilton's and Robins's versions of *My Little Sister* has to do with their respective endings. Ironically, Hamilton's version was more faithful to Robins's novel, ending with the grim death of Bettina, the younger of the two captured sisters, who never escapes sexual slavery. Hamilton's playscript ends with these sobering lines from Bettina's sister, Honor, who manages to flee from the brothel: "It's over then—it's over. . . . I shan't have to lie awake any more—I shan't have to lie in the night and think of her, think of her, think of her. . . . She's dead—and God has had mercy (*she falls on her knees sobbing*)."[19] Seeing death as liberation from the "living hell" of forced prostitution, Honor ends Hamilton's version of the play by reciting the opening lines from the Lord's Prayer.

Though it was faithful to her novel, Robins did not like this ending. She wanted a happier version that audiences would "tolerate," as she put it. In a letter to Jerome K. Jerome, a script doctor of sorts, Robins explains: "I tried myself to persuade her [Cicely Hamilton] she was mistaken to adhere so rigidly to the book. The unrelieved horror of the novel would never be tolerated by an audience. That was why I rewrote her version—of course with her permission."[20] Robins thus revised her own story so that Bettina is melodramatically saved just minutes before she is shipped abroad into sexual slavery. Robins's fourth act invents a new scene on board a ship, in which the detective, Bettina's fiancé, and Honor all confront the madam (called Grey Hawk) as she tries to sneak the drugged Bettina on board. Robins's ending is more melodramatic, allowing for a dramatic confrontation with the villains and a thrilling recovery of Bettina. It would have been perfect for the stage.

Yet Robins's repeated efforts to get her script staged ultimately backfired. Ironically, Hamilton's version, which was truer to Robins's novel, was the one that interested the Women's Theatre of London.[21] Members of the theatre were in fact unaware that Robins had a version herself until she presented it later on. The letters exchanged between Inez Bensusan of the Women's Theatre and Robins document delicate negotiations between the competing scripts.[22] Throughout the process, Robins balked at moving forward with the Women's Theatre, which had already circulated a press release announcing its production of Cecily Hamilton's adaptation. Wanting her version to be the one produced, Robins stalled the Women's Theatre and reached out to other producers.[23] In spite of her feminist inclinations, Robins hoped to find not only a "better" venue than the Women's Theatre, but also one that would take *her* script. After months of negotiations, however, Robins's agent, G. Golding Bright, had worked out concrete terms for *My Little Sister*, to which the Women's Theatre and Robins agreed.[24] The Women's Theatre then sent the play to the Lord Chamberlain for approval, fully anticipating that it would pass.[25] As if doomed from the start, however, *My Little Sister* was denied license on 10 August 1914, just five days after Robins secured her contract with the Women's Theatre.

Why did the Lord Chamberlain withhold approval? Joanne Gates suggests that the cause was the outbreak of the war, but I remain unconvinced that this was a primary reason.[26] Sue Thomas has speculated that George Bernard Shaw's *Mrs Warren's Profession*, which had yet to be licensed in the United Kingdom, was preventing other brothel dramas from being approved. "If *My Little Sister* were licensed," Thomas explains, "nothing would stop Shaw from arguing persuasively for Kitty Warren to take to the stage."[27] While I would agree in part, I would add another reason why *My Little Sister* was censored: it contained an extensive brothel scene. Whereas in the novel version the girls don't get nabbed by the madam posing as their aunt and tricked into the brothel until page 256 (more than three-fourths of the way into the book), the dramatic adaptations by both Hamilton and Robins set the brothel scene in the middle of the play. It occupies the entire second act. This second act contains a riveting exchange, culminating in a sensational escape scene in which one of the male clients in the brothel reveals to Honor that she is "in one of the most infamous houses in Europe" and facilitates her rescue. But in order to get out safely, she must leave her sister behind (see fig. 4). Given the widespread censoring of brothel interiors from white slave plays during the 1913–1914 season, this mise-en-scène was too volatile for the licenser and most producers to condone it. In addition to Robins's sensational portrayal of a brothel, *My Little Sister* also depicts the complicity of the police and a bourgeois male clientele in allowing brothels to flourish in the middle of the city—a detail also based on true accounts.

The limited scholarship on *My Little Sister* has focused almost exclusively on Robins's novel, not realizing that her dramatic version existed or was different.[28] Though never performed, Robins's drama provides crucial insights into international obscenity and sex debates. As a novel, *My Little Sister*'s capacity to ignite national pathos over white slavery was characterized by historian Mark Sullivan in 1926 as similar to the role that *Uncle Tom's Cabin* played in sparking national concern about slavery, although its reach was obviously much more limited.[29] The novel launched important discussions about white slavery throughout U.S. culture, including—most ironically—prompting the white slave genre of the 1913 season.[30] The ultimate irony is that Robins shaped Broadway's white slave season at the very moment that her script was rejected. If the theatrical staging failed, however, the dramatization did have some celluloid success. *My Little Sister* was made into a five-reel film in 1919 featuring Evelyn Nesbit, though no known version remains.[31] The script of *My Little Sister*, in print for the first time here, allows us to give this drama the scholarly and artistic attention that it deserves as an overlooked important antecedent to modern theatre and an artifact of the white slave panic.

• • •

Despite repeated efforts by Robins, *My Little Sister* (1913) was never performed.

# *My Little Sister*

by Elizabeth Robins

CHARACTERS:

MRS. DORRIEN
HONOR, *her daughter*
BETTINA, *her daughter*
RANNY DALLAS
ERIC ANNAN, M.D.
MADAME AURORE, a dressmaker
THE "GREY HAWK"
"THE TARTAR," *Mr. Guy Whitby-Dawson*
AN UNKNOWN MAN
MRS. HARBOROUGH
MRS. SELBY, *Ranny's sister, Janet*
HERMIONE HELMSTONE
AN INSPECTOR OF POLICE
MACDOUGAL, a detective
VALET, *to the "Tartar"*
HOLLIDAY, *Mrs. Harborough's butler*
FOOTMAN *at the "Grey Hawk's" house*
MARTHA, *a former parlour-maid*
CARRON, *the "Grey Hawk's" maid*
STEWARD, STEWARDESS, BEARERS, etc.

## Act I

SCENE: *The drawing room at "Duncombe." Long windows opening on to a country garden. The table is scattered with the paraphernalia of dress-making. As the curtain rises, Bettina is discovered standing in the middle of the room having a lining pinned on to her by Madame Aurore, who kneels beside her. Bettina's dress, which she has taken off, is thrown over the back of a chair.*[32]

MADAME AURORE: If you do not stand still, Mademoiselle Bettina, 'ow am I evare going to make your dress fit you properly?

BETTINA: Oh, I am standing still.

MADAME AURORE: *Mais non.* First one foot, den de other—nevare for one moment are you quiet.

BETTINA: Well, I'm sorry and I'll try to stand on both feet at once . . . I do hate having dresses tried on. Thank goodness, this is the last.

MADAME AURORE: Tank goodness eet is. First you sigh, and den you viggle—eet is like trying to fit a serpent. (*Despairingly*) And now you laugh to shake de pins out—Why?

BETTINA: I was only wondering what a serpent would look like having its clothes tried on.

MADAME AURORE: I don't know vhat eet vould look like but I know vhat eet would feel like under de hand— Joost like you.

BETTINA: Don't be cross! Be my kind, little Madame Aurore and talk to me about London—only, not too loud, please.

MADAME AURORE: Dis veek dat I have been here to make you clo'se, I have done nodding but talk to you about London.

BETTINA: Well, talk some more.

MADAME AURORE: Haf I not tol' you London ees a lovely place where you look in de shops all de afternoon, where you dance all de night and vhere de young men, dey mek loaf to you all de time.

BETTINA: But I know that much. What I want to know— (*She glances over her shoulder out of window.*)

MADAME AURORE: Vhy you viggle like dat?

BETTINA: Oh, was I? Well, go on. London.

MADAME AURORE: No need for me to talk now about London. On Tursday you see eet for yourself.

BETTINA: Yes, on Thursday I shall see it for myself. *(Business)* London Town, London Town, I am going to London Town.

MADAME AURORE: (*Despairingly*) And now she sing and dance.

BETTINA: (*Has put her hand over her mouth, conscience-stricken.*) I forgot Mother. And being tried on, too! But I will be good now. I really will. (*Stands erect and still.*)

MADAME AURORE: (*Grunts, sticks in pins.*) Den we go upstairs—you and I—and show your modair de gown ve feenish las' night.

BETTINA: We can't. She's asleep.

MADAME AURORE: Vell, so soon she vake up.

BETTINA: *(Hesitating)* I'd better go alone if you don't mind.

MADAME AURORE: (*Suspiciously*) Why you vill go alone?

BETTINA: (*Embarrassed*) She—my mother isn't well enough—to have many people in the room at once.

MADAME AURORE: (*Slight pause.*) Your modair not like me ver' mooch, *hein*?[33]

BETTINA: (*Still more embarrassed*) Oh Madame Aurore—why should you think that?

MADAME AURORE: (*Snorts.*) I am good enough for to mek clo'es for de daughter of Lady Helmstone—

BETTINA: Oh yes! Hermione is very proud of discovering such a genius!

MADAME AURORE: (*Slightly mollified*) Pity de only frien's you got, dey go 'vey! (*Lugubriously*) So terrible lonely, dis place.

(*The shoddy-smart figure of Martha appears lurking outside of window to which Bettina's back is turned. Aurore makes signs. Martha moves towards shrubbery.*)

BETTINA: Yes, it is frightfully lonely when the Helmstone's aren't here. (*Turns her head.*)

MADAME AURORE: (*Nervously*) Vhy you viggle like dat!

BETTINA: Oh I'm sorry.

MADAME AURORE: You expec' someone?

BETTINA: I only thought, maybe Ranny—Mr. Dallas . . .

MADAME AURORE: Dat de friend of Miss Hermione Helmstone?

BETTINA: He is my friend just as much.

MADAME AURORE: So.

BETTINA: You don't believe that?

MADAME AURORE: He haf to mek de grand marriage, *n'est ce pas*? He vill haf de title, *hein*?

BETTINA: Does that prevent his being my friend?

MADAME AURORE: Oh vell. (*Dismissing him*) He is joost a boy.

BETTINA: Ranny is older than he looks.

(*Martha reappears, hurriedly retracing her steps. Aurore makes furious signs. Martha signals back "some one coming."*)

RANNY: (*Heard off*) Bettina!

BETTINA: (*With scream*) There he is! (*Martha vanishes. Bettina slips from under Aurore's hands, pulls the white curtain round her, puts her head out of window.*) *Sh!* (*She points up.*) *Asleep!*

MADAME AURORE: (*Masking her own jumpy nervousness*) Ah, dis 'ouse! Eet is: "hosh! And go sof!—and please to not disturb my modair!" And den de scream and de . . . (*Makes a little hop and raves her arms.*) Oh, *mon dieu*!

RANNY: (*Voice from opposite direction in which Martha vanished*) Where are you, Betty?

BETTINA: In the drawing-room, on account of the long glass, but you mustn't come in.

RANNY: (*Nearer, but not visible*) Oh—why not?

BETTINA: I'm being tried on.

MADAME AURORE: Oh, ees dat so?

BETTINA: You must wait there in the garden.

MADAME AURORE: Come Mademoiselle! Ah!—let de pore young gentleman 'ave a seat in de 'all!

BETTINA: (*Calls.*) Yes, the hall!

RANNY: Garden will do me. I'll sit here on the grass till you're in a condition to receive visitors.

BETTINA: (*Drawing in her head*) All right, I shan't be long.

RANNY: I've got something to tell you—something important.

MADAME AURORE: Turn leetle—dis vay—

BETTINA: Mr. Dallas is going up to London too.

MADAME AURORE: (*Starting*) Mr. Dallas is—

BETTINA: Oh, you did prick me, you wicked woman—and I wasn't moving a bit.

MADAME AURORE: I am sorry—my hand slip—I do hope I haf not hurt you . . . What was dat you say about Mr. Dallas going up to London? Den he travel vid you, I suppose?

BETTINA: Oh no. He's going up to-morrow—we aren't going till Thursday.

MADAME AURORE: Ah— (*Acts condolingly*) den he vill not travel with you! But perhaps he vill meet you at the station—you have arrange zat, *hein*?

BETTINA: Oh dear, no—Aunt Josephine is going to meet us at the station. We've written to let her know the train.

MADAME AURORE: Dat good von—*hein*? De five-twelve at Victoria?

BETTINA: That's it.

MADAME AURORE: Lif' de arrum please. So, your Aunt Josephine she vill meet you vid her automobile.

BETTINA: If she has one.

MADAME AURORE: She 'as one, for certain. All rich people dey 'ave automobile in dese days.

BETTINA: I'm sure I don't know if Aunt Josephine is what you call rich.

MADAME AURORE: Of course she is rich. Dose ouses vhere she live—dat

Lowndes Sqvare—dey are not sheap, I tell you.[34] Besides, did you not say to me dat she pay for all your dresses to go to stay vid her? You take my vord—she have plenty of money, your aunt.

BETTINA: Well, even if she isn't rich she can't be poor like we are.

MADAME AURORE: Poor—you are not poor.

BETTINA: Oh—that's all you know.

MADAME AURORE: If you did not have a penny to your back you need not be poor—not you.

BETTINA: What do you mean?

MADAME AURORE: Ah, you know. Vhat is dat song you are always singing, *hein*? "My face is my fortune, sir, she said!"

BETTINA: (*Laughing, a little embarrassed*) Oh, that's what you mean.

MADAME AURORE: Yes, dat's vhat I mean . . . You 'ave a very good fortune and you know eet, you! . . . A man, he have his fortune in his head or his hands—a voman she have her fortune in her face. You are not like me . . . Vork, vork! Nodding but vork from breakfas' to bed-time. An' de rich ladies come and say: "Dear Madame Aurore, vill you mek me a gown for less dis time? Dis de off season," dey say. Or: "I loss my money at de bridge." *Hein*?

BETTINA: Well, we did not ask you to take less and we are not "rich ladies."

MADAME AURORE: Not rich! *Hein*? Dat's as you like. If I vas young and pretty like you, I vould not be sticking pins into linings—not me!

BETTINA: Well, if I've got such a valuable face I'd better sell it next time poor mummy's hard up.

MADAME AURORE: (*Drily*) Eet has been done.

BETTINA: (*Looking at her curiously*) You do say funny things sometimes.

MADAME AURORE: Do I? . . . I tell you vhat seems to me funny.

BETTINA: What's that?

MADAME AURORE: Dat your Aunt Josephine is your fader's sister and live only two—tree hour away in de train and dat you hav never seen her.

BETTINA: Oh—well—you see—

MADAME AURORE: She fin' your modair leedle hard to get on vid, *hein*?

BETTINA: Oh no, whatever happened it wasn't mother's fault.

MADAME AURORE: *Non non*, nevair!

BETTINA: And you can see she means to be kind—by her asking us to stay and paying for our new dresses. And Mother says she has no quarrel with her and we're to make up our minds to like her very much. And I'm going to.

MADAME AURORE: Qvite right. But still eet is funny to tink that you have nevare seen her. How vill you know her vhen you meet her at de station on Thursday?

BETTINA: Oh, she'll be looking out for us and we shall be looking out for her . . . Besides, we've got an old photograph of her somewhere.

MADAME AURORE: (*Alert*) 'Ave you? Vhere?

BETTINA: Would you like to see it? Where's mother's old album? . . . (*Puts out a hand to little table in front of open window piled with sewing—notices the bushes move; calls softly.*) Ranny you can't come yet— (*Hurriedly draws back.*) Gracious. Martha, again!

MADAME AURORE: Marta— Who is dat?

BETTINA: Ssh! An old parlour-maid of ours.

MADAME AURORE: Vell, vhat if eet ees "Marta"?

BETTINA: (*Gravely*) She oughtn't to come here.

MADAME AURORE: Vhy, she not ought to come?

BETTINA: Because my Mother had to dismiss her. Oh, it was dreadful. Mother gave her only an hour to get out of the house.

MADAME AURORE: (*In a hard voice*) Vhy she do dat?

BETTINA: (*A little anxiously*) I never quite knew. Our old cook said Martha "had gone down."

MADAME AURORE: (*Still surreptitiously watching the window*) Vell, she look like she hav come up.

BETTINA: Yes, didn't she? Such fine clothes! But I knew her the moment I saw her last Sunday. It was dreadful to go by without speaking.

MADAME AURORE: Not speak . . . ?

BETTINA: Mother said we weren't to. I never "cut" anybody before. It was horrid. (*Bettina cranes her neck.*) Don't you think I ought to ring the bell and let the cook know?

MADAME AURORE: Know vhat?

BETTINA: That Martha isn't to hang about here.

MADAME AURORE: (*Glancing out of window*) Oh, she go now—out de side gate.

BETTINA: (*Anxiously*) I do hope Mother won't see her.

MADAME AURORE: (*Maliciously*) Your modair get a shock, *hein*? (*Suddenly*) Vhy she send a girl off like dat vid no character?

BETTINA: Oh, I don't think she did that.

MADAME AURORE: (*Harshly*) Yes!

BETTINA: (*Surprised*) Why, how do *you* know?

MADAME AURORE: Did you not say—

BETTINA: No, I only said "at an hour's notice."

MADAME AURORE: Oh den, I mek a mistake. *Pairhaps.*

RANNY: (*Calls.*) I say, isn't that dress finished yet? It's beastly hot and there seems to be an ant's nest all over your lawn. I've had to move on twice.

(*Aurore glances out anxiously.*)

BETTINA: (*Calls.*) Oh, you poor thing—! (*To Madame Aurore*) Shall you be much longer?

MADAME AURORE: I haf feenish. (*Rapidly unpinning*)

BETTINA: That's a blessing. (*Gets out of lining.*) Tho' how you can let it get it done between now and to-morrow night—!

MADAME AURORE: Oh in dese days! Ve mek a dress vid tree yard chiffon (*Brisk cutting action in the air*) and four stiches (*Imitates lighting quick sewing*). *Hein?*

(*Business. Sound of door bell. Enter Honor, who runs through the drawing-room saying: "Dr. Annan." Exit to take him upstairs.*)[35]

MADAME AURORE: An de photographie.

BETTINA: Photographie?

MADAME AURORE: Of your Aunt—de von you vould show me.

BETTINA: Oh, yes. While you hook me, I'll have a look. (*Standing by little table, sweeps the work of the album.*)

RANNY: (*Voice quite near*) I say! I'm not going to stand it. If that fella Annan can come in, I can.

BETTINA: Why I never heard the like. *You're* not the doctor. Well, he *shall* come in, poor boy. Come and have a look at Aunt Josephine.

RANNY: (*Enter Dallas.*) Look at who?

BETTINA: Aunt Josephine. I'm showing her to Madame Aurore.

RANNY: With her best pearl earrings on.

BETTINA: I rather like long pearl earrings, don't you? I don't wonder Mother said she always wore them.

MADAME AURORE: (*Bending over the photograph*) Ah—always so?

BETTINA: And the way her hair's done too—rolled back.

MADAME AURORE: Dat is very distinctif—very.

RANNY: Pretty much of an antique. I don't expect she's like that now.

BETTINA: Perhaps not; it's nearly twenty years old.

RANNY: By the way, did you hear me call out that I'd something important to tell you?

BETTINA: Yes, what is it?

RANNY: You remember my sister, Janet—you met her once at the Helmstone's?

BETTINA: Mrs. Selby?

RANNY: (*Nods.*) I've just found out that she knows your aunt.

BETTINA: *Does* she? (*She shuts the album without noticing that Madame Aurore is still looking at the photograph.*) Not really. (*She moves away from the table with Ranny. Madame Aurore gathers up her work things slowly, listening to them as they talk.*)

RANNY: Yes, only just found it out! I mentioned your aunt's name in a letter of mine—said you were going to stay with her—and Janet's written back to say she knows Mr. Harborough quite well.

BETTINA: Ranny, how exciting. And does your sister like her?

RANNY: Ra-*ther*! What's more, Janet says she'll introduce me.

BETTINA: Oh!

RANNY: (*Lowering his voice*) And she says that while you're there, she thinks she can get your aunt to ask me to dinner . . . You wouldn't mind if she did.

BETTINA: Oh no—I shouldn't mind.

RANNY: We might be able to see a good deal of each other while you're in town.

BETTINA: Yes, we might.

RANNY: I know I can depend on Janet. She's giving a dance next month—

BETTINA: And will she ask Honor and me?— How lovely!

RANNY: Of course she will. That's to say if you'll promise—

BETTINA: What?

RANNY: Not to dance with anyone more than you do with me.

BETTINA: (*Laughing and turning away from him up to window*) I'll see about that when we get the invitation. There may be someone there who dances beautifully.

RANNY: I dance beautifully.

BETTINA: Oh, oh—who nearly fell down with Hermione at the Helmstone dance last week? (*Exit into the garden, laughing and running.*)

RANNY: Oh, I say—and whose fault was that—? (*He follows her into the garden.*)

(*While they have been talking, Madame Aurore has made a show of gathering together her linings, pins, etc., as if about to leave the room with them. As Bettina and Ranny go out, she puts down her bundle and follows them to the window and peers out after them. Then, returning to the table, she opens the album, hastily turns over the pages and is about to take out the picture of Aunt Josephine, when, hearing a step in the passage, she struggles to get the thing out and fails, swears, wheels about and catches up some ribbons—winds up in nervous jerks, eyes on the door. Enter Martha.*)

MADAME AURORE: (*Whispers.*) Oh! *You* 'ave de courage, you! (*Lowers her voice.*) Miss Honour, she in and out—vatching for de doctor—

MARTHA: (*Gently*) I should rather like to see Miss Honor.

MADAME AURORE: *Hein*! Maybe you like as vell if your old mistress catch you—

MARTHA: She shan't catch me! Tho' I wouldn't mind telling her before I die vhat I think of her.

MADAME AURORE: Vat good, dat? Better get even.

MARTHA: Get even?

MADAME AURORE: (*Nods.*)

MARTHA: How get even?

MADAME AURORE: (*Nervous, listening*) I tell you to-night. (*Returns to album, abstracts photograph.*)

MARTHA: Oh, to-night! I'm out of this dull hole by the afternoon train.

MADAME AURORE: No! London?

MARTHA: (*Nods.*) I only came to say good-bye.

MADAME AURORE: (*Feverishly*) You *moss* not go yet. I need you here, I tell you, *here*! Oh, I vill pay. Listen. I go vay. Young ladies go vay. Vhen dey gone you shall send telegram to London.

MARTHA: What shall I—

MADAME AURORE: Sh! Qvick! I come!

(*Bundles Martha out by kitchen passage and picks up pins as enter Honor and Hermione, the latter wearing a hat and somewhat extravagantly got up. Honor goes to table and picks up and examines the work.*)

MADAME AURORE: Mademoiselle!

HERMIONE: (*A little brusque*) How d' you do, Madame Aurore. What's the matter?

MADAME AURORE: De beautiful family party on de yacht, it ess not to be? Aw . . . (*Condoling*)

HERMIONE: (*Shortly*) We are all off to-morrow. (*Looks at her watch.*) I'm afraid I can't wait for your Mother to wake up.

HONOR: Yes, I know she would be disappointed. Still, if Mother is really ill—

MADAME AURORE: I tell you she count de hours. She tell me joost now dat de train vas settle, and she jump for joy. And de dresses all ready. And dere is your aunt—She 'ave arrange dat you go Tursday—she have wrote and settled—

HERMIONE: (*A little astonished at Madame Aurore's excitement*) Still, I don't suppose a day or two would make any difference to their Aunt.

MADAME AURORE: (*Noticing Hermione's surprise and pulling herself together.*) Even to her eet might be inconvenient. But eet is (*Addressing herself to Honor*) of your poor little sister dat I think—so impatient and so happy for de journey. I tell you she cry her pretty eyes out. Eet goes to my heart that she should be disappointed—I have took such a fancy to her . . . And I have vork so hard vith de dresses, me—dat dey should be all ready for Tursday.

HONOR: (*Kindly*) I'm sure you have.

HERMIONE: (*Half aside to Honor*) By the way, where is that photograph—?

MADAME AURORE: (*Exhibits consternation*)

HONOR: Aunt Josephine? It's here.

HERMIONE: No, I don't mean Aunt—

HONOR: Why, it's gone. Someone has taken it out. Has Bettina taken Aunt Josephine out?

MADAME AURORE: (*Cheerfully*) She vant to show eet to Mr. Dallas.

HERMIONE: I mean the photograph of Guy Whitby-Dawson.

MADAME AURORE: (*Relieved, withdraws with her sewing to other side of room.*)

HONOR: (*At mantelpiece*) Here it is.

HERMIONE: You hid it.

HONOR: Oh I—

HERMIONE: Well, I'll do better. (*Tears it across.*)

HONOR: Oh, Hermione.

HERMIONE: (*Tears it in smaller pieces.*) There's *that*!

HONOR: What does it mean? (*Pause.*) Have you broken with Mr. Whitby-Dawson? (*Hermione nods.*) Why have you?

HERMIONE: Oh, he thinks we won't have enough to live on.

HONOR: (*Takes her hand.*) I'm so glad.

HERMIONE: Glad? Why are you glad?

HONOR: Of course I've only seen his photograph but . . . I never dared tell you what an evil face we thought it—mother and I.

(*Enter Eric Annan. He smiles and nods at Honor; shakes hands with Hermione.*)

ANNAN: How do you do? I thought you'd all of you, gone—

HERMIONE: Still twenty-four hours grace.

ANNAN: Grace?

HERMIONE: Yes, time for you to change your mind and come too.

ANNAN: Oh, that's wildly impossible. Fathom's deep in work. (*To Honor*) Are you busy, or can I have a word with you? (*He glances at Madame Aurore.*)

MADAME AURORE: (*Gathering up her things*) I am joos going—joost—Tank you—tank you. (*Exit Aurore.*)

ANNAN: (*Closing door behind her*) Who is that?

HONOR: Madame Aurore, our dressmaker.

HERMIONE: —Little creature I picked up in London.

ANNAN: Don't like the look of her.

HERMIONE: We don't engage her for her looks. She can sew like an angel. And she's cheap. That's the great thing! She's extraordinarily cheap.

ANNAN: H'm. Well, (*Takes out his watch*) it wasn't the dressmaker I wanted to talk to you about. It's your Mother, Miss Dorrien.

HERMIONE: Well, look here. I'll stop in for a moment on my way to the station this afternoon. Good-bye, Scotch Granite. (*Exit Hermione. Eric and Honor take hands.*)

HONOR: Mother isn't so well I'm afraid.

ANNAN: No.

HONOR: Oh, Eric—

ANNAN: I don't know that there's any real cause for alarm; but, on the other hand, there may be. There have been symptoms lately that I don't like. I'm speaking to you plainly, dear.[36]

HONOR: (*Controlling herself*) I know; it's kinder.

ANNAN: But I don't want you to think she's worse than she is. When I say I am uneasy about her I am telling you the simple truth. That's my state of mind. Just that—neither more, nor less.

HONOR: She has so often been ill like this—and in a few days better again.

ANNAN: I know; and there isn't any reason why she shouldn't get better again this time.

HONOR: No? . . . Only . . .

ANNAN: Only there is always the danger . . . There has been before.

HONOR: . . . Of course we must put off London.

ANNAN: I think it would be better.

HONOR: Yes . . . I must tell Betty—and I must write to Aunt Josephine to-night.

ANNAN: Say as little as you can to Betty.

HONOR: As little as I can?

ANNAN: Don't frighten her—you know what Betty is—your mother would see it on her face. She would worry and try to find out—the worst thing possible for her. Only tell Betty she isn't so well and you don't like to leave her to the servants. Say that it is quite possible that in another week—

(*Enter Mrs. Dorrien. She walks feebly and leans on the door for support.*)

ANNAN: (*Going to her and helping her to sofa*) What, you've come down—when I advise no stairs to-day?

HONOR: Oh mother—how naughty!

MRS. DORRIEN: (*To Annan, laughing*) I thought you were out of the house.

ANNAN: A lot of respect you have for your medical adviser.

MRS. DORRIEN: One grows so tired of a bed-room—and the sofa here is quite comfortable. (*She lies down; Honor arranges cushions for her.*) I shall feel all the better for the change. And how are the dresses coming?

HONOR: Madame Aurore says everything will be ready to-morrow night.

MRS. DORRIEN: That's a good thing.

HONOR: But Mummy darling, I think we'd better put off London for a few days—don't you?

MRS. DORRIEN: Put off going to London!

HONOR: Eric thinks so, too— You're not a bit well.

MRS. DORRIEN: Oh, nonsense—

ANNAN: They can go next week, Mrs. Dorrien. When you're better to be left.

MRS. DORRIEN: I won't hear of it.

HONOR: But Mother—

MRS. DORRIEN: I won't have Betty disappointed. It would break the child's heart—she can hardly sleep for thinking of London.

HONOR: Only till next week.

MRS. DORRIEN: I tell you, I won't hear of it. This is your fault, Dr. Eric.

HONOR: Mother, dear—

ANNAN: (*Touches Honor and signs to her not to persist.*) Yes, I plead guilty; but you mustn't be too angry with me. I'm bound to make my patient's comfort my first consideration.

MRS. DORRIEN: I shouldn't be at all comfortable if I disappointed Betty; I should be very uncomfortable indeed . . . I'll forgive you only on the condition that you don't worry me about it any more.

ANNAN: Very well; you shan't be worried.

MRS. DORRIEN: (*Her good humour returning*) And I don't believe it was consideration for me at all—I believe it was a piece of pure selfishness on your part.

ANNAN: Selfishness?

MRS. DORRIEN: You want to keep Honor down here with you.

ANNAN: (*Laughs.*) So I do; you've seen through my motives exactly. (*He rises to go.*) Well, good-bye till tomorrow—I shall try to look in the morning. And try to remember what I told you—stairs as seldom as possible and make the others run about for what you want.

MRS. DORRIEN: A nice prescription, truly!— Good-bye.

(*Annan goes towards the door; Honor follows him.*)

ANNAN: (*Aside to Honor*) If you really wanted I could always let you know. Still, if you can manage—

HONOR: (*Nods. Exit Annan.*)

MRS. DORRIEN: (*Fretfully*) What put such an idea into his head? There's nothing really the matter with me—I'm a little run down, that's all.

HONOR: (*Trying to smile*) He knows you like to have me with you when you are "run down." You always say nobody looks after you as well as I do.

MRS. DORRIEN: And nobody does, darling, nobody does.

HONOR: (*Eagerly*) Then Mother, I don't want to bother you again but won't you let *me* stay with you? Let Betty go—she *would* be disappointed. But I'm not excited about London as she is—indeed, indeed I'm not. I'm quite happy here with you and Eric. Please let me stay—anyway let me stay for a week—and I'll write to Aunt Josephine to-night.

MRS. DORRIEN: No—you must go. For one thing I can't let Betty travel up alone.

HONOR: Why, Mother, what could happen to her?—I'd put her in the train.

MRS. DORRIEN: No, I shouldn't like it—she has never been anywhere alone. Nor have you, for that matter. Still—

HONOR: I'm older.

MRS. DORRIEN: Yes, and different . . . No, you must go with her darling, that's quite settled . . . But if I shouldn't be better by then—oh, I know I shall—

HONOR: Yes, but if you shouldn't—?

MRS. DORRIEN: Then—you can come back in a day or two—and leave Betty there—will that satisfy you?

HONOR: Yes . . . Dear little mother. (*Honor is seated on the floor beside the sofa caressing her mother's hand. There is a little silence and then Mrs. Dorrien speaks suddenly in an altered voice.*)

MRS. DORRIEN: I wonder if you understand why I don't want Betty to travel alone?

HONOR: Betty—oh she's rather scatterbrained—bless her! It would be just like her to get into the wrong train at the junction.

MRS. DORRIEN: (*Smiling faintly*) Yes, that's quite possible with Betty . . . Or—there are other things . . . Someone might talk to her in the train.

HONOR: Oh, yes—Betty's always ready to make friends with anybody. . . you mean?

MRS. DORRIEN: . . . Honor, you are a woman now, and Betty is almost one . . . I have thought lately there are things I ought to say to you—and now that you're going away . . . (*She stops.*)

HONOR: Yes?

MRS. DORRIEN: (*Speaking with a certain amount of difficulty*) You've never met anyone yet that you need be afraid of—you've never met any man . . .

HONOR: (*Astonished.*) No . . .

MRS. DORRIEN: But there are . . .

HONOR: (*Puzzled.*) . . . I don't understand—?

MRS. DORRIEN: I didn't till I was older than you . . . It's a thing that happens sometimes to women—only they don't say. . . It's like turning a corner in a garden and coming face to face with a wild beast! . . . That's what happened to me! And the wild beast was a man I had known and liked . . . I want you to understand that it may happen to any woman—that it's what you've got to guard against because you are a woman. You know something—instinctively and from books—but it hasn't come into your life . . . you've only known Eric—and the Vicarage boys—and Ranny. But I tell you there are some men with the beast in their souls and suddenly—suddenly—you see it looking out at you. It happened to me—and when it happened it was only by the grace of God that I escaped—only by the grace of God. But for that . . . It's a thing you never forget—it makes you afraid for yourself—it makes you afraid for your children . . . (*Her voice, which has been growing more and more excited, breaks suddenly and she sinks back exhausted on the sofa.*)

HONOR: (*Terrified*) Mother—mother—

MRS. DORRIEN: (*After a moment—weakly*) I've always meant to tell you—

HONOR: Lie still— Don't talk—don't talk—

MRS. DORRIEN: No. (*She lies for a moment with her eyes shut.*) I'll tell you about it another time . . . I've wanted you—to know . . . you do understand?

HONOR: (*Soothingly*) Yes, yes, I understand.

MRS. DORRIEN: And—you'll talk to Betty? I want her to see that it's enough to be young and pretty—that's quite enough. You'll talk to her?

HONOR: Yes, darling. Yes.

*(Enter Madame Aurore.)*

MRS. DORRIEN: That woman!

HONOR: Oh, it's Madame Aurore—do you want me, Madame?

MADAME AURORE: Oh, I deed not know dat your Modair vas here—I tought she vas in her bed-room . . . I hope you are better, Madame.

MRS. DORRIEN: Thank you—I'm not very well to-day.

MADAME AURORE: Ah, but I am sorry. Mademoiselle Bettina, she is joost putting on her evening frock to show you—de chiffon tilleul. I vill tell her you are down here.

HONOR: Perhaps you'd better rest now.

MRS. DORRIEN: No, no—I want to see Betty in her new frock.

MADAME AURORE: *(Going to door)* I vill tell her. *(At door signing to Honor)* Mademoiselle Honor—

HONOR: *(Going to her)* Yes, what is it?

MADAME AURORE: Is it settle dat you do not go Tursday?

HONOR: No—it's settled that we *do* go. Why?

MADAME AURORE: Oh, it vas only for de dresses—to know how mooch time I 'ave.

HONOR: But I thought you said they would be finished to-morrow?

MADAME AURORE: Oh yes, dey vill be feenish—but joost in case dey vas not . . . And I did so 'ope Mademoiselle Bettina vas not to be disappointed—it vas really on her account I ask . . . Oh, de dresses vill be feenish—don't you be afraid—day vill be ready for Tursday. *(Exit Madame Aurore.)*

MRS. DORRIEN: *(Rather irritably)* What did she want?

HONOR: *(Soothingly)* Only something about the dresses—nothing to matter.

MRS. DORRIEN: Get her away to-morrow. She poisons the air.

HONOR: Poisons the air!

MRS. DORRIEN: *(Apologetically)* With her horrible patchouli.[37]

*(Enter Ranny by window, whistling. He stops short.)*

RANNY: *(Surprised.)* I beg your pardon, Mrs. Dorrien. I had no idea—Betty told me you were in your bed-room.

MRS. DORRIEN: I was—shall be in a moment. Open the window, will you? *(Shaking hands.)*

RANNY: And may I stay? I was told I was to see Miss Betty's confection—that's the proper term, isn't it?

MRS. DORRIEN: The chiffon tilleul?

RANNY: The chiffon tilleul—whatever that may mean. Madame Aurore tells me to prepare myself to "be knocked all of a cap."

(*Enter Madame Aurore. She flings the door open with an air, and stands beside it.*)

MADAME AURORE: Mees Bettina Dorrien.

(*Enter Bettina in her evening dress—a wreath on her hair. She makes a little bow and looks round laughing. Ranny stares—doting.*)

BETTINA: Well?

RANNY: (*Pulling himself together*) I say! It *does*—you know, it does knock you all of a cap. (*Ranny collapses. Bettina claps her hands.*)

HONOR: It's lovely.

MADAME AURORE: Eet is *charmant—hein?*

MRS. DORRIEN: (*Unbending a little to Madame Aurore*) Charming—you've done wonders, Madame Aurore—you really have. Turn around, Betty—let us see the back.

BETTINA: (*Turns round to show herself off.*) Do you think Aunt Josephine will like it?

RANNY: Jolly hard to please if she doesn't.

BETTINA: You like it, don't you, Mummy?

MRS. DORRIEN: Yes, darling. (*Dreamily*) . . . What a baby she looks.

BETTINA: What? When I'm nearly seventeen! (*She kneels by her mother, kissing her.*) And isn't this a darling little wreath? (*Nods to Madame Aurore.*) She's a clever old thing, that Madame Aurore, isn't she? . . . (*She rises.*) And it's so nice and easy to dance in, too—I'm simply longing to dance in it. (*She makes a step or two and then begins to sing and dance around the room.*)

Where are you going to, my pretty maid?
Where are you going to, my pretty maid?
I'm going to London, sir, she said,
Sir, she said,
Sir, she said,
I'm going to London, sir, she said.[38]

(*As she sings, Ranny laughs and claps. Mrs. Dorrien and Honor look at her smiling and amused. Aurore standing behind the sofa watches her intently. At the end of the verse the Curtain comes down.*)

(*End of Act 1*)

## Act 2

*The Grey Hawk's house. A showily furnished room, arranged as a back and front drawing-room. It is brilliantly lit. In the back drawing-room is a grand piano. On the right is a door opening into the hall. Whenever it opens a footman is seen standing near it.*

*As the curtain rises the Grey Hawk is discovered. She is in evening dress, black, and much jeweled. She wears pearl earrings and her hair rolled back. She sits fanning herself.*

(*Enter Footman.*)

GREY HAWK: (*Looks up.*) Well?

FOOTMAN: (*He is French and speaks with a French accent.*) Madame Aurore—

GREY HAWK: Oh? Very well.

FOOTMAN: In here, Madame?

GREY HAWK: In here. (*She glances at clock.*) Yes . . . and—Edward—

FOOTMAN: Madame?

GREY HAWK: Tell Carron that the two young ladies who came in with me are not to come down just yet—not until I send for them.

FOOTMAN: Yes, Madame. (*Exit Footman—returning to usher in Madame Aurore.*)

MADAME AURORE: (*Waits for door to close.*) Vell?

GREY HAWK: Well?

MADAME AURORE: I mean—eet ees all gone off satisfactory?

GREY HAWK: Quite.

MADAME AURORE: And—dey are here?

GREY HAWK: Upstairs.

MADAME AURORE: Ah—I have been a leetle anxious . . .

GREY HAWK: There was no need.

MADAME AURORE: You had no deeficulty at de station? Dere vas no von to meet dem?

GREY HAWK: Of course not. Didn't you send the telegram to Lowndes Square?

MADAME AURORE: *Naturellement*! To say dey miss dat train—and dey come by de nex'.

GREY HAWK: Very well. Then they are not expected at Victoria till after 10.

MADAME AURORE: No, no. (*Nervously*) But it is not de common risk we run vid girls like (*Motion of head. Recovering her jauntiness*). Also it ees not de common price dey fetch, *hein*?

GREY HAWK: Ah. Exactly. (*Goes to writing table, unlocks drawer with key on her chain.*)

MADAME AURORE: (*Draws near with glistening eyes. Changes her crossing over as Grey Hawk looks up reflectively. Then with a snigger, but flattering, obsequious.*) You look vell, tonight, you! Dat funny way of dressing de hair—dat coiffure of Aunt Josephine. I tink he suit you—I tink he suit you down to de ground—and de pearl earring—just like de photographie. (*Sniggers.*) It has been useful, dat old photographie, *hein*?

GREY HAWK: (*Smiles grimly.*) They recognized the hair and the earrings before they were out of the train.

MADAME AURORE: And—dey suspect nodding yet?

GREY HAWK: Of course not.

MADAME AURORE: You will remember what I did say to you about dat young man—dat Ranny Dallas. De modair she is poor, she is ill and she cannot do anyting; but dat Ranny he is rich and he mek me—leedle nairvous, *hein*?

GREY HAWK: Oh, we'll have them out of the country before there is time to make trouble.

MADAME AURORE: Dat vill be best—dat vill be much de best—and you are satisfied? Dat little Betty? She is all I said, *hein*?

GREY HAWK: Oh yes, I'm satisfied with *her*. (*Pauses reflectively.*)

MADAME AURORE: Den—de balance of my account? If you please.

GREY HAWK: Oh—yes. (*Takes out cheque-book.*)

MADAME AURORE: (*Decisively*) Non. Bank notes dis time, if you please.

GREY HAWK: Oh, if you prefer— (*Counts out five notes.*) That is correct?

MADAME AURORE: Qvite correct. Tank you.

(*Grey Hawk rings bell. Madame Aurore puts notes in bag and takes out a card.*)

MADAME AURORE: I haf now de new address. I haf also de new name. I am Madame Rose a *votre* service!

(*Enter Servant.*)

GREY HAWK: Ah! (*Takes card and throws it into writing-table.*) Good evening, Madame Rose. (*To Servant*) Tell Carron to send the two new ones down to me at once.

(*Exit Madame Aurore with Servant. The Grey Hawk locks up her writing-table after making entry in book. There is a pause. Grey Hawk fans herself with her eyes on the door. It opens and Honor and Bettina come in, dressed in the clothes that Madame Aurore has made for them.*)

BETTINA: Here we are, Aunt Josephine. What a big room!

GREY HAWK: Are you rested after your journey?

HONOR: Yes, thank you.

BETTINA: I wasn't a bit tired. I really didn't want to lie down at all.

GREY HAWK: It was better for you—I hope they sent you up what you liked for dinner?

HONOR: Oh yes—we had a very good dinner, thanks.

BETTINA: They sent us up a lovely little tray each—only I felt too excited to eat. Do you like our dresses, Aunt Josephine?

GREY HAWK: Very much.

BETTINA: A French dressmaker made them for us.

GREY HAWK: She has very good taste— You like your rooms?

BETTINA: I should think so. We've never seen anything like them, have we? The darling little pink curtains! There's only one thing—you don't mind?

GREY HAWK: What is it?

BETTINA: At home, we always have a room together.

GREY HAWK: Your Mother's house is small?

BETTINA: Well, it isn't big.

HONOR: It isn't so much that; but we're used to being together.

GREY HAWK: I see. We may as well leave things as they are for to-night. I dare say I shall make other arrangements for you to-morrow.

BETTINA: Oh, thank you—you are good.

HONOR: But didn't you get my last letter? I am afraid I shall have to go home again to-morrow.

GREY HAWK: Oh!—a— Then your mother isn't any better?

HONOR: No, she is just the same as when I wrote.

GREY HAWK: Ah! That is a pity.

BETTINA: But Honor is so splendid at nursing, she'll soon have mother well; then she'd like to come back again, perhaps in a day or two—if you'll have her?

GREY HAWK: We can talk about that to-morrow. (*Bettina has moved towards the piano.*) You sing, don't you Bettina?

BETTINA: A little—but who told you?

(*Enter Footman. He stands just inside door and looks at the Grey Hawk.*)

GREY HAWK: (*Goes across to him and he says something to her in an undertone.*) Wait here till I come back. (*Exit Grey Hawk followed by Footman.*)

BETTINA: (*Aside to Honor*) Wait here! They seem to think we get lost if we stir a step without somebody. She has gone to speak to a man in the hall—a little fat man with a moustache, in evening dress.

HONOR: Betty, you shouldn't peer round doors at people.

BETTINA: As if Aunt Josephine minded our seeing her visitor. I suppose he's one of her friends that she said was expecting to come in after dinner. (*She wanders round the room looking at things.*) What a lovely motor Aunt Josephine has got; it's ever so much nicer than the Helmstone's.

HONOR: She must be rich.

BETTINA: Awfully—with all those footmen—I wonder what that piano is like. (*She goes up to it, strikes a chord or two and then strums on and off through the following speeches.*) Do you like that scent Aunt Josephine has on her things?[39]

HONOR: Not much. It's so strong.

BETTINA: It is rather—still, I think I like it. (*There is a moment's pause while she runs her fingers up and down the piano.*)

HONOR: It makes the room stuffy, don't you think? But they don't seem to mind stuffiness here—I can't get my bedroom window to open.

BETTINA: Won't yours open either?

HONOR: No, I tried hard, but it isn't made to unfasten. It has little iron bars across—painted iron. I'm afraid I shan't sleep with my window shut.

BETTINA: Oh, you're always so keen on draughts. I tried mine too, but the maid told me you never keep windows open in London because of the smuts—there were ventilators or something, she said. Isn't this a nice piano? (*She plays.*) I don't like that maid much who looks after us—that Carron. She's got a face like wood—a disobliging toad too—rather wanted to order me about.

HONOR: I expect Aunt Josephine has had her a long time and she thinks she can do as she likes.

BETTINA: Yes— She didn't want me to come round to you to have my hair done—actually wouldn't show your room when I asked her—pretended not to hear. I had to find it myself when she had gone off for something. That reminds me: there's a perfectly lovely woman staying here.

HONOR: Is there? How do you know?

BETTINA: Seen her—she's a foreigner—when I was looking for your room I opened the wrong door—just opposite yours—and she was there in her dressing-gown. Of course, I begged her pardon, and she said something but I don't know what. It wasn't French, it wasn't German, so I couldn't understand. But she *was* beautiful—queer looking, but beautiful—with the very reddest lips you ever saw. Carron was coming along the passage and was as cross as two sticks about it. I told her I was looking for you and hadn't done any harm; but she said the foreign lady wasn't to be disturbed. I asked if she was ill and Carron did like this "oh"—(*Impatient acquiescence*)

HONOR: Well, if she's ill, I hope it isn't anything infectious.

BETTINA: That's just like you; always worrying over infection— You're worse than ever since you've been engaged to a doctor. Anyway, she couldn't have been very ill. She *looked* quite well, wasn't even in bed—only in her dressing-gown. That man we met on the stairs—he must have been the doctor!

HONOR: The young man—going up with the footman?

BETTINA: Yes.

HONOR: (*With the air of one familiar with the medical profession*) *He* wasn't a doctor.

BETTINA: Well, that's where you're wrong, because I saw him go into her room.

HONOR: Oh—then he must have been. He didn't look to me like a doctor.

BETTINA: You mustn't think they all look like old Eric. (*She comes down and sits beside Honor.*) I wish you weren't going home to-morrow, darling.

(*Enter the Grey Hawk.*)

BETTINA: (*Surprised to see her alone.*) Oh, your friends haven't come?

GREY HAWK: (*Carelessly*) I dare say they'll be here directly; we don't keep such early hours here as you do in the country.

BETTINA: No. Down at Duncombe we should be thinking of going to bed by this time. I love sitting up late.

(*Enter the Colonel and the Unknown Man.*)

GREY HAWK: How do you do. (*Greetings*) These are my nieces, Colonel. (*To the Unknown Man*) My nieces.

COLONEL: (*Effusively*) Delighted.

BETTINA: How do you do. (*She shakes hands with him.*)

(*The Unknown Man bows to the two girls, murmurs something and leans against the mantelpiece, looking at them. While Bettina talks to the Colonel, Honor stands a little awkwardly alone.*)

COLONEL: You've only just arrived, eh?

BETTINA: Only just—that's to say we got in soon after five.

COLONEL: Tired?

BETTINA: Not a bit; and I'm longing for to-morrow.

COLONEL: Longing for to-morrow—what for, eh?

GREY HAWK: To see London, of course.

COLONEL: That's a large order. (*Talks in dumb show to Bettina.*)

MAN: (*To Grey Hawk—looking at Bettina*) *Je vous fais mes compliments, Madame.*

GREY HAWK: (*Following his eyes*) Yes. But— (*She glances at Honor and shrugs her shoulders.*)

MAN: Oh!—I see nothing particularly wrong. A different type.

GREY HAWK: You like it! Oh, very well—(*She shrugs her shoulders again, and turns away.*)

MAN: (*Looks at Honor thoughtfully for a moment, takes out a cigarette and is about to light it —then as if changing his mind walks across to her, indicating sofa.*) Sit down—won't you?

HONOR: Thank you.

MAN: (*Offering case*) And smoke?

HONOR: No thank you—I don't.

MAN: Really? (*He lights his own cigarette and sits beside her.*)

COLONEL: (*Laughing*) Capital! Capital! (*Turns to Grey Hawk.*) What about the Tartar?

GREY HAWK: I think it's all right.

COLONEL: Well, I don't know. If he does turn up, you shouldn't be surprised if he's in a devil of a temper.

GREY HAWK: Oh!

COLONEL: He must have lost a pot of money to-day. All the same, (*with a meaning glance towards Bettina*) it would be a thousand pities if—a—if the party wasn't complete.

BETTINA: Oh, yes—I meant to ask Aunt Josephine—how is the invalid?

GREY HAWK: The invalid?

BETTINA: The lady upstairs—the foreigner. I knocked at her door by mistake—for Honor's. I'm so sorry. I do hope you'll apologize for me. I tried to, but I don't think she understands English.

GREY HAWK: No—she doesn't understand English.

COLONEL: What made you think she was ill?

BETTINA: Carron, the maid told me so. Besides we saw the doctor going into her room.

COLONEL: (*Obviously amused*) Oh—you saw the doctor did you? Then of course she must be ill.

GREY HAWK: There is nothing much the matter with her.

BETTINA: I'm glad. She *is* pretty . . . I suppose she won't come down tonight?

GREY HAWK: No.

COLONEL: You see, she's the sort that rather expects people to go up to her. (*He chuckles.*)

BETTINA: (*Puzzled by his evident amusement.*) Oh . . . is she?—that sort?

COLONEL: Yes, *that* sort.[40] (*Laughs.*)

(*The Man at Honor's side has turned his head to listen to Bettina; then he looks back at Honor intently.*)

MAN: Our friend, the Colonel is a bit of a wag.

HONOR: He seems amused about something.

MAN: I don't think your sister quite grasps the point of the joke.

HONOR: No—I'm afraid I didn't either—what—

MAN: It hasn't much point. The Colonel's jokes aren't usually worth explaining.

(*Enter the Tartar.*)[41]

COLONEL: Hallo, Tartar, there you are. What sort of a day?

TARTAR: Rotten.—I say, isn't there anything to drink?

COLONEL: Coming. (*He rings bell.*)

GREY HAWK: My nieces.

TARTAR: Oh. (*He nods, stares at them, and fixes his gaze on Bettina.*)

BETTINA: Oh! Why how do you do?

(*General astonishment—a pause.*)

BETTINA: (*Continues.*) I've only seen your photograph, but I knew you at once. (*A pause.*)

TARTAR: Oh, you think you know me, do you?

BETTINA: (*A bit bewildered*) You're Mr. Whitby-Dawson, aren't you?

TARTAR: (*Scowling. Glares at Grey Hawk. She makes covert sign of disapproval.*) Sorry to disappoint you. My name's Jackson. (*Turns away, furious, and flings himself down. To Colonel.*) How much do you think I dropped? Damned beastly, rotten luck—that's what I've had the whole blessed day.

(*Enter Footmen with trays, wine and glasses.*)

COLONEL: Well, here's to better. What's yours?

TARTAR: Champagne, and plenty of it. (*To Footman*) Here—hurry up, you there. (*He drinks. Footmen go out leaving trays.*)

BETTINA: (*To Grey Hawk*) I'm so very sorry I made that mistake. (*Prettily*) Please ask him to forgive me.

TARTAR: (*Has been looking at her across his glass; sets it down.*) *That's* better. There's one woman in London who's got a decent cellar (*Nods to Grey Hawk*) and I approve of the new coiffure too— Rippin'!— What's the niece's name?

GREY HAWK: Bettina.

TARTAR: Well, isn't Miss Bettina going to have any champagne?

BETTINA: I'm glad you've forgiven me, but I—oh no—

COLONEL: Of course she will—they both will.

HONOR: No, thank you, we—(*No one pays any attention to her.*)

TARTAR: (*Handing Bettina a glass.*) Here you are.

BETTINA: I don't think I ought—really—

TARTAR: Why not?

BETTINA: I've never tasted champagne.

TARTAR: Never tasted champagne! Time you began then.

BETTINA: It might go to my head.

TARTAR: And a very nice place for it to go to. Come along.

BETTINA: Aunt Josephine . . . ? (*The Grey Hawk nods. Bettina is rather astonished.*) Shall I? (*The Grey Hawk nods again.*)

(*Honor makes a movement in her chair and seems about to speak. The Grey Hawk turns and looks at her coldly. Honor shrinks back a little—nervous and astonished. At the same moment the Colonel approaches offering her champagne. Bettina has not seen Honor's movement; she takes the glass and sips at it cautiously—the Tartar laughing at her.*)

COLONEL: (*To Honor*) You won't? Oh, nonsense.

HONOR: I'd rather not, thank you.

COLONEL: Take an old man's advice and try it. A glass of good wine is one of the best things you'll get out of life—you take my word for it. It's a chancey sort of a world, you know—better make sure of a bitter certain bliss.

GREY HAWK: (*Coldly*) Why don't you take a glass, Honor?

HONOR: (*Looks up and meets her eye—then, firmly.*) I'd rather not, thank you.

COLONEL: Well, well. (*Turning away to Man*) Here, what are you—?

MAN: Thanks. (*He goes up with the Colonel to the table with the wine. Honor is left alone on the sofa; she looks anxiously at Bettina who is too much engaged with the Tartar to notice her.*)

TARTAR: Well, what's it like?

BETTINA: It prickles.

TARTAR: Prickles. Is that all you can find to say about one of the best champagnes in London?

BETTINA: No . . . it's—rather nice.

COLONEL: That's right.

TARTAR: Makes you feel jolly, doesn't it?

BETTINA: Yes . . . At least, I do feel jolly—I don't know if it's that.

TARTAR: Makes you feel you'd like to finish the glass?

BETTINA: (*Laughing*) Ye—es.

TARTAR: Finish it, then.

BETTINA: (*Looks instinctively toward the Grey Hawk who nods again.*)

HONOR: (*Nervously*) Betty—

TARTAR: (*Drowning her voice*) Come on—finish it. (*Betty drinks, then sets down glass laughing.*) Bravo. Makes you feel you'd like to have another?

BETTINA: No—no—

TARTAR: (*Filling glass*) Yes, it does.

HONOR: (*Rises.*) No, Betty—certainly not!

BETTINA: (*Speaks with her little formal air.*) No, I don't want any more, thank you. I don't, really—I mean it.

(*Honor sinks back in her seat, relieved. The Footman has just entered the room and signed to the Grey Hawk. Same business of her speaking to him and leaving the room with him. As she does so, the Unknown Man, who has been watching Honor, strolls back to her and takes his former place at her side, lighting another cigarette. The Colonel with his glass in his hand joins the other two further upstage.*)

MAN: I see you've got a will of your own.

HONOR: A will of my own?

MAN: We can take a horse to the water but we can't make him drink. In the same way you can offer a girl champagne—

HONOR: (*She laughs a little nervously.*) I didn't understand what you meant. Betty wants to make up for her mistake—I saw that resemblance too!— And she wants to please Aunt Josephine. I'm sure Aunt Josephine hadn't any idea that we never drink wine.

MAN: She has not had enough to do her any harm.

HONOR: Still, when you never have it? I expect it will give her a headache.

MAN: You look as if you had one now.

HONOR: (*Apologetically*) I have a little.

MAN: I believe you aren't accustomed to smoke. I beg your pardon. (*He puts out his cigarette.*)

HONOR: Oh—please don't—

MAN: Nonsense, I ought to have noticed it before—I'm sorry.

HONOR: I don't really think it's the smoke. It's the heat perhaps—and the scent. I suppose Aunt Josephine must be fond of scent—there's so much of it about . . . Do you think we might ask to have a window open?

MAN: Well—I'm not sure.

HONOR: Are the downstairs windows barred with iron too?

MAN: (*Looks at her—then*) I believe so.

HONOR: It makes it rather oppressive having them always shut—when you're used to a lot of fresh air . . . Is Aunt Josephine afraid of burglars? (*Man stares.*) She seems to have a great many valuable things?

MAN: I don't fancy it's that.

HONOR: Then I wonder . . . (*She looks around almost as if she were about to ask someone else.*)

MAN: (*Quickly*) Oh—I've heard this place used to be a private madhouse.

HONOR: *This* was a private madhouse?

MAN: I've heard so . . . You needn't say I told you.

HONOR: Oh no . . .

(*There is a loud laugh from the others—loudest from the Colonel. Honor glances at him.*)

HONOR: (*With a little hesitation*) Who is the Colonel?

MAN: Who is he?

HONOR: Yes. I don't even know his name.

MAN: His name's Jones.

HONOR: Colonel Jones. What I mean is—is he any relation of Mr. Harborough's?

MAN: Mr. Harborough's?

HONOR: Perhaps you didn't know my aunt's husband? He's been dead a long time—ten years, I think.

MAN: No, I never met him . . . What makes you think the Colonel is a relation of his?

HONOR: Well, I don't think he can be any relation of my aunt's—of ours—or I should have heard of him; but he seems very much at home here, doesn't he? He gives orders . . . ?

MAN: That's only his way.

HONOR: Oh! . . .

MAN: You don't like him?

HONOR: Not very much.

MAN: I should not think much of your taste if you did.

HONOR: (*After a pause*) There's another thing I don't understand.

MAN: (*Nervously*) Don't ask me any more questions! It—it reminds me of passing an examination, and I never could pass an examination in my life. Besides I'm afraid I haven't any time to answer them. (*He pulls out his watch.*) I've got an engagement to keep in exactly three minutes from now.

HONOR: Oh—have you?

MAN: Yes—(*He rises.*) Good-bye.

HONOR: Oh dear, *must* you go?

MAN: (*Curtly*) Afraid so . . . (*With a change of tone*) Why did you say that?

HONOR: (*Taken aback*) I—

MAN: Why did you ask me to stay?

HONOR: You'll think me very silly, but—I don't feel as if I could get on with the others.

MAN: You're frightened of them?

HONOR: I don't mean that—

MAN: Oh, yes, you do . . . your sister isn't frightened.

HONOR: She's different. Betty gets on with everybody. You can't imagine anyone not getting on with Betty, can you?

MAN: Then you would like me to stay.

HONOR: Yes— No—that is, I hadn't any right to ask you.

MAN: Oh, you've every right to ask. The question is—

HONOR: (*As he pauses*) What?

MAN: Have I any right to listen to you.

HONOR: I don't understand.

MAN: Obviously. (*He stands for a moment silent; then*) I'll see it out since you've asked me. (*He sits.*) But you'll remember you *have* asked me.

HONOR: Perhaps you oughtn't—your engagement—

MAN: Can go to the devil.

HONOR: Isn't it important?

MAN: I've forgotten . . . I suppose you feel rather strange here, eh?

HONOR: I suppose I do. (*Looks around and puts her hand to her temple.*) Or only headachy, perhaps.

MAN: Well, lie back and rest for a minute or two. Cushion comfy? (*He arranges it behind her head.*)

HONOR: (*A little surprised*) Oh, thank you.

TARTAR: (*Calling across the room to the Colonel who is pouring out another glass*) Colonel, you'll be glad to hear that Miss Bettina likes London and thinks we're all delightful people here.

BETTINA: I didn't say so. I should certainly never think of calling you a delightful person.

COLONEL: Hear, hear—one for you, Tartar.

TARTAR: You'll have to take me in hand and improve me, Miss Betty. Besides, I'm much nicer than this generally; this isn't one of my good days.

BETTINA: (*Pertly*) Yes, *I* thought something was the matter with you.

TARTAR: Oh, you did, eh? (*Roars; they all laugh, except Honor and the Man. The Tartar sobering.*) Dammed rotten luck I've been havin'.

BETTINA: Oh! That's twice you've sworn.

COLONEL: You see, he's had his horse scratched.[42]

BETTINA: Scratched—oh poor thing! Was it scratched very badly?

(*The Tartar and the Colonel roar with laughter.*)

BETTINA: What have I said?

TARTAR: Something very nice indeed.

BETTINA: Tell me, what is it? What is the joke? I shan't talk to you any more unless you tell me what it is. (*The two men laugh and tease her.*)

MAN: You don't like London as much as your sister does?

HONOR: I can't talk much about "London" yet. I've only seen this house and the streets from the station . . . I'm glad Betty seems to get on so well. (*A little sadly*) But she won't mind my leaving her to-morrow. I was afraid she might.

MAN: (*Looks at her—then*) Did you say you were going away to-morrow?

HONOR: Yes—going home again. My mother is ill.

MAN: Oh, your mother is ill.

HONOR: Very ill I'm afraid. I oughtn't to have left her at all. I shan't feel happy unless I go back to her to-morrow. I shouldn't have come to London at all if she hadn't insisted.

MAN: You came all this way just for a few hours?

HONOR: Mother would make me—you see, she wanted me to take care of Betty. Betty has never travelled alone.

MAN: And you—have you travelled much alone?

HONOR: No—to-morrow will be the first time. But then I am older.

MAN: I see.

(*Enter the Grey Hawk. She glances at the pair on the sofa but does not approach them; then goes up and speaks to the Colonel. The Man watches her for a moment; then goes on.*)

MAN: Then you live with your mother in the country?

HONOR: Yes.

MAN: No father?

HONOR: He died when we were babies—in India. He was a soldier.

MAN: So—there's just you two and your mother?

HONOR: Just us two.

MAN: And the man you're engaged to—who is he?

HONOR: He is a man of science—a doctor. But how did you know I was—?

MAN: I saw your ring.

HONOR: Of course. Do you know my aunt's maid wanted me to take it off—said it wasn't the sort of ring people wear in London.

MAN: That was odd of her—it's a nice ring.—So you're engaged to a doctor down there . . . And your aunt—you don't generally see much of her, I suppose?

HONOR: I have never seen her in my life until she met us at Victoria to-day.

MAN: Really.

COLONEL: I'm sure you sing and dance, Miss Betty?

GREY HAWK: Oh yes, Bettina sings and dances.

BETTINA: I sing—just a little. But I can only dance waltzes, and that sort of thing—that's not what you mean, I'm afraid.

TARTAR: Do you mean to say you can't do anything in the "Maud Allan" line or even a skirt dance?[43]

HONOR: Who's Maud Allan?

TARTAR: Oh, I say—she's worthy of a seat on the bench.

HONOR: And what is a skirt dance?

TARTAR: Look, here, Colonel, you'd better give her a lesson.

*(They go up stage towards the piano around which they stand laughing and talking —the Grey Hawk follows them and joins the group, eventually sitting down to the piano. The Man has been watching Bettina covertly. When the others are round the piano he turns, looks hard at Honor for a moment and then speaks.)*

MAN: How good are your nerves?

HONOR: VERY good.

MAN: Sure?

HONOR: Sure. Why do you ask?

MAN: I've a reason . . . Have you ever fainted?

HONOR: *(Indignantly)* Never.

MAN: Could you hear something very unexpected—even horrible—and not cry out?

HONOR: *(Half starting up)* Something has happened to my Mother!

MAN: Careful!

HONOR: My Mother's worse!

MAN: You told me you had good nerves.

HONOR: *(Struggling for self-command)* I have.

MAN: That's better; but it's not good enough yet . . . you must keep perfectly still. If you can't, I won't go on. You must look just as usual . . . that's right. Lean your head on your hand, as if you were chatting to me—so.

HONOR: Is it about my Mother?

MAN: No, it's not. Now, do you understand what I say? You've got to keep steady, you've got to keep yourself in hand—because everything—more than life, depends on your self-control, during the next few moments.

HONOR: (*Staring*) Yes—I understand.

MAN: You don't; you think I'm mad. That's the idea that has just come into your head, isn't it?

HONOR: I—

MAN: Never mind—as long as you don't act upon it during the next few minutes. Just sit there and look pleasant while you talk to the poor lunatic: remember he has to be humoured when he asks you silly questions.

HONOR: Oh, of course I don't—

MAN: Very good . . . And now—have you any idea where you are?

HONOR: Any idea where I am?

MAN: That's what I asked you.

HONOR: At my aunt's—Mrs. Harborough's.

MAN: At your aunt's, Mrs. Harborough's. And where does your aunt live?

HONOR: At 160 Lowndes Square.

MAN: At 160 Lowndes Square . . . You are twenty minutes from Lowndes Square by taxi. That woman over there is not your aunt and you are in one of the most infamous houses in Europe.

(*By this time the Grey Hawk has sat down to the piano. She plays a waltz and the Tartar, catching Bettina in his arms, begins to dance with her round the room.*)

BETTINA: (*Laughing*) Not so fast—not so fast. Oh, clumsy, treading on my foot—I won't dance with you if you jump me about like that.

MAN: Take your time—they're enjoying themselves. I suppose you know there are such places? Or are you still under the impression that I am an escaped lunatic? For God's sake, disabuse yourself of that idea—if you want to save your body and soul alive. Tell me, do you believe me?

HONOR: I—

MAN: I suppose you can't—straight off—put two and two together. You've only been in this house a few hours, but there are things you must have noticed. You *did* notice the barred windows.

HONOR: You said it was a mad-house—

MAN: I had to say something; it was the first thing that came into my head. Then that woman your sister saw upstairs—the man who went into her room—

HONOR: The doctor—

MAN: The doctor!—You innocent! And the men—you must have noticed that *she* goes out to speak to! What do you think they come for? What— (*Suddenly bringing his face close to hers*) What do you think we all come for?

HONOR: You!

MAN: (*After a little pause*) Now you believe me?

HONOR: (*Looks at him—then lowers her hand over her eyes speechless.*)

MAN: Very well, then, pull yourself together; I'll give you time—Here. (*He opens an illustrated paper and lays it on her knee.*) We're looking at this together; you see there are pictures—Remember, a careless look or a move or a word would mean ruin—*ruin*! Do you understand?

HONOR: Go on—I'm listening.

MAN: Can you grasp what I mean?

HONOR: I'm trying to.

MAN: You've lived the ordinary sheltered girl's life, but you must have heard that there are houses—I won't say like this. This is a masterpiece of devilry and masterpieces are never plentiful— But you must have heard or read of places where men and women meet?

HONOR: I—have heard—something.

MAN: Something—next to nothing, I suppose—Well, you're in one of those places. Just get used to the idea. You've plenty of time—they haven't even rung for the cognac and liqueurs yet. Do you know what will happen when they do?

HONOR: What will happen?

MAN: Sooner or later they'll press you to have one.

HONOR: To have—?

MAN: A liqueur. They'll make it very difficult for you to refuse—press it on you and laugh at you if you won't drink it. Then, if you hold out, they'll send for coffee—a thimbleful—if you won't take anything else—and it won't matter whether you drink coffee or whether you drink liqueur. They'll both be doctored—drugged.

HONOR: Drugged—But I've had coffee already—I had some after dinner.

MAN: (*Puts out his hand.*) Steady. That was all right. They wouldn't give it to you so early. Careful—careful, don't look at me like that—! Remember I'm running a greater risk in telling you—a risk you have no idea of. But you are facing a ghastly certainty if I don't . . . Try to sit easily—that's better . . . If you keep your head, there's no reason why you shouldn't get out of this unscathed—both of you.

HONOR: What am I to do?

MAN: Nothing in a hurry. I can't give you up just yet without arousing suspicion.

HONOR: Then you will?

MAN: I believe I shall be fool enough . . . For the next few minutes we have got to seem friendly—very friendly. You understand?

HONOR: And then?

MAN: She's looking! (*He throws himself back on the sofa and laughs loudly.*) No you won't make me believe that!

HONOR: (*Taking her cue from him*) And why not?

MAN: (*Under his breath*) Capital—and now look down at the paper. (*He leans forward and appears to whisper into her ear, smiling.*)

BETTINA: (*Who is sitting on the music-stool which the Grey Hawk had left—laughing and fanning herself.*) No, how can I possibly sing yet? I'm all out of breath.

TARTAR: Oh? You're not going to put us off like that. We'll give you two minutes to get your breath again and then you've got to sing for us and do us a skirt dance. Or if it comes to that we're not particular about the skirt.

BETTINA: I haven't done what you all a skirt dance since I was a little girl.

COLONEL: Oh—and what are you now?

BETTINA: I think the Colonel's rather rude—don't you, Aunt Josephine?

MAN: It's all right—I thought she was trying to hear.

HONOR: Why are you doing this?— Telling me?

MAN: (*Shrugs his shoulders.*)

HONOR: You didn't mean to when you came here to-night—

MAN: Good God, no.

HONOR: Then why?

MAN: I don't know. (*Looks at her.*) Unless it is—your eyes make me think of someone I used to know.

HONOR: Tell me—oh, quickly, what I am to do?

MAN: They'll make your sister sing or dance directly. When she begins, I shall give you a signal and you are to get up—can you? (*She nods.*) No haste—you must do it quite quietly and go out of that room.

HONOR: But shan't I be asked where I am going—and why?

MAN: You would be if you went alone, but I shall come with you.

HONOR: You will—?

MAN: I shall have to. I shall let them imagine—they will leave you to me.

HONOR: Please. I'd rather go by myself.

MAN: You would never be allowed out of this room alone.

HONOR: I could say I must post a letter.

MAN: They would ring for a servant.

HONOR: If I once got as far as the door, I could run.

MAN: As far as the front door, perhaps. You would find it locked. No servant would open it for you.

HONOR: Will they for you?

MAN: I can manage it. I am afraid you have got to trust me. I shall not be offended if you refuse; but for your sake I shall be sorry.

HONOR: I beg your pardon.

MAN: You need not— Then, it is agreed; when I tell you, you will come?

HONOR: I *can't* leave my sister!

MAN: Haven't I made it clear to you? If you don't leave the room with me, she'll leave it with the Tartar.

HONOR: No—No.

MAN: Hush . . . She won't know why—but she'll do it. Don't you remember what I told you—about the liqueurs and the coffee? . . . And she won't come back again. She would probably be on her way to Paris this time to-morrow—Bend low—look at the paper! (*She bends down as the Colonel strolls up and leans over the back of the sofa.*) Now, Colonel, no poaching on my preserves. We are deep in a discussion about art and you are not to interrupt.

COLONEL: Oh, art is it? —A very engrossing subject.

MAN: I agree with you. There's a lot to be said about art. (*The Colonel winks at him and moves away.*)

HONOR: (*When he has gone, looks up—takes in the picture: Bettina and the Tartar.*) I'll do what you tell me.

MAN: That's right. Everything depends on your nerve. If the Grey Hawk has the slightest suspicion of what is in your mind when you get up to go, then God alone can help you— Incidentally I may mention that if she had the slightest suspicion of what I have been saying to you, she would call in her bullies to beat me to a jelly.

HONOR: I think my mind's going.

MAN: No—you've had a shock that's all . . . All things considered you're wonderfully steady.

HONOR: Then, I can go?—

MAN: Wait a moment. If you went now everyone would turn and look at you—and if your sister saw your eyes—she would want to know— . . . They're more and more absorbed in her. You have your sister to thank for giving you time. She's a success. These people here won't hurry her. They know their business.

(*Enter Footmen with tray of liqueurs. They go towards the Tartar who is leaning over Bettina at the piano.*)

TARTAR: (*Waving tray away*) Oh, leave that a bit . . . Look here, she says she'll sing and dance if anyone will play for her.

COLONEL: Bravo!

BETTINA: Oh, it's only a ridiculous, babyish song.

COLONEL: Anything *you* sing—

GREY HAWK: What's the tune?

BETTINA: You know it. Everybody knows the nursery rhyme—"Where are you going to?"

GREY HAWK: Sing it over to me and I'll try.

(*The Footmen have come down to the sofa with the tray.*)

MAN: (*Loudly*) Ah, that's right. Put it down there on the table. (*Exeunt Footmen.*) Ready now—(*Aloud*) What will you have—eh? Well, try some crème de menthe! (*He busies himself with the tray.*) Steady.

(*The others are all grouped around the piano. Bettina hums and occasionally dabs at a note with her fingers while the Grey Hawk picks out the tune.*)

MAN: (*Handing Honor a glass*) Drink this—it's only a cognac—it will pull you together.

HONOR: (*She takes it but does not drink; spills some.*)

MAN: You won't? It's all right—but perhaps I can't expect you to believe me! (*He takes the glass from her and drinks it off.*) You see . . . I'm going over now to speak to her. When I leave her I shall go to the door and open it—and you'll come.

HONOR: And then?

MAN: Then—I'll see you get outside the house.

HONOR: And when I'm outside?— How shall I get help?

MAN: By going straight to Lowndes Square. I'll take you.

HONOR: Oh no, no, *please* let me go alone.

MAN: (*Swallowing his discomfiture*) Oh, very well; turn to the left and run as hard as you can. Perhaps I needn't tell you that. There's a cab rank not so very far away—or you may pick up a taxi before you reach the rank. (*He strolls across the room to the piano. The Grey Hawk has just played the tune through.*)

GREY HAWK: Is that the right time?

BETTINA: Just a shade slower.

GREY HAWK: Like this?— (*She plays a bar or two.*)

BETTINA: Yes—quite right.

(*The Man leans across the piano and says something inaudible to the Grey Hawk. She looks up at him, smiles mockingly, glances across the room at Honor and nods. Honor, with bent head, seems to be looking at a picture.*)

BETTINA: (*Impatiently*) What are you waiting for? I'm all ready—I thought you were going to begin.

TARTAR: Strike up, strike up!

GREY HAWK: I'm ready now. (*She strikes a chord. Bettina begins to sing and dance.*)

MAN: (*To Honor*) The picture I mean is in the hall—(*He opens the door; Honor rises.*)

BETTINA:

Where we you going to, my pretty maid?
Where are you going to, my pretty maid?
I'm going a-milking, sir, she said,
    Sir, she said,
    Sir, she said,
I'm going a-milking, sir, she said.

(*The Man crosses to the door and stands holding it open. Honor rises, walks slowly across the room and goes out. The Man follows Honor and closes the door behind them. Bettina's back is turned; she does not see them. At the conclusion of the verse the Colonel and the Tartar clap their hands noisily and cry "Bravo."*)

BETTINA:

Shall I come with you, my pretty maid,
Shall I come with you, my pretty maid?
Oh, yes, If you please, kind sir, she said,
    Sir, she said—

(*Servants' voices, low at first, steadily rising. Grey Hawk signs over her shoulder to Colonel who goes towards door as it is hurriedly opened by the Butler very red in the face, struggling for composure, and goes to Grey Hawk and whispers. Colonel has disappeared into the hall. Bettina still singing.*)

GREY HAWK: (*Crashing notes to discord.*) *WHAT*! (*Leaps to her feet. Bettina pauses, amazed.*)

GREY HAWK: (*Wheels around upon Butler, her face distorted with passion.*) *GONE*?

BUTLER: But a single moment, I am downstairs— (*Colonel and other servants seen crowding and gesticulating at the door.*) I leave that young fool—the new one—

(*A Babel of tongues. Tartar seizes one of the men servants and interrogates him—dumb show.*)

BETTINA: What's happened? Honor! Where are you? Honor! Tell me where my sister is—please—

GREY HAWK: There, sit down, child. There's nothing to be frightened about. (*Pushes her into a chair. To Footman*) Bring some— (*Passionately*) Yes, *now*, fool!

BETTINA: Where is she—where has Honor gone?

GREY HAWK: Only upstairs. Her head aches— And you too, all of a tremble. Take this.

BETTINA: No, No—Honor!—

GREY HAWK: Hush! Do as you're told.

BETTINA: (*Trembling, bewildered*) Please, I don't want any more.

COLONEL: You haven't had any of this— This is different.

BETTINA: No, already the room is going round.

COLONEL: This will stop any room from going round.

BETTINA: (*Thrusts it away and rises.*) No, I won't. (*Screams.*) Honor!

GREY HAWK: (*Pushing Colonel aside*) Oh, get out of my way.

BETTINA: Where are you?—Honor! (*Still trying to get out of the room; at every fluttering attempt finding one or other barring her way.*)

GREY HAWK: Damn you! Take this and be quiet! (*Forces the stuff down her throat. Bettina bursts into tears. She still makes little attempts to leave the room but her motions grow more and more confused and feeble.*)

(*Meanwhile the Tartar has hauled in the new Footman.*)

FOOTMAN: I didn't. The gentleman himself opened the front door.

TARTAR: What for?

FOOTMAN: To show her something. *I* do not know what.

TARTAR: (*A storm of imprecation.*)

(*The Colonel and Grey Hawk try to quiet him and get the facts.*)

FOOTMAN: (*Shaking with fear*) It is as I say. De lady stand dere a second, and look out. De gentleman turn to speak to me. "François," he say—and before we know where we are de lady is not dere. "Where—where is she?" he say, and look round like he not awake. Den he pick up his hat and run out.

(*Confused talking*)

COLONEL: They say the kitchen maid saw the lady turn to the left.

FOOTMAN: I swear, the gentleman run the other way.

ALL TOGETHER: How much did she know? What happened?— She'll go straight to Lowndes Square. How did she know?

TARTAR: Look here! What she'll do will be to stop the first policeman!

GREY HAWK: Go bolt the doors! (*Servants scatter.*)

TARTAR: No you don't! I'm out of this damned mess! (*He bolts.*)

(*The Colonel and Grey Hawk stand one on either side of the unconscious Bettina.*)

COLONEL: What are we to do now?

(*Curtain*)

## Act 3

(*Drawing-room at Lowndes Square. Mrs. Harborough, a rather heavy, stately old woman, and Ranny Dallas are playing Bezique.*[44] *Mrs. Selby, who has been looking over Ranny's shoulder, rises and wanders about the room looking at the old prints or what-not—evidently unsettled.*)

MRS. SELBY: (*Pausing in front of the clock*) In half an hour they ought to be here—no less—

(*Dallas looks up quickly, compares clock with his watch, glances at Mrs. Harborough and goes on with game.*)

MRS. HARBOROUGH: (*Absently, thinking of her cards*) Half an hour, yes—and four kings. (*Takes up marker and marks. They play a card or two.*)

RANNY: Four aces! I'm going to beat you after all, Mrs. Harborough.

MRS. HARBOROUGH: Wait a moment. (*Plays.*) Don't be too sure. (*He plays. She plays.*) Double Bezique! Game!

RANNY: By George! I never saw anything like your luck; really.

MRS. HARBOROUGH: *Luck*!

RANNY: N-o, no, I don't mean that. Fact is I haven't played Bezique since we were youngsters—(*Turning to Janet*)—getting over measles. Whenever I was beaten I used to tell Janet she cheated.

MRS. HARBOROUGH: I'm glad to see that you behave better now. I wonder Bezique isn't more played. It is quite a good game—(*Angrily*)—if it *isn't* bridge!

RANNY: One gets fairly fed up with bridge— (*Turns and looks at the clock.*)

MRS. HARBOROUGH: (*Evidently ready for another game*) Are you going to have your revenge?

RANNY: Oh—delighted! If you think we'll have time.

MRS. HARBOROUGH: Well, perhaps not—they'd be coming in the middle; that is so upsetting. (*Puts cards in case.*)

MRS. SELBY: I wonder what happened to make them lose their train?

RANNY: Oh, forgot their tickets or some of their luggage, I should think.

MRS. HARBOROUGH: Silly creatures! I don't consider this a good beginning. I don't like people who miss their trains.

RANNY: (*Apologetically*) Oh, well, it's their first visit to London, or anywhere, I believe.

MRS. HARBOROUGH: By the way, I wonder if my maid has started to meet them. What did I do with that telegram? Would you hand me my little bag? Thank you. (*She takes out telegram and reads.*) "Don't meet five-twelve. Missed train. Cannot arrive till ten-fifteen." Ten. Fifteen.

RANNY: (*Anxiously*) Isn't it after ten?

MRS. HARBOROUGH: No, five minutes to—and the station's so very near. Still, I'll just ask if Watson's gone; she isn't as dependable as she used to be. Just ring the bell, will you? (*As he is about to do so enter Butler with tray to clear away coffee cups.*)

MRS. HARBOROUGH: Oh, here's Holliday. Watson has started, I suppose?

HOLLIDAY: Not yet, M'm.

MRS. HARBOROUGH: Well, tell her to go at once, or she won't be in time. She ought to be on her way now.

HOLLIDAY: Yes, M'm.

RANNY: She's cutting it rather fine, don't you think? Your maid, I mean. Why not let me go?

MRS. HARBOROUGH: To meet my nieces?

RANNY: Well, you see, I could slap off in a taxi—bring them back here and pick up Janet.

MRS. HARBOROUGH: Oh, no, thank you. Watson . . .

RANNY: But she hasn't started—

MRS. SELBY: Ranny's such an old friend of theirs. Better let him.

RANNY: That's just it—they know me and they don't know your maid—they'd have to hunt for each other. I can look after their traps and see they don't lose everything.

MRS. HARBOROUGH: (*Meditatively*) There is that! I've never forgiven Watson for losing my travelling footstool. We were coming from Mentone—

RANNY: So you don't mind if I—?

MRS. HARBOROUGH: Very well. (*To Holliday*) Tell Watson she needn't go.

(*To Mrs. Selby*) Ever since she lost my travelling footstool—it was the kind that has a foot warmer inside.

HOLLIDAY: (*At the same time as Mrs. Harborough*) Shall I whistle a taxi, sir?

RANNY: No thanks; I shall get one quicker off the rank— (*Exit Ranny, followed by Holliday with the cups.*)

MRS. HARBOROUGH: In my time it wouldn't have been received that a young man should escort girls from the station.

MRS. SELBY: Oh, I think it's all right, nowadays.

MRS. HARBOROUGH: Nowadays, yes, I dare say. "Now-a-days" is the conclusive argument! If a woman of my age objects to young girls going to balls without a chaperon, or going to live in a flat because they hate their mother—or wriggling about as if they had a serpent in their back instead of an honest spine—I'm told "Now-a-days" and there is no more to be said.

MRS. SELBY: (*Laughing*) Well, I won't use that argument. Anyhow I have a better one. This is a rather special case.

MRS. HARBOROUGH: And why, pray, is this case special?

MRS. SELBY: (*Hesitating a little, then comes and sits by Mrs. Harborough.*) Because my brother, I think, feels there is a particular reason why *he* should go to meet—Bettina.

MRS. HARBOROUGH: Oh, really.

MRS. SELBY: He's very hard hit, I'm afraid.

MRS. HARBOROUGH: (*Takes up white wool crochet.*) He has talked to you about it?

MRS. SELBY: Hardly that. You know what brothers are. But I gather—indeed I am quite sure.

MRS. HARBOROUGH: And the little Bettina?

MRS. SELBY: I can't be quite sure about her. I've only seen Bettina once.

MRS. HARBOROUGH: I gather they will have your blessing?

MRS. SELBY: I hope they would have yours.

MRS. HARBOROUGH: If it's any comfort to your Ranny to know it, you may assure him that I haven't taken a dislike to him—rather the other way. As I am Miss Betty's aunt and chaperone, he may be pleased with my favourable impression.

MRS. SELBY: (*Laughing*) I'm sure he will.

MRS. HARBOROUGH: But I have only set eyes on him once—and as yet I haven't so much as set eyes on my niece at all. The only things I know about her is that she is charming and *not* seventeen—and I can't help thinking that in the child's own interests—being charming and *not* seventeen—an immediate engagement—might be—shall we say a little unfair?

MRS. SELBY: Oh—of course.

MRS. HARBOROUGH: Your young man will understand that, I'm sure. He's a very pleasant young man, my dear, and your brother—so I don't want to be hard on him. But I think he ought to let the child look about her for a little. It's the wisest thing—for his sake as well as for hers . . . That (*A little constrainedly*) is what I gather her mother would wish.

MRS. SELBY: Oh, naturally! Any mother would—it is only fair. You haven't seen Mrs. Dorrien, for some time, have you?

MRS. HARBOROUGH: I haven't seen her for twenty years—since she married my brother.

MRS. SELBY: Really? . . .

MRS. HARBOROUGH: You mustn't imagine a feud; there has never been a quarrel in the ordinary sense of the word. It was just that I thought my brother was marrying the wrong woman. It does happen sometimes—when you're very fond of the brother. That was all—except I foolishly took it upon myself to offer advice with the usual results. So there was coldness. They married and went out to India; the children were born and he died—and when she came home as a widow, I understood, from other people, that she did not care to insist on the relationship. So I left it at that and kept away; until a few weeks ago when an advance came from the eldest girl—from Honor. I won't deny that I was glad enough to respond to it. You see (*Mrs. Selby turns her head and listens*) I am growing an old woman now, and I have no children of my own, and Frank was my very dear brother. I hope we shall be better friends in the future—the children, their Mother and I.

MRS. SELBY: Was that a ring?

MRS. HARBOROUGH: It sounded like it.

MRS. SELBY: And I thought I heard a taxi stop—

MRS. HARBOROUGH: It surely can't be—

MRS. SELBY: Oh no, they can't possibly be here yet. Ranny has hardly had time to get to the station.

MRS. HARBOROUGH: Besides—the train isn't due yet.

MRS. SELBY: (*Drawing aside curtain*) There is a taxi at the door.

(*Voice in passage—"Mrs. Harborough! Where is Mrs. Harborough!"*)

MRS. HARBOROUGH: (*Astonished, stiffening*) Who is screaming my name out like that?

(*The door is flung suddenly open and Honor stands panting on the threshold.*)

MRS. HARBOROUGH: Why—what's this?

MRS. SELBY: Good Heavens! It's—

HONOR: Are you Aunt Josephine? Mrs. Harborough—you *are*.

MRS. HARBOROUGH: Oh—are you Betty?

HONOR: No, I'm Honor. Betty—you must come and save her! For God's sake come with me and save her— D'you understand—save her—save her— (*Leans panting breathless against the door.*)

MRS. SELBY: Save her!

MRS. HARBOROUGH: What do you mean?

MRS. SELBY: An accident—there has been an accident?

MRS. HARBOROUGH: Where—how—is Betty hurt?

HONOR: No, no, not an accident—it's worse a thousand times. She's in a place—a place—we've got to get her out. I'll show you—come with me —quick.

MRS. HARBOROUGH: You must calm yourself.

HONOR: Come with me, come—and I'll tell you on the way.

MRS. SELBY: (*Taking her by the shoulder*) You remember me, don't you? I'm Ranny Dallas's sister, and you know I want to help you. But how can we do anything till we know what has happened?

HONOR: (*Repeats, shuddering*) What's happened?—not yet—oh God—not yet— But we must be quick.

MRS. SELBY: You must pull yourself together; you must try and talk reasonably. Now—tell me—where is your sister?

HONOR: I've told you already, she's in a place—a place—like hell—shut up there.

MRS. SELBY: Shut up?

HONOR: The doors are locked and the windows are barred and I tell you she can't get out. A man helped me to get out but he couldn't help her—he didn't dare. Betty's shut up there alone—with men, and a woman who is a devil! And if you don't come—if you don't come this moment—

MRS. HARBOROUGH: My dear, what does she mean—what is she talking about?

HONOR: Betty—I'm talking about Betty. My little sister! She's there and I had to leave her—I had to get help.

MRS. HARBOROUGH: But where—where—?

HONOR: I've told you! I've told you! In a house where they do worse than murder. That's where Betty is—and now do you understand, now will you come and help her?

MRS. HARBOROUGH: In a house where—

HONOR: (*To Mrs. Selby*) Oh, make her understand—can't you make her? No, no, don't—wait, don't talk to her; if we wait any longer, it might—might *be too late*! If you're Ranny's sister, you'll come for Ranny's sake.

MRS. SELBY: She can't mean—

HONOR: Do you want me to say it again? Can't you hear—can't you listen when I tell you? (*Controlling herself and speaking slowly*) She's in a house where women are sold to men. Betty—Betty who doesn't know anything. "One of the most infamous houses in Europe." That's what he said. That's quite plain isn't it? You can understand now?[45]

MRS. HARBOROUGH: But it can't be—we're—we're in England!

MRS. SELBY: If it's true!

HONOR: "If" it's true!—she says, *if it's true*!

MRS. SELBY: Hush, don't be afraid, I believe you. Oh, if Ranny were only back. (*She runs to bell and rings it.*)

HONOR: (*Following her*) If you believe me what are you waiting for?

MRS. SELBY: I'm coming, don't be afraid. (*To Mrs. Harborough, who is sitting as if stupefied, staring straight in front of her.*) We must go with her at once—but I think the police ought to how. Your butler, couldn't he?

MRS. HARBOROUGH: (*Places her hands on the arms of her chair, about to rise.*) Yes, yes, anything—

MRS. SELBY: Where is this place—how far?

HONOR: Twenty minutes in a taxi, he said—twenty minutes in a taxi from Lowndes Square. It seemed hours and hours.

MRS. SELBY: But where is it, child—what part of London?

HONOR: Wh—what part?

MRS. HARBOROUGH: (*Standing her full height and speaking presumptuously*) Yes—the name of the street and the number?

HONOR: Name? Number? (*She opens her terrified eyes wide and utters a cry.*)

MRS. HARBOROUGH: (*Hand on table leaning forward*) It is not possible you have forgotten the address!

HONOR: (*Her lips are again parted, but at first no sound*) I never heard it. (*She falls on a chair and covers her face.*)

MRS. HARBOROUGH: (*To Mrs. Selby*) Ring, ring, again. (*She chafes Honor's hands.*)

(*Mrs. Selby rings and rushes back to find Holliday in the room.*)

MRS. HARBOROUGH: Water, bring some water—bring brandy. There, there. (*As Honor opens her eyes*) Now, child. Tell us what you can remember.

HONOR: (*Holding her temples and trying to recall*) I ran out—I ran and ran; I never looked at the street—it was dark—I looked for a cab—I found a cab—and I— (*Starts up crying out*) Thank God—thank God—it's waiting! Come! He knows. The cabman knows! I forgot that I kept him to save time. He'll take us to the street and then we'll find the house—

MRS. SELBY: We'd better have a policeman along with us.

MRS. HARBOROUGH: (*To Holliday, who has brought a tray, water, etc.*) Get the policeman in our Square. And tell Watson to give you my cloak—bring an armful of wraps—

HOLLIDAY: (*As he goes out*) And call a taxi, M'm?

MRS. HARBOROUGH: There's one at the door.

HOLLIDAY: (*Stops.*) No, M'm—

MRS. HARBOROUGH: Yes, yes,—the one Miss Dorrien came in—

HOLLIDAY: He's gone, M'm.

MRS. HARBOROUGH and MRS. SELBY: Gone!!

HONOR: He can't have gone—I never paid him—

HOLLIDAY: I paid him, Miss, and sent him away—

HONOR: You—you—what have you done? Stop him. Stop him— (*She rushes to the door. Mrs. Selby seizes her.*)

MRS. SELBY: No, no, not you, not you— Go after him, man—run, run!

(*Exit Holliday.*)

MRS. SELBY: (*Holding Honor's hands*) It's no use your running out in the street—you'd only lose yourself. Holliday knows where the cab rank is.

HONOR: But if my cabman isn't there! What's going to happen if he isn't there!!

MRS. HARBOROUGH: Sit down, child—sit down. You didn't notice his number?

HONOR: Number—what number?

MRS. SELBY: The number of the taxi?

HONOR: Was there a number?

MRS. SELBY: They all have numbers—we might have found him that way.

HONOR: If he doesn't catch him—if he doesn't catch him—

MRS. SELBY: Don't—don't—he will—he will.

(*There's a moment's silence, while they all listen intently.*)

HONOR: (*Turning suddenly on Mrs. Harborough*) Oh, why didn't you come to meet us at the station, as you said? You said you would; why didn't you keep your word?

MRS. HARBOROUGH: I should have—but when you telegraphed—

HONOR: Telegraphed?

MRS. HARBOROUGH: That you'd lost your train and were arriving so late. (*Pauses.*)

HONOR: We never—(*Honor makes motion of bewilderment, then jumps up and goes to window, looks out.*)

MRS. SELBY: But how—you must have come by the 5:12, after all.

HONOR: Yes, yes, of course. (*Wrings her hands.*) I must go and find the cab man myself. (*Runs towards door.*)

MRS. SELBY: Oh, if Ranny were only here!

HOLLIDAY: (*Enters breathless.*) He wasn't on the rank, M'm. I couldn't see him anywhere.

(*Honor collapses in a chair. After an instant's horrified silence—*)

HONOR: (*In a whisper*) Sent away! Sent away the only one in London who knows!—(*Then with a choked cry*) Betty!! (*She tries to struggle to her feet.*)

MRS. SELBY: Hush— (*Forcing her back into her chair*) Keep your head—we must think.

HOLLIDAY: And the policeman, M'm, am I to—

(*Enter Ranny.*)

HONOR: (*Staggering towards him*) Ranny!

RANNY: What's the matter?

HONOR: Ranny! Save her!

RANNY: Save who? Why, what in heaven's name— (*He catches Honor in his arms.*) Where's Betty? (*Honor half fainting*)

MRS. HARBOROUGH: (*To Ranny*) Put her down on the sofa. (*To Mrs. Selby*) I'll look after her. Tell him.

RANNY: Janet, where's Betty?

MRS. SELBY: Come here. (*She draws him up stage and speaks to him rapidly.*)

MRS. HARBOROUGH: (*Bending over Honor*) Honor, my poor child, you mustn't despair—you must keep up your courage. Thank God he has come back—he'll know what to do.

HONOR: (*Clinging to her*) Yes, he'll find her, he'll go out and find her. Ranny will do it—Ranny loves her, too!

RANNY: (*Upstage with Mrs. Selby, gives a sharp, horrified cry.*)

MRS. HARBOROUGH: (*Soothing Honor*) I'm sure you can trust him. He'll do what he can—all there is to be done. He won't leave a stone unturned—he won't leave a stone—(*Mrs. Harborough and Honor watch Ranny and Mrs. Selby for a moment; then Ranny breaks away from his sister.*)

RANNY: (*To Mrs. Harborough*) —Telephone! Where's your telephone?

MRS. HARBOROUGH: In the dining-room—by the bookcase.

MRS. SELBY: (*As he rushes to the door*) What are you going to do?

RANNY: Ring up the nearest police station. Wait here— (*Exit Ranny.*)

MRS. HARBOROUGH: You see, he knows what to do. We can leave it in his hands. He'll tell the police and they'll know how to set about looking—they'll know where to find her.

HONOR: Yes, but how soon—how soon? They've got to be quick. Did you tell him that—do you think he understands that?

MRS. SELBY: Yes—yes.

HONOR: The things that man told me—she might be drugged—that's what they do. He said they might take her to Paris—and it's been so long since I left her—

MRS. HARBOROUGH and MRS. SELBY: No—no—quite a short time.

HONOR: But every minute matters—every single minute that goes by.

MRS. SELBY: He knows that—Ranny knows it. Oh, you needn't be afraid that he will lose a minute. Do you think he feels it less than you do?

HONOR: No—I think he loves her— Has he told you that?

MRS. SELBY: I've guessed it.

HONOR: So have I—for a long time. He's like me—he'd rather die than let any harm come to Betty. If I could save her, I'd die—I'd die this minute—And yet I left her—I slipped out of the house and left her—while she was singing to those men—I don't know how I did it—I don't know how—If she had looked at me I couldn't have done it—but the man told me it was the only thing to do—the only way there was any hope of saving her. So I went out end left her—and she doesn't know why—I wonder how soon she found out I wasn't there any longer—and what she thought. She must have found out by now. Perhaps she has found out—other things.

MRS. HARBOROUGH: Hush. Hush.

MRS. SELBY: No, no, sit still. Ranny—

HONOR: I can't. Just think of her alone there. My little sister, my Betty. What would you feel if it was your sister?—Those men. And that devil—that devil. You can see in her eyes that she doesn't know what it is to have any mercy or pity—that whatever you said or whatever you did—I ought to have seen from the first—but how was I, how was I to guess?—and Betty was just singing to them and dancing—Not at all afraid—quite happy, and not knowing, anything . . . and I couldn't say a word to her—not a single word to warn her. I went out and left her—alone with them—singing and dancing. . . What is she thinking of me now? What will she think of me if we don't get there in time?

MRS. SELBY: But we shall—we shall.

HONOR: You're only saying that to quiet me.

MRS. SELBY: No, no—indeed I'm not.

HONOR: You're sure? You believe?—But we don't know where to go! How can we get there in time when we don't know where to go?

MRS. SELBY: Ranny has sent for the police—they'll be here directly.

MRS. HARBOROUGH: Yes, there's a station quite near.

HONOR: But the police don't know either—how can they tell?

MRS. SELBY: Oh, they will—they will. They know a great many things that we don't, about—that sort of people. It's their business.

HONOR: Why does Ranny stay away so long?

MRS. SELBY: He is downstairs telephoning.

HONOR: I must go and hear what he says—if he tells them right. I don't know what you said to him. (*She tries to rise and the others detain her.*)

MRS. HARBOROUGH: No, no.

MRS. SELBY: Ranny said: wait here. He'll be back in a moment. Indeed I told him everything.

(*Enter Ranny followed by a Police Inspector.*)

MRS. SELBY: Here he is.

RANNY: This is the young lady, Inspector—the one who escaped. Honor, he wants to know everything—you must tell him exactly.

HONOR: Yes—only you won't be long. We ought to be starting now.

INSPECTOR: I'll do my best if you'll answer my questions, Miss. (*He takes out his note-book and licks his pencil.*) I understand that you and your sister arrived at Victoria this afternoon by the five-twelve? Is that correct?

HONOR: Yes.

INSPECTOR: And what happened then—after you had got out of the train?

HONOR: A lady came up to us—she waved to us just as the train was stopping. We thought she was our aunt.

MRS. HARBOROUGH: They had never seen me in their lives.

INSPECTOR: I see . . . By the way, Mr. Dallas said something about a bogus telegram—have you kept it?

MRS. HARBOROUGH: (*Fumbling in her bag*) Yes—here it is.

INSPECTOR: (*Reads telegram to himself.*)

HONOR: (*To Mrs. Selby*) How slow he is; doesn't he understand?

INSPECTOR: I'll keep this, Madam—it may give us a clue. (*He places telegram in pocket-book.*) And now—this lady who met you on the platform—what did she say to you?

HONOR: She asked if we were Honor and Betty.

INSPECTOR: You're sure?

HONOR: Yes.

INSPECTOR: Sure she mentioned your names?

HONOR: (*Impatiently*) Quite, quite, quite.

INSPECTOR: (*Makes a note—then*) Will you tell me what she was like to look at—as accurately as you can, please.

HONOR: She is tall und dark—with grey hair—rolled back. She was dressed all in black—with a hat full of ostrich feathers—black too—and all her clothes smelt of scent. I think you'd call her handsome but I don't know—(*She shivers.*) She wore pearl earrings—like Aunt Josephine in the old photograph we had. She took us in her motor.

INSPECTOR: Did you notice the number of the car?

HONOR: No.

INSPECTOR: What sort of car—what make?

HONOR: (*Passionately*) Oh, I don't know! (*Controlling herself*) Yes. A large car—green—dark green (*To Ranny*) like the Helmstones'—

RANNY: A limousine.

INSPECTOR: (*Writing*) Dark green limousine. Did you notice the chauffeur's livery?

HONOR: Dark—with brass buttons—and the footman's too.

INSPECTOR: Ah. (*Writing*) Two men on driver's seat . . . I understand that you don't know London at all?

HONOR: I've never been to London before.

INSPECTOR: Can you describe at all the way you went—after you turned out of the station?

HONOR: (*Uncertainly*) I—

RANNY: Try to remember—try.

HONOR: I think there was a kind of a garden first—or a patch of green—and then a long wall on one side and some high houses on the other.

RANNY: Grosvenor Place?

INSPECTOR: (*Writes—nods.*) And afterwards—can you remember what came next?

HONOR: What came next?

INSPECTOR: Think—it's important.

HONOR: I'm not sure—my head seems . . .

MRS. SELBY: Wasn't there a big open space—very wide. With lots of traffic—and two large arches.

HONOR: Yes, yes, that came next—I remember. The policeman held out his arm and we stopped in the middle of the road.

INSPECTOR: (*Writing*) Hyde Park Corner.

RANNY: And then—

HONOR: We went on into a park—with flower beds— . . . Oh, my God, we keep talking, talking, talking! Aren't we going to—

MRS. SELBY: Honor, Honor.

INSPECTOR: I'm very sorry, Miss, but it's the only way we shall get a clue.

HONOR: (*Weakly*) I'm sorry. What was I telling you?

MRS. SELBY: You said you went through a park with flower beds.

HONOR: Yes— Flower beds—and houses beyond them.

INSPECTOR: Houses on your right hand side.

HONOR: Yes.

INSPECTOR: And did you go straight through the park till you came to a large arch with a street beyond it—or did you turn off—

HONOR: Yes, we came to a large arch—another large arch.

INSPECTOR: (*Writes.*) And then?

HONOR: Then?—I only remember streets and streets—and streets.

RANNY: For the love of God, Honor, try and remember—think! When you left the Park—when you came out of it by the arch—which way did the car go? To the right—to the left—

HONOR: (*With her hands to her head, trying to fix her thoughts*) I think . . . straight on—or nearly straight.

RANNY: North of Oxford St., then.

INSPECTOR: Or North of Bayswater Rd.? She said *nearly* straight on.

HONOR: Nearly straight on—for a time . . . and then we turned—yes, we turned two or three times . . . I can't remember how the turns came.

INSPECTOR: And you can't remember the name of any street you passed? You didn't see a name written up at any of the corners?

HONOR: No, we were watching the people and talking. We never thought of looking at names . . . We thought we were going to Lowndes Square.

RANNY: Lord, have mercy! (*He covers his face with his hands.*)

INSPECTOR: And the street you were set down in—what was it like?

HONOR: There were large houses—very large. With gardens in front of them. The houses had porches—porticos.

INSPECTOR: Yes—You can't remember anything else about them—any detail?

HONOR: No—we went in as quickly. (*She looks at him hopelessly.*)

RANNY: Listen Honor. After you left the park, how long was it before the car stopped?

HONOR: Not long. Only a few minutes.

INSPECTOR: How many minutes—ten?

HONOR: I should think not more than ten. (*Puts her hands over her face.*)

INSPECTOR: H'm. And now the young lady's description, please. Her name?

MRS. HARBOROUGH: Bettina Dorrien.

INSPECTOR: (*Writing*) Bettina Dorrien—double R?

HONOR: (*With a sudden outburst*) Oh, does it matter how you spell it?

MRS. SELBY: Dear, he has to—

MRS. HARBOROUGH: Double r.i.e.n.

INSPECTOR: Thank you. Age?

MRS. HARBOROUGH: Nearly seventeen.

INSPECTOR: Height and appearance?

MRS. HARBOROUGH: Honor, you'll have to—

HONOR: She's not so tall as I and younger. She looks younger than she is—younger than seventeen. She has fair hair and a complexion like a baby's.

INSPECTOR: Eyes?

HONOR: Grey— Large eyes—like a baby's too.

INSPECTOR: Thank you. (*He closes his note-book—draws Ranny aside.*) We'll do all we can, sir—you can rely on that.

RANNY: And what she has she told you—does it give you any clue?

INSPECTOR: (*Aside*) Well—not so very much. Somewhere north of Oxford St. or Bayswater Rd.—ten minutes from the Marble Arch. And even that's vague. There are a good many houses of that sort within a ten minute's radius of Marble Arch. It's possible one of our men may have noticed the car at Victoria—the woman's obviously an old hand and we get to know most of these people by sight. That's about our best chance . . . Then, there's the taxi that picked up the young lady and brought her here—I'll have enquiries made for him. (*Writes again in note-book.*) Lady in evening dress Marylebone, Bayswater, Paddington or St. John's Wood district—dropped at 160 Lowndes Square . . .

HONOR: What's he saying to you Ranny? What's he going to do?

RANNY: God knows—I shall go mad, I think.

HONOR: What do you mean, Ranny? Isn't he going to do something? (*To Inspector*) What are you waiting for? Don't stand there.

INSPECTOR: (*Soothingly*) We'll do all there is to be done.

HONOR: And what is there to be done?

INSPECTOR: Well, we'll make all—

HONOR: Enquiries—But aren't you going to look for her—aren't you going to begin this instant?

INSPECTOR: It wouldn't be much good starting out to look for her until we've identified the house—would it now?

HONOR: But how long will that take? When will you identify it—when?

INSPECTOR: Well, it's difficult to say—but we'll do all we can—and sooner or later we're bound to identify it.

HONOR: Sooner or later! Does that mean now—to-night?

INSPECTOR: Well, we've got to make our enquiries . . . but, as I say, we're bound to identify it in the end. It's sure to be on our list. Then we'll apply for a search warrant—

HONOR: Your list—what list?

INSPECTOR: Why, the list we have—the police list—of—of that sort of house.

HONOR: (*Lifting her face*) That sort of house? Do you mean that there is more than one . . .

INSPECTOR: Well . . .

HONOR: Do you mean that there are many . . . ?

INSPECTOR: I'm afraid there are, Miss—you see, young ladies like you—

HONOR: (*Staring at him*) Many houses where they take girls and— So many that you can't tell which—and you know it, and you *keep the list*! . . .

(*There is a moment's pause.*)

INSPECTOR: (*Awkwardly to Ranny*) I think I'll be off—I seem to have all the information the young lady can give me. We shall do our best—and as soon as news comes in, I'll ring up—or send round.

RANNY: (*Mechanically*) Thank you.

INSPECTOR: Not at all, sir. Good-night. (*Exit Inspector.*)

HONOR: (*Slowly and staring in front of her*) Sooner or later . . . And now—this very night—perhaps this very minute . . .

RANNY: God in Heaven—stop. (*He falls suddenly into a chair, sobbing.*)

(*Mrs. Selby makes a movement towards him, then turns away despairingly. Mrs. Harborough is sitting silently rocking herself backwards and forwards a little, with her eyes closed and her hands clasped as if in prayer. Honor does not notice any of them; she just sits staring before her. When she speaks her voice is slow and level, and as if talking to herself.*)

HONOR: Then we really can't do anything except sit and wait while the police make enquiries—about which of the places on the list . . . (*She sits silent until a little-moan from Mrs. Harborough catches her ear; she turns and looks at her as if just aware of her presence.*) You didn't know it, did you—that a girl could be taken like that—a girl who was good like Betty?

MRS. HARBOROUGH: No, no—who could have thought—

HONOR: (*In the same tone*) Yes, I remember you couldn't believe it at first. I had to keep on telling you. If anyone had told me yesterday, I shouldn't have believed it either . . . But that man—he knew—he has known it all along. But (*To Ranny*) you didn't know, did you?

RANNY: (*Makes no answer. His face is still hidden.*)

HONOR: (*Waits a moment for Ranny to reply—and then goes on as before.*) You knew! That a girl like Betty!

RANNY: (*Springs up.*)

MRS. SELBY: Where are you going?—

RANNY: I don't know—

(*Enter Holliday with a man.*)

HOLLIDAY: (*Stopping Dallas*) If you please sir, a gentleman says he must see you at once—

RANNY: Who are you? Can't stop now.

DETECTIVE: I'm MacDougal.

RANNY: Mac. Dougal?

DETECTIVE: You telephoned for me, sir. (*Adds something sotto voice.*)

RANNY: Oh, the Detective. Of course—I'd forgotten—(*Talks very fast in a whisper. Pause.*)

HONOR: (*Who has paid no attention, staring rigidly into vacancy*) And Eric—I suppose, he knows too—

MRS. SELBY: (*Gently*) Every man—that is, most—know to a certain extent.

HONOR: And they do nothing—they let it go on. But we didn't know—Betty and I—no one had ever told *us*—

RANNY: (*Turns sharply.*) What can you remember about the other people who were at that place?

HONOR: (*In a mechanical, toneless voice—still staring in front of her*) Three men. One old, one who opened the door for me, and the one we both took for Hermione's fiancé—for Guy Whitby-Dawson.

RANNY: Why, I thought you'd never seen Whitby-Dawson.

HONOR: Only his picture. The man was like the picture. But he was angry when Betty took him for Mr. Whitby-Dawson.

RANNY: Angry, was he? (*To himself*) It would be like Whitby-Dawson— (*Suddenly*) Look here. (*Shakes Honor slightly by the arm.*) Was he a big fellow, bullet-headed, black moustache, with a scar?—

HONOR: (*Nods vaguely.*) Yes, a scar. (*Lifts her hand feebly and draws it across her chin and lets her hand fall in her lap.*)

RANNY: (*Turns with sudden conviction, whispers to Detective.*)

DETECTIVE: Of course he would deny it. Any gentleman *would.*

HONOR: (*Starts up.*) Mother, mother! (*The two women close about her, try to soothe and hold her.*)

DETECTIVE: (*To Ranny*) *He* won't know, none of 'em will—that the young lady had no idea of the address. They'll be expecting a raid.

RANNY: By the police?

DETECTIVE: (*Nods.*) As to what's going on at that house, you can make yourself easy so far as to-night's concerned.

RANNY: Easy?

DETECTIVE: It'll be the one house of *that* sort where there'll be nothing doing to-night.

RANNY: You mean Whitby-Dawson and the rest—

DETECTIVE: Busy, proving alibis.

RANNY: Getting out of the country?

DETECTIVE: Can't do that till to-morrow.

RANNY: No boats! That's so.

DETECTIVE: At their clubs or— (*Looks at his watch*) gone home. Strikes me, your clue is the gentleman.

RANNY: (*Face lights up—drives his left fist into right palm.*) Look here, Whitby-Dawson's chambers are in Mount Street! (*Calls sharply.*) Janet! Telephone book—Whitby-Dawson's number— Quick! (*Mrs. Selby flies out.*)

DETECTIVE: You wouldn't telephone to him!

RANNY: No, but I want his number. (*Takes the Detective by the arm, draws him further away from Honor and Mrs. Harborough.*) Listen! There's such a thing as tapping the wires . . . ? (*They whisper.*) Well, anyway you could go to the Exchange and bribe, bully—what you like. D'you understand? Money is no object in this. *Whatever it costs*, find out what number is rung up to-night by Mr. Guy Whitby-Dawson.

MRS. SELBY: (*Coming in with telephone book open, finger pointing. Reads out:*) "Empress 1622."

RANNY: Empress 1622.

RANNY: (*To Detective*) Wait for me at the Telephone Exchange. I'll come on there after I've . . . (*Accompanies Detective to door, whispering. Exit Detective. Ranny hurries back to his sister.*)

RANNY: You and Honor have got to come with me. Give her some wine —yes, brandy—(*As Holliday appears at door*) Another taxi please! We'll be in Mount Street in eight minutes.

(*Curtain*)

## Act 4

### *Scene 1*

SCENE: *The sitting room at Whitby-Dawson's Chambers in Mount Street.*

(*Whitby-Dawson, flushed, perspiring, coatless, waistcoat undone, is by telephone, receiver at ear.*)

WHITBY: (*Angrily to his valet who waits by bathroom door*) Damn you! What are you standing there, staring at?

VALET: Just came to tell you it's ready, sir.

WHITBY: What's ready?

VALET: The shaving water you ordered, sir.

WHITBY: I didn't order water. I told you to give me a clean shave—quick too!

VALET: Yes, sir. (*Hesitates.*) You don't—er—mean in here, sir—?

WHITBY: That the Exchange? I've asked twice for the clerk in charge. Oh, you are! Well, don't let's have any tomfoolery *this* time, or I'll make a deuce of a row. If a call comes for 1622 this line is *not* "engaged." I "*can* be found." I've warned you! (*Listens.*) I tell you I shan't be three feet away from this receiver for the next three hours. (*Listens. Valet disappears, comes back with dressing gown, shaving mug, etc.*)

WHITBY: All right. (*Hangs up receiver, pours out brandy, flings himself in chair.*

*Valet in and out.*) Well, now as I was saying: rotten day at races—up four nights running—worn to a thread paper. Got that?

VALET: Yes, sir.

WHITBY: (*Half to himself*) Now where did I dine?

VALET: You said at the Club, sir.

WHITBY: I didn't dine at the Club.

VALET: Oh, didn't you, sir?

WHITBY: (*Reflective*) I dined here. (*Looks sharply at Valet, as he doesn't instantly endorse the statement.*) What the devil is the good of keeping a cook, if I never dine at home?

VALET: Very true, sir—but you told the cook she might—

WHITBY: What if I did! Are you such a fool you can't grill a sole, or set a cold fowl on the table?

VALET: No, sir. (*Puts towel round Whitby.*)

WHITBY: Very well, that's what you've done, see? (*Holds off the shaving brush an instant.*) I telephoned you I was coming home, after all.

VALET: Yes, sir, but—

WHITBY: Damnation! Don't tell me again it's the cook's night off. You've already made that illuminating remark three times. You got me something to eat. As you don't usually, the fact impressed you. You remember I didn't like your salad. I've been reading the papers in this room since half past eight. Remember?

VALET: Yes, sir. (*Lathers him.*)

WHITBY: You're sure you understand?

VALET: I think I do. (*Faint trace of malice*)

WHITBY: Well—look here, Billings. This . . . this time . . . (*He seizes the man's arm and looks him in the eyes.*)

VALET: Yes, sir; quite so, sir.

WHITBY: (*Drops his hold, assumes a careless air.*) What I was going to say was—(*A ring. Dawson jumps up.*) I've gone to bed. (*Turns at bathroom door—speaks low.*) Money in your pocket not to forget how I've spent every moment of the time since 8 o'clock.

VALET: (*Imperturbable*) Yes, sir.

WHITBY: (*Comes back, pulls Billings round and points to mug, towels.*) You born idiot! Clear that away! (*Exit.*)

(*Valet clears away, shuts bathroom door. Second ring. Valet goes to the door which opens into passage. He is heard indistinctly making excuses.*)

RANNY: (*Outside*) Why, Billings, have you forgotten me?

VALET: Oh, it's you, sir! We 'aven't seen you for such a while. I—

RANNY: Mr. Whitby-Dawson in?

VALET: Yes, sir. Been in all evening. Gone to bed sir. A bit done. All day at the races.

RANNY: Glad he's in. (*Tries to enter.*)

(*The two ladies are seen behind him. Mrs. Selby with Honor's arm drawn through hers.*)

VALET: Very sorry, sir. I 'ad particular orders, sir. Mr. Whitby's been sleeping bad. I was on no account to disturb him, sir.

RANNY: Yes, but he'll see me, you know.

VALET: Well, sir, any other time, I know he would, but he won't see anyone to-night, sir.

RANNY: I tell you, Billings—

VALET: Very sorry, sir—

RANNY: If you don't want to take the responsibility—

VALET: I really couldn't, sir.

RANNY: Then I'll announce myself. (*Towards the bathroom door*)

VALET: (*Hurriedly intervenes*) Just a moment, sir. I'll tell—I'll wake Mr. Whitby. (*Leaves bathroom door open, returns, eyes on the ladies.*) Who shall I say, sir?

RANNY: Just say Mr. Dallas. (*Exit Valet.*)

(*Mrs. Selby has led Honor to a seat and stands beside her. Ranny is sharply scrutinizing the room as he walks about—makes sure the bedroom door—opposite the open bath-room is shut, etc.*)

RANNY: (*Frowns as he looks about. Under his breath*) He must be the one. (*Mrs. Selby makes a sign that the telephone is behind high-backed chair, or screen. Ranny nods relieved. Goes close to Honor.*) Remember, we accept his denials. You are convinced he's not the man.

HONOR: (*Shakes her head—tries to speak.*)

MRS. SELBY: She thinks she will never—never be able—

(*Sound of Whitby-Dawson opening the inner door*)

HONOR: (*Unstrung, shaking, unmindful of the instructions, before she sees more than his height, bulk and bullet head, cries out.*) Betty! What have you done with her—? (*As the Tartar without the marked moustache, his sleek hair ruffled, faces her, she draws back, crying.*) Oh, no, no—this isn't— (*Drops into Mrs. Selby's arms.*)

(*Ranny is motionless, watching Dawson closely.*)

WHITBY: Hello—what's up?

RANNY: My sister, Mrs. Selby—and— (*As he draws Whitby-Dawson aside*) Look here, Dawson, a ghastly thing has happened—this girl's sister has been decoyed—

(*His voice low—words indistinguishable, speaking two or three quick sentences.*)

WHITBY: Sounds a cock and bull story to me—

RANNY: (*Sternly*) I vouch for the truth of it.

WHITBY: Well, what if it is? What in thunder do you come to me for?

RANNY: I hoped if I were to describe the house you might help us to find it.

WHITBY: I help you? I? What in the name of Satan do I know about your house?

RANNY: (*Looking at him very straight.*) You are, or were, when I used to see more of you, pretty well up in such matters.

WHITBY: (*Glances at Mrs. Selby. Low, to Ranny.*) Strikes me you deserve to be kicked down the stairs. I don't know why I don't kick you down stairs.

RANNY: I do. Among other reasons, it would look a little odd, if at my mere stating the case, you were so unstrung as to want to murder me.

WHITBY: Damn you! (*Recovers himself.*) To have you coming here and—Isn't it enough to make a man—?

RANNY: Not at all—you shouldn't jump to damaging conclusions.

WHITBY: (*Scowls.*) Coming here and asking *me* . . . !! You seem to take me for a policeman!

RANNY: No, for a more useful person. As to why we came to you—these ladies are friends of a particular friend of yours. Of Hermione Helmstone. Also they saw a man there they took for you.

WHITBY: Took for me—how could they take me for anybody? (*Violently*) I tell you I don't know them! You heard her say herself she'd made a mistake. By the Lord, Dallas—

RANNY: (*In a conciliatory tone*) Yes, but she couldn't have known what she does now—if she hadn't come here and seen you. Be reasonable.

WHITBY: (*Prowling angrily about, catches sight of telephone—his agitation increases.*) Look here, I'm sorry to seem rude—

RANNY: You've got the jumps, Dawson. The case is this:

WHITBY: (*Nervously circling about the telephone*) "The case," whatever it is, isn't my job. I'm sorry—I'm afraid you must excuse me. (*He looks angrily in the direction of Mrs. Selby and Honor.*)

RANNY: (*Sharply*) Oh, very well—I dare say we'll get on without you. They may be there by now.[46]

WHITBY: What are you going to do?

RANNY: It's no use your knowing, if you won't help.

WHITBY: You haven't told me how I can.

RANNY: (*Sharply*) Would you help if I showed you how? The point is:

WHITBY: (*With sudden misgiving*) Who's there? Where—?

RANNY: The police. They know enough as it is to land several people in gaol to-morrow.[47] (*He moves towards the ladies, takes up the cloak Honor has dropped.*)

WHITBY: (*Follows—under his breath*) You said she was half out of her head and couldn't give the address.

RANNY: I said—couldn't give the exact address.

WHITBY: How much of it do you know?

RANNY: Oh, enough, enough. The only thing was . . . (*Moving away. Whitby-Dawson following*) . . . was whether we could act to-night, and have no scandal, or to-morrow, and have the names in everybody's mouth. (*Looking at Whitby very straight.*) For the girl's sake we don't want that.

WHITBY: No, of course not. For the girl's sake. Wait a bit— Let me think! If I could help you in any way—

RANNY: (*For one moment losing some of his self-control—speaks hoarsely.*) *Time*, man! The whole question is one of time!

WHITBY: What's the girl to you?

RANNY: (*Hesitates an instant, then suddenly*) Pretty much the whole show.

WHITBY: (*Gives a low, horrified whistle.*)

HONOR: (*Honor stands up shakily; Janet puts cloak around her, nervously.*) You'd better just tell me what's the plan.

RANNY: Plan?

HONOR: Yes, what are the bally police at? You intimated they weren't being too brilliant.

RANNY: Oh, they'll run the foxes to earth—sure as Fate!

HONOR: Ah!

RANNY: But to do any good to (*Break in voice*) *us*, the business would have to be put through quietly.

HONOR: And not to-morrow—to-night, Ranny. *Now*. (*Janet soothes her—Leads her out of the door.*)

RANNY: She's right—it's no time for words. (*Bolts after the two women.*)

WHITBY: (*Pours out brandy, walks up and down, goes to telephone, stands looking at it, puts out his hand to receiver, draws it back, goes to bathroom door, stands *listening, opens door suddenly.*) Billings. (*Billings is washing out shaving mug or what not.*)

VALET: Yes, sir? (*Comes out.*)

WHITBY: (*Plainly at a loss to invent some errand.*) Ah—yes—I—a—I must get a letter into the pillar box to-night.

VALET: Yes, sir.

WHITBY: (*Comes back, takes up a blank sheet of paper, facing audience with blood-shot, vacant eyes; folds the blank sheet, puts it in envelope, licks it down.*) Here you are—*quick*, Billings!

VALET: (*Valet goes and returns.*) There's no address, sir.

WHITBY: Damn! (*Scribbles on envelope.*) Look lively! D'you hear? (*As soon as Billings exits the outside door, Whitby rushes to telephone—is about to take up receiver when Billings returns second time.*) Damnation!

VALET: Shall I get a stamp, sir?

WHITBY: Good Lord, no! Let the other fella pay. (*Exit Valet.*) (*Walks up and down, listens to sound of footsteps dying—to telephone again. Stops, goes softly to door, listens, throws it open suddenly—no one. Satisfied, returns to telephone. Hesitates again.*) What risk can there be? Less than letting them be nabbed. (*Rings up a number.*) Who's that? Oh, that you, Colonel? You know who's speaking? No names, understand? Well—is—a—the lady of the house—What? In her car? How long ago? Who with? What? Did she take anybody else? Who's Carron? What? Speak plainer—this damn line— Taken Carron and the meat? Hah! Got off with the meat, eh? Good, good! Where're they going? To Hell! Oh, Hull for Hamburg? Capital! You and I'd better go to Hell Hull too, eh?[48] I'll come and talk to you about it to-morrow. Yes. Good-night. (*Has nearly hung up receiver—reconsiders.*) Oh, I say—Yes? (*Hears the different voice.*) Who's that? Who are you? (*Nearly drops receiver.*) Dallas! Why, I—I haven't been talking to you! But you've what? You have had the benefit of it! (*Drops receiver.*) Good God! He knows! ! !

*Scene 2*

SCENE: *Passage and Campion Way, SS. Fritz, in Hull Harbour, bound for Hamburg.*

(*Enter Ranny with Porter.*)

RANNY: (*Giving tip to Porter or Deck Steward*) Tell some one to ask the Purser to come and speak to me. Say it's important. I can't possibly leave this lady.

(*Turns to see that Janet is following with Honor. To Steward.*) You know about the stateroom that was telephoned for?

STEWARD: (*Stopping at door*) I've got one reserved for three ladies.

RANNY: (*Hesitates.*) Is this the only reservation you have?

STEWARD: Yes, sir—so far.

RANNY: (*With decision*) Then it's ours.

STEWARD: I was told three—

RANNY: The other lady's coming.

HONOR: (*Half under her breath*) Pray God she is coming—!!

RANNY: (*To Mrs. Selby*) You two go in—and shut the door.

HONOR: I must stay and watch.

MRS. SELBY: In there—yes. Come. (*Honor resists.*)

RANNY: Don't you understand? You mustn't be seen. Not at first.

HONOR: How *can* I wait behind a shut door—not knowing?

MRS. SELBY: Ranny's right, he must go warily. A desperate woman like that— (*Draws Honor towards the state-room.*)

RANNY: (*Aside to Mrs. Selby*) Whatever you hear, don't come till I call. (*He shuts the door, pays Porters, saunters about watching.*)

(*Two or three Passengers enter.*)

FIRST PASSENGER: Hurrying the life out of me!

SECOND PASSENGER: I told you there was oceans of time. (*Exit into a cabin in opposite corridor.*)

(*Enter the Detective, shaking off Steward.*)

STEWARD: What number, sir?

DETECTIVE: Only came to see some people off.

RANNY: (*Aside*) Well? She's got the girl?

DETECTIVE: (*Nods. Aloud, for the benefit of a Passenger*). That's a good car of yours, sir. (*Lower*) Followed easy, in spite of all her doubling.

RANNY: (*Anxious*) Why have you left them? She might change her plans.

DETECTIVE: I've got two men outside. (*Looks out, and slips back hurriedly.*) She's coming up the gang-plank.

RANNY: Which?

DETECTIVE: Both women. There are two.

RANNY: No girl?

DETECTIVE: They're carrying the girl.

RANNY: "Carrying!" (*Agonized*) Why do they have to carry her?

DETECTIVE: Look out! (*Vanishes down corridor. Ranny draws back out of sight.*)

(*Enter Carron, talking to Stewardess. Carron dressed as a nurse, carrying wraps and jewel case, evidently instructed to do the talking.*)

CARRON: The large state-room for three. I shall have to be in there too. We've got an invalid. (*Looks back at sign from Grey Hawk. Grey Hawk enters, dressed in mourning, heavily veiled.*)

GREY HAWK: (*In angry whisper*) Not so fast, fool. We mustn't lose sight—(*Glances back.*)

(*Enter two Porters with Bettina in a carrying chair. She is also in mourning, closely veiled and lies in a stupor. Bearers pause, Stewardess about to open Honor's door. Ranny steps forward.*)

RANNY: That room is taken.

STEWARDESS: Yes, by this lady.

RANNY: No—by Miss Honor Dorrien.

GREY HAWK: (*Staggered, pulls herself together with lightning quickness.*) I thought this was the wrong side of the ship. Come. (*Hustles Carron.*)

RANNY: (*Intervening sternly.*) No, this is the right side. (*To the Bearers*) Bring the lady in here.

GREY HAWK: (*Sharply to Bearers*) He is not speaking to you. He has nothing to do with us.

RANNY: I have everything to do with this lady. Carry her in.

GREY HAWK: (*Lays her hand on the chair. She and Ranny confront each other. She draws herself up, lifts her veil and speaks with dignity.*) There is some mistake. I don't know you.

RANNY: What's of more importance, I know you. (*Very low*) The only safe thing you can do is to get out of this.

GREY HAWK: Bring my daughter away—this is a madman!

RANNY: (*Bars the way.*) This woman is wanted by the police.

GREY HAWK: (*Covert glance, takes in the fact that there are no police in sight, speaks with deadly calm.*) I told you he was mad. (*Lower to Bearers*) For my child's sake, I must not risk a scene. (*Slips gold in Bearer's hand.*) Quietly! (*To Carron*) A taxi—anywhere out of this—

RANNY: (*Intercepts Bearers; calls.*) Betty! She doesn't answer!!

GREY HAWK: Why should she? A perfect stranger. Alice, dear, don't be alarmed.

(*Ranny quickly lifts Betty's hand and lets it fall, to feel her pulse.*)

GREY HAWK: (*With an outburst of indignation*) How dare you touch my daughter! My child is dangerously ill.

CARRON: 'Sh, Madam, 'sh! She has fainted with the excitement.

GREY HAWK: This person has nearly killed her already. Have you men no spirit? To be intimidated by this boy! (*Turning*) Where is the Captain? Send the Captain here. Send any of the ship's officers. (*Stewards run about. Aside to Bearer.*) £50 if you get her off the ship.

(*Carron has run towards the exit to be ready.*)

RANNY: (*Intervening, turns sharply to Grey Hawk.*) Can't see when the game is up? (*Carron has brought the Stewardess; Someone else brings Purser.*)

GREY HAWK: (*Hastens to him, speaks with great dignity and plausibility.*) Ah! At last! My daughter has fainted—the shock of being attacked by this poor madman—give him in charge. Here, you men . . .

RANNY: (*Speaking through this last*) A notorious character trying to abduct this girl. I want quietly to—

PURSER: (*Suspicious*) Want to settle it quietly, eh?

GREY HAWK: You see, quite demented. You must help me to get my child off the ship. (*Ranny talking to Purser unheeded.*) Deal with him afterwards. My child's life hangs by a thread.

PURSER: (*Impressed*) Stand aside, sir. (*Ranny resists. Purser has him seized. Bell clangs.*)

VOICE: Visitors ashore!

(*Grey Hawk and Party are hastening off. Ranny, growing more excited and "lunatic," struggles fiercely.*)

RANNY: (*Very loud.*) Honor! (*Cabin door bursts open. Honor rushes out, followed by Mrs. Selby.*)

GREY HAWK: (*Storming*) Carry her ashore, you fools! She is being done to death!

HONOR: (*Rushes toward Betty. Carron holds her off.*) Oh, my dear—my dear—

RANNY: This is the young lady's sister. (*To Purser*) You have very nearly connived at an abduction.

PURSER: I don't unders— Call the police!

RANNY: (*Wrestling himself free. To Grey Hawk*) You want the police called even less than I do. Tell him so!

GREY HAWK: (*Unstrung—shaking*) All I ask is to get her away. Save her—save her!! (*Wildly*) I'll give any man £1,000 who gets her safely away. (*Enter the Detective. Coming up quietly behind Purser*)

DETECTIVE: This woman— (*Shows badge—speaks in an undertone.*)

RANNY: (*To Grey Hawk—aside*) You ought to suffer the full penalty. But you can't suffer the penalty alone. And she has suffered enough. No, I'm not going to do duty to Society. I mean to let you go. This will be one more of those cases "not verified." But if this case isn't known, you are. Your race is run. England is going to be too hot, thank God, for such as you!

GREY HAWK: (*Interrupting*) Carron! (*Lifting eyeglass, speaks as calmly and haughtily as if nothing unusual had occurred.*) Was this the cabin I reserved?

PURSER: Yes, Madam.

GREY HAWK: Bring my things. (*Exit into cabin, shuts and bolts the door.*)

(*Tableau*)

# "A Shanghai Cinderella" (*East Is West*) by Samuel Shipman and John B. Hymer

"A SHANGHAI CINDERELLA" (renamed *East Is West* in 1918) was one of the longest-running comedies of the Progressive Era, with 680 performances.[1] *Hearst's Magazine* selected it as Play of the Month in June 1919, printing excerpts and six production photographs.[2] Although *East Is West* mimicked traditional white slave tracts, it was among the first plays to portray interracial desire and include dramatic pleas for racial equality—progressive elements that are ultimately undermined by the play's final plot twist. The lead character, Ming Toy, is sold by her father to a Shanghai "love-boat" where girls work as courtesans (or sing-song girls) and are also resold as take-home concubines. The son of the U.S. ambassador to China, Billy Benson, stumbles upon the love-boat and is shocked by its "barbaric" practices. Smitten by Ming Toy, he asks his friend Wong Lo to buy her and bring her to San Francisco, where she eventually joins the Benson family as their maid. Once in the Benson home, Ming Toy undergoes a miraculous transformation. Like Eliza Doolittle in *Pygmalion*, she quickly learns the behavior of the well-to-do; but perhaps even more important is how swiftly she is Americanized. Within months she can mix a cocktail like Mae West and dance the Shimmy Wiggle like Josephine Baker, and yet she remains charmingly naïve. As Billy's sister Mildred points out, "Do you know she's quite a talented little thing. And how she picks up our ways. I've never had a white maid so intelligent." Ming Toy begins to fit in so well that she seems to be a member of the family, which is to say, *not* Chinese. "Isn't she the dearest thing?" asks Mildred. "I am just wild about her. I can't put her in the same category with the ordinary Chinaman. She just takes to things naturally." And one of the things she naturally takes to is Billy Benson.

When Billy in turn takes to her, there is, as *Theatre Magazine* put it in 1919, "a perilous racial problem to solve."[3] In spite of its liberal leanings and embassy work in China, the Benson family does not at first approve of Billy marrying Ming Toy. His mother warns him: "Do you know that she is a girl out of your class? Caste and color?" Ming Toy herself, however, increasingly identifies as American: "Ming Toy no China girl. Ming Toy was American girl even when she was in China. Got nothing China. Don't speak China. Don't know why for hell God put me in China." Ming Toy in fact loathes her Chineseness, exclaiming, "Why didn't God make all people white!" Here the play seems to recognize the racial limits of the *Pygmalion* (and Cinderella) plots—Ming Toy might be able to change her class, but she seemingly cannot alter her "yellow blood." In a bizarre plot twist, however, it turns out that Ming Toy *can* change her race. In the play's final act, just before the lovers elope to avoid societal scorn, Ming Toy learns that she is in fact "a perfectly good white girl, who, when a baby, was kidnapped by Chinese bandits from her American missionary father and her Spanish mother."[4] This astonishing revelation explains (surprise!) her command of English, rejection of Chinese culture, love of Christianity, and good manners. Upon hearing of Ming Toy's "true" identity, Billy's mother is palpably relieved: "Oh! I am so happy, Ming Toy. You are one of us. You could not be anything else—such a sweet soul could not simply be anything not white." Discarding one's racial otherness has never been so easy, or so unbelievable, in American theatre: "Would you believe it," *Theatre Magazine* quipped, "the maiden stolen in her childhood, wasn't Chinese at all?"[5] *New York Times* critic John Corbin railed against this unbelievable plot line by invoking Kipling's well-known "Ballad of East and West": "it thus appears that maugre Kipling, the Orient has become the Occident."[6] As the play's revised title suggests, East really *is* West. The drama's progressive message—"love has no race"—is underscored by a disavowal of true miscegenation. "A Shanghai Cinderella" gets to have it both ways: it builds a plot about racial tolerance but ultimately reinforces ideas of white supremacy and taboos about miscegenation. These notions became more visible when the play became revised, and performed, as *East Is West*.

Central to the conceit of mistaken racial identity in *East Is West*, and its all-white cast, is the practice of yellowface performance. Much like blackface performance and minstrelsy, yellowface was ubiquitous in U.S. theatre, vaudeville, musical theatre, and silent film. Chinese stereotypes became codified through yellowface, as Krystyn Moon puts it in her book of the same title. Makeup books for actors playing "Orientals," as Josephine Lee has documented, provided explicit instructions for developing racial typographies, complete with guidelines for body coloring, hairstyles, fingernail length, posture, and so on.[7] Production photos for *East Is West* demonstrate adherence to many of these typologies, with male actors wearing Chinese "coolie pants," ponytails, and dark grease paint, while Fay Bainter, the actress playing Ming Toy, wears traditional gowns, plays Chinese instruments, and poses in submissive postures (see fig. 5 and 6).

Launched into stardom with this role, Bainter was so popular that she appeared as Ming Toy on the cover of the sheet music for "Chinese Lullaby," the hit song from *East Is West*.[8] She received rave reviews for what commentators repeatedly called her "authentic" portrayal of the Chinese type. "Miss Bainter gives the best reflection of a Chinese sing-song girl yet shown on the stage in dramatic form," wrote the *Forum*. "Her work is faithful, dainty and at all times fascinating and true to type—a revelation in the characterization of the Oriental on the American Stage."[9] *Theatre Magazine* reported: "Fay Bainter plays this pseudo Chinese role with perfect conventional pertness."[10] Ming Toy became an identifiable type, inspiring a 1919 song, a 1949 musical comedy, and a George and Ira Gershwin musical (which was planned to open in 1929, but was never performed).[11]

If some audiences perceived *East Is West* as "true to type," others complained that it trafficked in stereotypes. Heywood Broun of the *Dramatic Mirror* pronounced it the worst play ever been written: "velly lotten," he wrote, mocking (but repeating) racist depictions of Asian accents.[12] John Corbin of the *New York Times* faulted *East Is West* for recycling the familiar female Chinese type: "The heroine is just another version of the pretty, coquettish, adorably slangy, and wearing little heathen in trousers which has been familiar to our musical comedy stage for a quarter of a century, and which was exploited dramatically."[13] The *Nation* railed against the "shoddy" writing and "cheaply bright lines," adding: "Still more insidious is the labeling of characters with false tags."[14] Bainter herself expressed concern at being typecast as a yellowface actress. In an interview in September 1919, she said: "I shall never take an oriental part again. I have made up my mind definitely to that. I don't care what sort of a part I have so long as it is different, so long as it is not oriental."[15] And she never did.

Advertised as a "Touch of the Orient," *East Is West* offered an encounter with the East, but what kind of contact was achieved? What kind of aversions and fascinations, to use Moon's words, were negotiated by Bainter in performing the role of Ming Toy in yellowface for over a year and a half, for thousands of audience members? Was anyone, as Corbin from the *Times* wondered, "misguided enough to take *East Is West* as a sincerely meant rep-

FIGURE 5. "A Shanghai Cinderella" (produced as *East Is West*): Forrest Winant as Billy Benson, Fay Bainter as Ming Toy, and Lester Lonergan (standing) as Lo Sank Kee. Photo by Ira D. Schwartz (1919). David Shields's private collection.

FIGURE 6. Fay Bainter as Ming Toy in "A Shanghai Cinderella" (produced as *East Is West*). Photo by Louis Fabian Bachrach Jr. (1919). David Shields's private collection.

resentation of life?"[16] The answer to these questions lies not in the ontology of authentic mimesis but rather in how this production negotiated fantasies within the national imaginary through performance.

Performing a racialized other has been central to the construction of U.S. identity both on and off the stage, from "playing Indian" in the Boston Tea Party to portraying yellowface icons like Fu Manchu in Hollywood. As Jill Lane has observed, "racial impersonation—acting in the name and place of the other through such practices as blackface, redface, yellowface, cross-dressing, and drag—has played a particularly important role in the imagination and aesthetic articulation of national communities across the Americas."[17] Karen Shimakawa has identified this tension as a process of abjection whereby we can read "Asian Americanness in relation to and as a product of U.S. Americanness—that is, as occupying the seemingly contradictory, yet functionally essential, position of constituent element *and* radical other."[18] Using Julia Kristeva's notion of abject as both a rejected state and a process, Shimakawa demonstrates how performance becomes central to articulating an identity that is never stable, constantly moving, and continually in touch with the national imaginary. U.S. Americanness thus makes Asian Americanness abject "by making it other, foreign, abnormal, not-American."[19] In the case of *East Is West*, however, the process of identification is complicated: Ming Toy occupies a liminal, multiethnic identity, signifying as Chinese, Spanish, and American. In this light, she is both foreign *and* American.

"A Shanghai Cinderella" and its production as *East Is West*, like many other yellow slave dramas, hinges on Orientalist fantasies regarding a Chinese sing-song girl. Like white slave tracts, it features "foreign"—figured here as Chinese—men ruining women and white men rescuing them, even when rescue puts them into domestic service. *East Is West* transported audiences across racial boundaries, if only momentarily, while also invoking racial stereotypes. Yet its enduring success on Broadway for almost two years and its adaptation into two musicals and two Hollywood films demonstrate that the lure of the opium den and the prostitute were never far from the national imaginary.

• • •

"A Shanghai Cinderella" was first performed under the title of *East Is West* on 25 December 1918 at the Astor Theatre and ran for 680 performances, one of the longest running plays of the Progressive Era. It had the following cast:

| | |
|---|---|
| Love Boat Attendant | William J. Kline |
| Lo Sank Kee | Lester Lonergan |
| Hop Toy | Harry Huguenot |
| Chang Lee | Charles Mussett |
| James Potter | Hassard Short |
| Mildred Benson | Ethel Intropidl |
| Thomas | Martin Wells |
| Andrew Benson | Frank Kemble Cooper |
| Mrs. Benson | Martha Mayo |
| Mr. Davis | Walter Hart |
| Billy Benson | Forrest Winant |
| Customer | William Tennyson |
| Ming Toy | Fay Bainter |
| Servant | Arthur Ginson |
| Charlie Yang | George Nash |
| Miss Claybrook | Louise Seymour |
| Miss Fountain | Marta Spear |
| Mrs. Davis | Eva Condon |
| Proprietor of Love Boat | Edwin Maxwell |

It was staged by Clifford Brooks with sets designed by Livingston Platt.

# A Shanghai Cinderella" (renamed *East Is West*)

A COMEDY DRAMA IN A PROLOGUE AND THREE ACTS

by Samuel Shipman and John B. Hymer

CHARACTERS:

ANDREW BENSON—*Ambassador to China, 60 years*
MRS. ANDREW BENSON, *his wife, 55 years*
WILLIAM BENSON, *his son, 25 years*
MILDRED BENSON, *his daughter, 21 years*
JAMES POTTER, *Mildred's fiancée, 28 years*
MISS CLAYBROOK, *guest, 20 years*
MISS FOUNTAIN, *guest, 19 years*
MRS. DAVIS, *guest, 60 years*
THOMAS, *Butler, 40 years*
WONG LO, *a San Francisco merchant, 50 years*[20]
CHARLIE YONG, *a Chinese Beau Brummel, 35 years*
HOP TOY, *a Chinese religious fanatic, 45 years*
MERCHANT, A PROPRIETOR OF THE LOVE-BOAT, *a trader in women, 40 years*
ATTENDANT, *55 years*
MING TOY, *18 years*
GUESTS, CHINAMEN, etc.

TIME: 1910

PLACE: Prologue takes place in China. The remaining three acts are staged in America.

## Prologue

(*At rise of curtain attendant enters excitedly from left.*)

ATTENDANT: (*In Chinese*) Hurry up—play something—quickly—someone is coming.

(*Girls start to play sing-song song on shamisen.*[21] *Merchant enters hurriedly from left gorgeously dressed in Chinese robes, as he is the proprietor of the boat and buys and sells girls.*)

MERCHANT: (*In Chinese*) Is everything all right?

ATTENDANT: (*In Chinese*) Yes.

MERCHANT: (*In Chinese*) Go quick and get customer.

(*Attendant leaves boat, exits up steps right. Merchant goes up to top deck of boat, looks at each girl as he passes to see that she is at her best for prospective buyer. He pantomimes to one or two that their hair or something with their raiment requires attention.*[22] *The girls to whom he speaks immediately rearrange their hair and raiment as the case may be. He sits in chair on top deck towards right end of boat where he can overlook wharf and steps leading to wharf. Takes Chinese pipe from pocket—fills with tobacco—lights same. Girls are all playing sing-song on shamisen.*[23] *Billy Benson and Wong Lo enter down steps right, stand on right side of wharf, looking at love-boat.*)

BILLY: So this is the love-boat?

WONG: My most honorable friend, it is the love-boat.

BILLY: Is there going to be a sale here tonight?

WONG: Many of the most beautiful girls in this flowery kingdom are bought and sold here, both night and day. All these maidens whom you see there upon the boat will be sold to him who pays the highest price.

(*Billy Benson lights cigarette, stands smoking and looks at boat. Wong lights pipe and starts humming softly the song which the girls are playing. During this business, attendant and another richly dressed Chinaman of middle age enters down ladder right and go on love-boat. When from his position on top deck the Merchant sees attendant and Chinamen entering right, he comes down to lower deck of boat and moves forward to greet Chinamen.*)

BILLY: (*To Wong*) Who is this Chinaman?

WONG: A customer; he has come to buy—you will see.

MERCHANT: (*In Chinese*) Fine assortment today.

CUSTOMER: (*In Chinese as he looks girls over*) Yes, beautiful flowers of the Orient you always have.

MERCHANT: (*In Chinese*) They are the budding blossoms from the best families in China.

BILLY: (*To Wong*) What did he say?

WONG: All these girls on boat come from best Chinese families.

CUSTOMER: (*Pointing to one of girls, speaks in Chinese to merchant*) I want that girl.

MERCHANT: (*Motions girl to come forward. Speaks in Chinese.*) Come here. (*Girl comes forward—customer looks her over as if buying a horse; inspects teeth and counts them. Also looks at her feet very carefully; apparently he is not satisfied with this girl, motions her away.*)

CUSTOMER: (*In Chinese*) She is not so good—let me see another.

MERCHANT: (*Stepping to foot of stairs, which leads to upper deck of boat called

*Yellow Rose. One girl from top deck comes down and goes with Merchant to where customer stands, turns to him, and speaks in Chinese. She is the most precious one on the boat. Customer goes through the process of examining girl's teeth, feet, etc.; seems pleased with her.*)

CUSTOMER: (*In Chinese*) How much?

MERCHANT: (*In Chinese*) 1,000 yen—1,000 yen I ask for her, but I know you as good friend, and you can have her for 750 yen. (*Customer again inspects girl carefully.*)

BENSON: (*To Wong*) What did he say then?

WONG: He tell the customer the girl is worth 1,000 yen, but as customer is his good friend, he sell her to him cheap, for 750 yen.

BENSON: Wonderful business.

(*Customer pays Merchant, takes hand of girl and leaves boat. Exits up steps right. Benson and Wong stand watching the proceedings. Merchant goes back up stairs to former position in chair, refills pipe, and lights it.*)

BENSON: (*Motioning off right*) Where is he taking her?

WONG: He take her to his home; he bought her.

BENSON: You mean to say he just buys her for money—like one would buy a horse or a dog?

WONG: Horse, dog, sing-song girl. All the same.

BENSON: Did she want to go with him?

WONG: It does not matter. She must go—he bought her.

BENSON: What is he going to do with her?

WONG: Maybe sometime he kiss her—maybe sometime he beat her—all the same he feel like.

BENSON: Is it all right for us to go on the love-boat?

WONG: It would be my most august pleasure to show you, my dear friend, the love-boat. He who owns the boat, in years gone by, enjoyed the hospitality of my celestial friendship.

BENSON: Well, I guess that will make it all right then.

WONG: Come. (*They start for boat—just before stepping on, Merchant sees them and comes down lower deck to meet them. Wong and Merchant bow most profusely to each other.*) Many summer suns have kissed the sea since last we met.

MERCHANT: The hospitality of my abode is ever welcome to you and your most august friends. (*Looks at Billy Benson who starts to take Merchant's hand—but bows instead.*)

WONG: This is my august friend, Mr. Billy Benson, son of Mr. Andrew

Benson, the American Ambassador to our most celestial Court. Mr. Billy Benson, he make China rich with American money—he make American banks in China.

MERCHANT: The greetings I extend to you shall live from now until the end of my celestial days. (*Bows to Billy. He bows also.*)

BENSON: You speak English pretty well.

MERCHANT: The man who deals in women successfully must speak many languages.

BENSON: Yes, I guess you are right. You do a good business here? Pardon my being as personal—but this is all rather new to me, and I am interested.

MERCHANT: If my girls are beautiful, they bring me many yen.

BENSON: You don't get so much then for an ugly girl? No of course not, naturally you would not.

MERCHANT: What one man call beauty in one girl—to another man she might not appear to be charming. It is the curse of man no matter what a woman's face may be—she got a chance.

BENSON: Yes, I notice that feet and teeth have something to do with the sale.

MERCHANT: Small feet in our maidens denote high caste, and the girl who has beautiful face, captivating manner, good teeth, and small feet is very easily sold in this country.

BENSON: Yes, a girl like that would not have much trouble in my country either. What makes their parents sell them?

MERCHANT: A girl is a curse upon the household.[24] When she marry, family name all lost—that why girls no good. When family got lots girls, always sell them.

BENSON: Oh, then it's an economic reason?

MERCHANT: Girls no good—sell for any reason.

BENSON: What's the highest price you ever got for a girl?

MERCHANT: I get 8,000 yen—highest price for one girl. She very near like white woman. Chinaman always pay high price for girl that looks like white woman.[25] Chinaman like you—he like variety.

BENSON: You get many of this kind?

MERCHANT: Hop Toy, he have fine girls. His wife very yellow—much Chinese, but he always bring here fine daughters. I don't know how Hop Toy have such nice daughters. Maybe his wife look at pretty American lady picture.

BENSON: How many has he brought you?

MERCHANT: Oh, Hop Toy he bring lots. He got finest wife. You want to buy girl? You friend of Wong, I sell you nice girl cheap.

BENSON: Never found a girl cheap.

MERCHANT: You see my girls—but Hop Toy he come any minute just like I tell you. Always he bring nice girl. He have fine daughters. (*Ming Toy and her father Hop Toy enter down steps right and come on wharf. Ming Toy is walking under protest, her father almost dragging her along. She is crying. At the last step he pulls her down, almost flinging her from him, but she catches her balance and remains standing in the center. The girls on boat laugh. Merchant scolds them in Chinese, and they become very quiet. Merchant to Billy.*) That's the girl I told you about.

BENSON: She is to be sold?

MERCHANT: Yes.

HOP TOY: (*In Chinese*) It was a hard job to bring her—but I got her here.

MING TOY: (*To Merchant*) Don't buy me.

BENSON: (*To Wong*) What did she say?

MING TOY: (*To Benson in English*) I say "I run away." I no stay.

BENSON: I don't blame you, kid.

HOP TOY: (*Hop Toy grabs Ming Toy's arm and shakes her violently. In Chinese.*) Don't you say anything.

MING TOY: (*In Chinese*) Let me alone. (*Hop Toy releases her arm.*)

BENSON: (*To Wong*) Ask why her father is selling her.

MING TOY: I tell you Mr.— (*Benson steps forward.*)

BENSON: My name is Billy Benson.

MING TOY: My name is Ming Toy.

BENSON: That's a sweet name.

MING TOY: You like name Ming Toy?

BENSON: A beautiful name. Who is this man who brought you?

MING TOY: My most august father.

BENSON: Your own father?

MING TOY: Yes, Mr. Billy Benson.

BENSON: And he wants to sell you as a slave?

MING TOY: Yes.

BENSON: Why?

MING TOY: He want to buy new pig.

BENSON: You mean your father wants to exchange you for a pig?

MING TOY: Yes, pig much better than daughter. My father have sixteen daughters and only fourteen pigs. He have too much daughters and not enough pigs, he sell one daughter and he buy one pig and have fifteen daughters and fifteen pigs.

BENSON: You mean your father has sixteen daughters?

MING TOY: Yes, Mr. Billy Benson.

BENSON: How long is your father married?

MING TOY: I don't know. He married long time before I born. He say he married nineteen years.

BENSON: Nineteen years and sixteen daughters?

MING TOY: Four quartets.

BENSON: (*To Wong*) Ask him if any children are dead.

WONG: (*Asks Hop Toy in Chinese if any children dead. Hop Toy answers five.*) He say he got five dead.

BENSON: (*To Merchant*) Nineteen years, twenty-one children. Great man for your business. (*Hop Toy looks at Benson—speaks angrily at Benson.*) What does he say?

MERCHANT: He say you want to know too much about his business.

BENSON: (*To Ming Toy*) Suppose I buy him a pig. Will he let you go?

MING TOY: I don't know. He like pigs.

BENSON: (*To Wong*) Tell her father I will buy him a pig if he will not sell Ming Toy. (*Hop Toy told this by Wong in Chinese.*)

HOP TOY: (*In Chinese*) I would not have Ming Toy in house if you buy me a thousand pigs. (*Wong tells this to Benson in English.*)

MING TOY: My father, he got buy clothes for me and feed me; much trouble. Pig—he eat slop, and then father eat pig—then he have fine time.

MERCHANT: (*To Benson*) What Ming Toy tell you is true—but there are many other things she did not tell you.

BENSON: What, for instance?

MERCHANT: She is in the Mission and learn many of the foreign devil ways. She disgrace in her honorable father's household. It is the custom of our country that women bind their bosoms tight.

MING TOY: No, I will not do it, for Christian lady at Mission tell me I have pretty bosom. I should not spoil it.

MERCHANT: But it is the custom of your country, and you should obey your father.

MING TOY: Christian lady tell me must obey father, but also must obey God. God he give me nice bosom, nice feet and God he want me to keep it. God been good to me. He give me nice form like Christian lady. I got be good and not spoil it. My father try to make me put on shoes that can't go on my little finger.

HOP TOY: (*In Chinese*) You are the most accursed of my many daughters. All the bad devils dwell within you.[26]

BILLY: (*To Wong*) What did he say?

WONG: He said Ming Toy was the most accursed of his many daughters —that all the bad devils dwell within her.

HOP TOY: (*In Chinese*) When I sell you, man make you do what he say.

MING TOY: (*Stamping her foot*) I do nothing—I don't want.

BILLY: (*To Wong*) What did he say?

WONG: He say any man that buy her make her obey custom of China.

MING TOY: Chinamen want women have little feet so they cannot follow men fast to see what he do. When I get man, I get good man. I got good feet. I go where he go.[27]

MERCHANT: Christian dog's Mission have put devils in your head. I'm afraid when I sell you, you will close your mouth and do what man say.

MING TOY: Man make me shut my mouth little while maybe—but I no tie up my feet tight for no man.

MERCHANT: We will see. In short time you belong to me. (*Speaking Chinese to Hop Toy*) How much you want for her?

HOP TOY: (*In Chinese*) 3,000 yen.[28]

MERCHANT: (*In Chinese*) I'll give you 1,200 yen.

HOP TOY: (*In Chinese*) All right, I take it. (*Merchant takes large wallet from pocket inside of coat, opens same very carefully, takes out several bills, counts them over three and four times.*)

WONG: (*To Benson*) Hop Toy ask 3,000 yen for her, but Merchant say only give 1,200. Hop Toy say, "all right, quick I take it."

MING TOY: (*To Merchant*) Oh, please no buy me; if you no buy me, he no can sell me.

MERCHANT: A little devil like you must be sold, and I don't do good business today, and you are good buy, and I make big profit on you.

MING TOY: I am devil and you want make profit from devil? If I am devil you no make profit—you no can sell me.

MERCHANT: Many men like devil in women.

MING TOY: You sell me to such mean men?

MERCHANT: I sell you to any man.

MING TOY: You sell me to Bing Bang Boo?[29] He beat his girls—he beat two women to death.

MERCHANT: Sure, I send for him; I tell him good stock today.[30]

MING TOY: You buy me, I raise hell on sing-song boat.

MERCHANT: You raise hell and Lum Go give you twenty lashes every day. (*Pays Hop Toy 1,200 yen—Hop Toy looks at money, walks over to Ming Toy and spits at coat.*)

HOP TOY: (*In Chinese*) Oh, Christian dog, Buddha will bless my household today.

BENSON: What does that beast say?

WONG: He say, "Christian dog, Buddha bless his household today."

BENSON: Ask him for me why will Buddha bless him for selling his own children?

WONG: (*In Chinese*) Why will Buddha bless you for selling your own children?

HOP TOY: (*In Chinese*) He bless me because I do fine thing for him. I sell these girls for Buddha.[31]

WONG: (*To Benson*) Buddha bless him because he do fine thing for him. He sell these girls for Buddha. (*Wong questions Hop Toy again in Chinese and Hop Toy angrily replies; he repeats to Benson in English.*) No foreign devil's business. Tell him to go to hell. (*Hop Toy exits right counting his money.*)

MING TOY: Tomorrow he eat so much pig his belly swell so. (*Clasps hands in front of her showing how fat his stomach would be.*)

MERCHANT: (*To Ming Toy*) You sit down. (*She walks over to a low stool and winks at Benson. Merchant turns just in time to see her do this.*) Where you get this? You learn this at foreign devil Mission? Sit down. (*He sees customer coming down steps to wharf, takes instrument and hands it to Ming Toy. Old Chinaman enters. Merchant notices and turns to Ming Toy.*) Quick, you play beautiful sing-song lullaby. (*He turns and sees Bing Bang Boo entering down steps to Wharf—speaks to him in Chinese.*) My most august friend, the beautiful fair one, of whom I told you is here. (*Ming Toy starts to play Yankee Doodle—Merchant turns to her.*) What you play?

MING TOY: Doodle Yankee. I hear it at Christian Mission.

MERCHANT: You play beautiful sing-song melody for Bing Bang Boo. (*Old Chinaman now steps on love-boat. Ming Toy starts playing sing-song song and blends into it the tune of Yankee Doodle. Catching sight of Old Chinaman, she stops.*)[32]

MING TOY: Girl beater. Bing Bang Boo.

MERCHANT: (*In Chinese*) All these girls good stock. (*Old Chinaman Bing Bang Boo, beckons to one girl who comes up—looks her over, throws her off roughly and resumes inspection of girls, walking around until he reaches Ming Toy. He motions her to rise.*) Ah! I see my most august friend has a most wonderful eye for the most beautiful one in all our flowery kingdom.

BING BANG BOO: (*In Chinese*) How much is she worth?

MERCHANT: (*In Chinese*) 3,000 yen.

BING BANG BOO: (*In Chinese*) I take her. (*Ming Toy smashes instrument on stool. Merchant goes to her, pulls her over to Chinaman, twisting her wrist and hurting her. She cries out.*)

BENSON: Let go of her arm.

MERCHANT: (*Steps up to Benson.*) You keep away, white devil.

WONG: (*To Merchant*) Mr. Billy Benson is honorable son of American Ambassador to our celestial Court. (*Merchant bows to Billy humbly.*)

BENSON: It's all right, old man, but don't pull any rough stuff with the young lady while I'm around. It makes me awfully nervous.

MING TOY: Oh, Mr. Benson, you nice man. You buy me.

BENSON: I would love to, but what could I do with you?

MING TOY: You do anything. You buy me, I be nice; I no be devil.

BENSON: I know you would. We don't do these things. It is not customary with us.

MING TOY: Oh, please buy me. He beat me dead, sure. Please no let him take me.

BENSON: I'm sorry, but I can't help you Ming Toy. Honest I'd love to, but I can't.

MING TOY: You ain't got money?

BENSON: Oh, my dear Ming Toy, the yen don't bother me, but we don't deal in women.[33]

MING TOY: Too bad. You Americans no civilized like Chinamen.

MERCHANT: (*Taking hold of Ming Toy*) Come on—go ahead.

MING TOY: Oh, you bad man, you mean man. You sell me to Bing Bang Boo, he treat me like dog; he shut me up in little room all day and come full of (*Chinese drink*) beat me like devil.[34] (*Breaks down crying. Bing Bang Boo starts to pay Merchant.*)

BENSON: (*To Wong*) Why don't you buy her?

WONG: I go back to San Francisco next week. What would I do with her?

BENSON: Take her with you.

WONG: I am honorable merchant in San Francisco. I am too busy and it is against your American law that I should have sing-song girl.

BENSON: I know, but we cannot let her go to this brute. She is such a sweet little thing.

MING TOY: Thank you, Mr. Billy Benson—you sweet man. Why you no can buy me?

BENSON: Will it be all right if my friend Wong buys you?

MING TOY: I like you—I like your friend. I know if he your friend, he sweet man too.

WONG: Would you like to go to America?

MING TOY: Oh! I like go to America. Lady at mission tell me America very fine. Women free to wear any kind of shoes. I want Statue of Liberty hold punk stick.[35]

MERCHANT: You go with Bing Bang Boo—he buy you.

WONG: Please, a moment—wait. I give you 500 yen more for her.

MERCHANT: She belong to Bing Bang Boo now. I have nothing to say. (*Wong speaks in Chinese to old Chinaman, asking how much he wants for Ming Toy.*)

BING BANG BOO: (*In Chinese*) 5,000 yen.

WONG: 5,000 yen is what he ask for her.

MING TOY: Don't give him. Why he want 5,000 yen? 2,000 more than he pay?

WONG: Well, he may be brute, but he know sweet little girl when he see one.

MING TOY: And you pay so much money for me?

WONG: I am afraid we must if we want to take you from him. He bought you and 5,000 yen was his last price.

MING TOY: That heap money to pay for Chinese devil like me.

BENSON: Nothing is too much for you. Pay him, Wong. (*Wong pays money to Bing Bang Boo.*)

MING TOY: (*Kneeling in front of Benson*) Oh! Mr. Billy Benson, you sweet man. You save me from what you say—monster. In all my life I no forget Billy Benson. I always remember you like humming bird that come and speak to one little lonely rose and then fly away.

BENSON: I did not do it. Wong did it.

BING BANG BOO: (*Old Chinaman steps in front of Ming Toy—sarcastically in Chinese.*) You are not worth one of these. (*Shows money in his hand.*)

(*Ming Toy spits on coat of Bing Bang Boo. Girls begin playing on shamisens*).[36]

(*Curtain*)

## Act I

### *Scene 1*

SCENE: *Room in Wong's house in Chinese quarter, San Francisco.*

(*At opening Wong enters from door back, bows and kneels in front of altar. He lights punk sticks and places them in sand bowls. While he is placing punk sticks, Ming Toy is heard singing "Song of Contented Wife" off left. Wong turns, stands, listens a moment, goes to door, and speaks off stage in Chinese. The singing ceases. He turns with satisfied smile. Takes counting machine and sits at table counting diligently in Chinese. Chinese servant enters, followed by Potter.*[37] *Wong Lo rises ceremoniously.*)

WONG: The blessings of ten thousand ancestors upon your house and mine.

POTTER: Same to you and many of them.

WONG: You Americans just so about your ancestors.

POTTER: Well, believe me, Wong, some of mine were funny—and saying this I beg ten thousand ancestral pardons.

(*Wong goes back to the table where he has been counting and offers cigarettes to Potter. He takes one and lights it.*)

WONG: Mr. James Potter, you will not think ill of my hospitality if I finish my accounts.

POTTER: Go to it, Wong—you're lucky to have accounts. Don't mind me —I'll puff this and wait. (*Wong sits and counts on machine, making notations in book. Potter walks over—looks out window—walks back and looks over Wong's shoulder.*) When are you going to move that red one in the corner? (*Indicating red key on machine. Wong pays no attention but continues counting. Potter walks over to window again and comes down to altar. Potter salutes Joss.*) Good morning, Judge. (*Potter leans over—places nostrils in line of smoke from joss stick and sneezes twice.*[38] *Wong goes right on counting.*) Wong, I've always had an idea there was pepper in those things. How about it? (*Wong counts a little louder—Potter listens a moment.*) Oh, that's what's in 'em—(*Looking over Wong's shoulder. Wong scratches his head—speaks one word in Chinese very loudly and moves large bead on counting machine.*) Oh that's the one—thought you'd get it in a moment. (*Wong closes book—lays down pen—folds hands on stomach—looks up at Potter and smiles.*)

WONG: Mr. James Potter, my house and all I possess is at your disposal. How are my honorable friends, the Bensons?

POTTER: Fine—thank you.

WONG: I hear they come back from China last month—eh?

POTTER: Yes, our Ambassador has resigned.

WONG: Too bad—he do much good for China.

POTTER: Oh yes—well, I guess he has had enough of it. But Andrew Benson is getting on in years and he needs a rest.

WONG: Mr. Billy Benson—he come too? And Billy's esteemed sister—Miss Mildred—she come back too?

POTTER: Yes. I wrote her to come back. There are too many good-looking men in China.

WONG: (*Laughs.*) Oh, she fine girl. I congratulate you on your taste.

POTTER: Thanks.

WONG: Won't you sit down, Mr. Potter. (*He takes seat. Wong sits beside him.*)

POTTER: Wong, I am here on a rather embarrassing mission.

WONG: So?

POTTER: Wong, I have known you to be one of the most honorable Chinamen I ever met.

WONG: Thank you.

POTTER: As a merchant you are the last word in honor. Wong, there is gossip about you.

WONG: Gossip! You mean bad talk?

POTTER: Put it as harshly as you can.

WONG: So! I always pay my debts. I got no debts.

POTTER: Well, it is not exactly that.

WONG: Well—what?

POTTER: Wong, you know that I have been mixed up in what they call social work among your countrymen.

WONG: Of course. You make good Chinamen out of many bad one.

POTTER: Nonsense. I don't believe you can reform anyone. However, dad has left me a lot of money, and the least I can do for him is try to do some good.

WONG: Oh—you do lot of good.

POTTER: I don't agree with you. However, I hope dad thinks so. Now then, let's come back to the point. Very few bachelors have good reputations —but I have always thought that you were one of the few.

WONG: I have always presented a clean face to the world.

POTTER: Oh yes—a credit to your razor and your morals.[39] Wong, as a social worker, I get all the gossip there is in this quarter. Wong, the Mission workers are complaining that there is a little Chinese girl who sits at that window and flirts with every man who goes by.

WONG: (*In anger*) Anyone say that—it is lie!

POTTER: I hope so.

WONG: I beg you to inform me who it is that put shame upon my face.

POTTER: Your own countrymen. The girl here—whoever she is, is said to stand at the window and make goo-goo eyes at everyone from hatchet man to coolies.[40]

WONG: (*Angrily*) It is a lie!

POTTER: Knowing you as I do, I did not believe it at first. But only last night I stood outside of that window myself and— (*Hears singing off stage*) What is that song? A Chinese love song?

WONG: We have very few love songs in China. That is "Song of Contented Wife."

POTTER: Oh—you married?

WONG: No—not married.

POTTER: Not married. Yet that's a woman's voice, isn't it?

WONG: Sure.

POTTER: You are not married? What are you doing, feeding a Chinese chicken?[41]

WONG: No—no chicken—nice little bird. I brought her back from my flowery kingdom two months ago.

POTTER: Then the Mission was right.

WONG: I did not bring her for my own pleasure like many others that buy sing-song girl.

POTTER: Well, what did you buy her for?

WONG: Same reason that you might pick up little crippled bird—take it in—put it in nice cage—give it good feed.

POTTER: Well, it will be pretty hard to make the folks at the Mission believe that.

WONG: What they think? I trade in women like some of my other countrymen that make shame on their face? I deal only in staple goods—no women—no profit in women anyway.

POTTER: But this chicken—crippled bird—is living here, isn't she?

WONG: Yes. She live in same house I do.

POTTER: Well, don't you think that the gossip is very natural? These things are prohibited by the Mission. It is just things of this sort that the Mission has endeavored to eradicate among the Chinese.

WONG: Did I not hire what you call—a chaperone?

POTTER: Who?

WONG: Miss Mary West—nice fine American lady—she teach Ming Toy high top English. See—look— (*Opens door.*) In that room is two beds—in one bed sleep Ming Toy—in other bed sleep Miss Mary West. Mission got no right to say I do wrong.

POTTER: That means nothing to the Mission, Wong. A chaperone may only be a screen.

WONG: What you mean a screen?

POTTER: A blind.

WONG: You mean I have chaperone to make Mission blind?

POTTER: That is just what it may mean. Or at least the Mission thinks it means.

WONG: Ming Toy good girl—and I good man.

POTTER: That's true—you are good. And you better be sure that everyone else thinks that.

WONG: I can't help what Mission think.

POTTER: You can help. Now, if you are a good man, you will get rid of this girl. As long as she remains here, it is bound to cause talk, and if you are jealous of your good name, take my tip and my good advice: get her out of your house.

WONG: I have been planning this without your advice, but I cannot bring myself to do it.

POTTER: Well, if you are on the level with this girl, you will get rid of her, and if you don't, you cannot blame people for talking about you, and acting accordingly.

WONG: I try to do what you say, Mr. Potter. I know you good friend of mine.

POTTER: Fine. Meanwhile keep an eye on her—and don't let her out too much.

WONG: She never go out—all time she stay in that room—except sometime she come in here little while and sit by window and get fresh air, (*Ming Toy starts singing again*) and then sometime she sing and play.

POTTER: Is that all? Well, according to that, I don't see what she has to sing about.

WONG: Well, you know, even if you take crippled bird and feed him nice—he sing.

POTTER: Doesn't she ever want to go out?

WONG: The bird who has never flown has no desire to try his wings. (*Claps hands and Ming Toy enters.*)

MING TOY: What is my lord's august pleasure? (*Looks coquettishly at Potter.*)

POTTER: You have trained her well, Wong. You are sure she never flirts?

WONG: Her eyes are full of me—her ears hear but my commands.

(*She again looks at Potter.*)

POTTER: You're right. I guess she has an eye full of you all right.

WONG: You will sing for my most august friend, Mr. James Potter.

(*Ming Toy sings. Wong is very much upset because she sings "Song of Contented Wife."*)

POTTER: That's great—such an appealing melody. That's the "Contented Wife Song"—isn't it?

WONG: Yes. She knows others, more befitting her station. (*Ming Toy sings "Song of Sing-Song Girl." She starts to dance, moving her shoulders. Wong is furious and stops her abruptly.*) Where did you learn this swaying movement of the body?

MING TOY: It is my most august lord's desire that I learn the foreign ways, and so I sit by that window in the evening and look across—and there I see men and women at the tables—eat and drink—then the music play—and they go through many funny movements—so. (*Starts to dance. Wong claps his hands twice—Ming Toy exits hurriedly through door. Wong then goes over to window, and slams same shut angrily.*)

POTTER: I must say she is a charming little thing. Is it possible that this girl could be bought by a man?

WONG: Well, in China women are the slaves of men. But in this country, it is different—man is slave of woman.

POTTER: You are quite right. Well, I will report to the Mission that you intend to get rid of her. You'll make good—won't you, Wong?

WONG: I'll try. (*Potter exits and Wong follows him out.*)

(*Ming Toy enters and looks around cautiously. She goes to window right and opens window. Business of flirting with someone below. She jumps back from window and giggles. She takes flower from hair and throws to street. Wong enters just as she throws flower.*) (*Severely*) Ming Toy!

MING TOY: (*Runs to him—drops on her knees before him.*) Oh lord of my every action—I await your command.

WONG: What you doing at the window?

MING TOY: (*Evasively*) Most august lord, when I raise the little window, the air tastes much sweeter.

WONG: You were making faces like the foreign devil woman.

MING TOY: I thought that my honorable lord would be pleased I had learned to do it so well.

WONG: Do what so well?

MING TOY: Like the foreign women when the handsome man go by—so. (*Winks one eye—then the other and nods her head coquettishly.*)

WONG: Do you know the meaning of these distortions?

MING TOY: I know not the meaning, my most august lord, but yesterday I did—so—(*winking again*) and one beautiful foreign devil man who was passing said, "some chicken."

WONG: And you like to be called "chicken"?

MING TOY: I do not know the meaning—but it sound cute—"chicken."

WONG: You took from your hair the flower that only maidens wear, and threw it in street.

MING TOY: Not in street. Foreign devil that call me "chicken" catch flower.

WONG: (*Walks over to window and slams same angrily shut. Says angrily*) Ming Toy—no more shall your actions at that window cause foreign devils to look shamefully at my household.

MING TOY: But I can bring no shame on your house. I am only a sing-song girl.

WONG: The foreign devils do not know that. They only know that you are a woman.

MING TOY: No woman—"chicken."

WONG: Tomorrow you go to Portland.

MING TOY: (*Elated for a moment*) Oh—Miss Mary West say Portland beautiful place. My honorable lord have nice house there like this. You let Mary West stay here—we go alone.

WONG: I do not go. You go to house of Charlie Yong.

MING TOY: You sell me?

WONG: You bring disgrace on house of Wong Lo, one of most honorable merchants in San Francisco.

MING TOY: Charlie Yong nice man? Not fat? (*Looks at Wong.*) Not very fat?[42]

WONG: Charlie Yong is fat like well-fed pig and the wrinkles in his face are like dry water courses that run down from the hills and his feet totter seventy years toward his ancestors.

MING TOY: Charlie Yong, fat and seventy years—he'll like chickens. All right, I go. (*Goes back to Joss, kneels and bows her head. She then rises and starts left singing "Song of Sing-Song Girl."*)

WONG: Ming Toy, you are pleased to leave my honorable household with such a song upon your lips?

MING TOY: I sing a song of pleasure, for it is my most august master's desire that I should go away—and to please him, I leave with a smiling song upon my lips.

WONG: You have no sorrow in your heart in leaving my household?

MING TOY: But my lord, I am not of your household. I am like goods upon your shelves. I have no place before your family altar. I shall go. (*Naïvely*)

WONG: I am sorry, Ming Toy, but American ways are not like Chinese ways. You pray to Joss and ask him to make Charlie Yong be good to you. (*Exits.*)

MING TOY: (*Kneels as though preparing to pray to Joss. Rises suddenly and runs to door where Wong exits. She listens for a moment, comes down, opens small door in altar, and takes out cross. Ming Toy comes down, kneels on cushion—front—facing audience and holds the cross up and closes eyes. She prays.*)[43] Nice white man's God, my Chinese father always make me pray to Joss. I no like Joss. He got funny face. I always give you first chance. Chinese father catch me pray to you, he spank me good. Whole lot spankings I get for you, God. Little Ming Toy ask you here please to make Charlie Yong be good to Ming Toy. You make Charlie Yong—or he go to hell! (*Kisses cross and places in her bodice. Jazz band heard playing off right. Ming Toy walks back to Joss.*) Oh! Honorable Joss—hear Jazz band. (*Starts to dance—she turns down collar of dress.*)

(*Potter enters back door and sees latter part of dance. Ming Toy does not see him at first, then she suddenly glances around, notices him, drops to floor, kneeling and placing draperies around her so it covers limbs. With her left hand she pulls up collar to cover her neck.*)

MING TOY: You bad man—you go away. What you come back for?

POTTER: I was standing over at Kelley's and I saw you flirting at this window.

MING TOY: I no flirt. I only wink eye.

POTTER: Don't you know that it is not ladylike for you to sit at that window and wink your eye at men as they go by?

MING TOY: Men wink eye at me. Like American I want to be polite and wink eye back at man. Now you go way so I can get up.

POTTER: Oh—you can get up. I will go over and talk to Joss. I won't look! (*Walks up stage and pantomimes as if talking to Joss. Ming Toy rises hurriedly to exit. She reaches door when Potter quickly turns.*) Don't run away so soon.

MING TOY: (*Drops on cushion left.*) You bad man.[44]

POTTER: Why do you call me a bad man?

MING TOY: You come in quick and see me dance with short skirt and neck open.

POTTER: Well, if I had a pretty neck like you, I would not try to hide it.

MING TOY: It wrong for China girl to show neck.

POTTER: But you are in America now and our best girls here show their neck and wear dresses rather short.

MING TOY: You don't think wrong for girl to show neck and some leg to man?

POTTER: Why, certainly not!

MING TOY: All right. (*Rises.*) I look like American girl now.

POTTER: You look wonderful.

MING TOY: You think wrong for girl to dance?

POTTER: Certainly not.

MING TOY: You teach me dance I see at Kelley's?

POTTER: Which one?

MING TOY: (*Goes over to window right.*) Look—see what dance they do!

POTTER: That's called the Shimmy Wiggle.[45]

MING TOY: You show Ming Toy how to dance Shimmy Wiggle?

POTTER: With pleasure.

MING TOY: All right—what I do?

POTTER: (*Placing his arm around Ming Toy.*) Now put your right foot forward and bend—so. (*Bends her over.*)

MING TOY: Don't break Ming Toy!

POTTER: No danger—now—glide. (*Takes gliding steps with Ming Toy.*)

MING TOY: Ming Toy dance fine—huh?

POTTER: Great. (*Does waltz step with Ming Toy. Wong enters back. Wong looks angrily at Ming Toy. She drops quickly on floor, covering her legs with raiment.*)

POTTER: That's all right, Wong. I was just teaching her a little dance.

MING TOY: He teach me Shimmy Wiggle.

WONG: Honorable Mr. Potter, I am surprised. You want Chinese be good and you teach Chinese girl Shimmy Wiggle.

POTTER: Oh—that's all right. That's harmless pleasure.

WONG: I see bad women at Kelley's do what you call Shimmy Wiggle.

POTTER: Why, it's a popular dance; our best people do it. We have established dancing schools as a recreation for working girls.

WONG: Maybe I don't know your custom, but I do not think it right that girls work all day and do Shimmy Wiggle all night. Now—what you come back for?

POTTER: Well, I was over at Kelley's and saw Ming Toy flirting at the window and I came back to tell you about it. But I have changed my mind. Wong, I think Ming Toy is a very nice little girl. I guess it will be all right for you to keep her. I will talk to the Mission so you can keep her.

WONG: So you can come teach her Shimmy Wiggle dance every day—eh?

POTTER: Not every day. I might come once or twice a week. You keep her cooped up too much. I think a girl should have a little recreation.

WONG: Well, maybe I let her out in the street too?

POTTER: Well, that would not be a crime!

WONG: Well, maybe you take her to theatre!

POTTER: Well, that would not be a crime either. She is a young pretty little thing. She should have a little harmless pleasure. It won't hurt her. I, as a reformer, advocate it.

WONG: If you go to theatre with Ming Toy, what Miss Benson say—eh?

POTTER: She would be delighted to think I take a little interest in a poor little thing like Ming Toy. I very often do that.

WONG: Oh—you take girls out to reform them, eh? But you tell me to keep girl in to make them good.

POTTER: Well, I thought Ming Toy was a different kind of a girl when I said that. But she is all right. Just keep her away from that window, and stop her flirting.

WONG: No, Mr. Potter. I do what you say the first time.

POTTER: All right—suit yourself. If it is more advisable that you give the people no cause for gossip. (*Turning to Ming Toy*) Good-bye, Ming Toy, and good luck to you.

MING TOY: Good-bye, Mr. Potter—you nice man. I like Shimmy dance.

POTTER: Good day, Wong Lo.

WONG: Good-bye, Mr. Potter. (*Potter exits door back.*) Ming Toy, you bring more disgrace to me. You show your neck and show your leg to honorable Mr. Potter. Chinese girl never do that.

MING TOY: I don't want to be Chinese girl. I American girl. In China I American girl. Mission lady always tell me that. I never like Chinese girl.[46]

WONG: Yes, I know. That is reason your father, he sell you.

MING TOY: I am not sorry. Got better father now.

WONG: Who?

MING TOY: Wong Lo. (*Tries to put her arms round his neck.*)

WONG: Ming Toy, you just same like American vamp.

MING TOY: What you mean vamp?

WONG: Vamp is woman bee. You go get honey—you get stung.

MING TOY: But I try to give you honey—and you sting me.

WONG: But I should beat you for what you did. (*Points to legs.*) Look—see—your dress undone. I should not beat you—I should kill you.

MING TOY: All right. You may kill, but a beautiful flower shall die.

WONG: Now again you like vamp. Ming Toy, you cannot vamp Wong Lo. You go to your room. This is last night you sleep here. No more will you sit by window and wink eye.

MING TOY: All right. Maybe Charlie Yong got window. (*Exits.*)

(*Old Chinese servant opens door in back and shows Charlie Yong in. He is a Beau Brummell—a man of the world—and proprietor of several chop suey restaurants.*[47] *Yong is about 35 years old, is in modern fashionable clothes, and wears a que in a coil under his hat.*[48] *He seems to have absorbed superficial and petty traits and American customs. Yong carries a small cane. He is also a regular rounder; wears a boutonnière and speaks with very little accent. Marks of worldliness characterize his dress.*)

CHARLIE YONG: Good afternoon, Wong. What you phone for me?

WONG: I think I give you what you ask me.

CHARLIE YONG: I no ask anybody give me anything. When I see what I want, I take it.

WONG: Charlie Yong—you sit down. (*He obeys.*) How business, Charlie Yong?

CHARLIE YONG: My business always good. American people eat chop suey when stomach empty—all same late at night when stomach full, eat chop suey. Eat it when stomach good—eat it when stomach bad. I open another place—big place. Now I got three fine Chinese restaurants—never work an hour. (*Rises and pats himself with cane, with an air of bragging.*) Smart—eh? How your business, Wong?

WONG: My business not so good—but I do lot of work.

CHARLIE YONG: Well, it always so—man who do lot hard work, get nothing. (*Again pats himself with cane. Pause. Puffs cigarette.*)

WONG: Charlie Yong, you know girl you see from Kelley's sit at that window?

CHARLIE YONG: Sure! Girl's faces to me all same—but not one that sit at your window.

WONG: Many time you ask me for this girl. I always say no—now you can get her if everything all right.

CHARLIE YONG: Fine! I take her if she all right.

WONG: All right. Charlie, you got wife?

CHARLIE YONG: No.

WONG: What's the matter—she die?

CHARLIE YONG: No—I never have pleasure to bury wife.

WONG: No woman?

CHARLIE YONG: Have not one wife, but got three girls. If I got wife, maybe she boss me. Girls—Charlie Yong boss.

WONG: Well, what you want with more girls?

CHARLIE YONG: I want no girl—girls I got. I have for too long. They are what Americans call passé.

WONG: What passé?

CHARLIE YONG: Passé women like broke automobile standing in mud—nobody ride. I got get new machine.

WONG: What you do with machine in the mud?

CHARLIE YONG: I make them go in restaurant—bring chop suey to my customers. Good enough for them. Save me hiring waiters. When they no good for customers, I put in kitchen to help chefs. When they no good for chefs no more, I kick them out.

WONG: They wait so long? Don't they run away from you before?

CHARLIE YONG: Charlie Yong big man in town—got lots of power. Policeman takes hat off to Charlie Yong. Big Tong Society make him President.[49] No girl want to run away from such man. Once one girl run away from Charlie Yong—he tell Tong—they see girl—she have another man. One morning girl back—man buried. Charlie Yong no fool. Don't kick nice girl in street. She appeal to me, all right, I keep her long time. It is up to girl.

WONG: If you like her much, you marry Ming Toy?

CHARLIE YONG: Charlie Yong, he never marry. Wife kill all pep in man. If I like her, she be good as wife—but marry—NO!

WONG: You swear by Joss if Ming Toy nice girl, and you like her you always treat her nice, Charlie Yong?

CHARLIE YONG: She nice—I like her. Charlie Yong nice always—I swear. (*Wong rises and starts to door left.*) You wait, Wong. Now I ask you something! How long you got Ming Toy?

WONG: One year.

CHARLIE YONG: Where you get her?

WONG: Love-boat.

CHARLIE YONG: Oh—sing-song girl!

WONG: Yes.

CHARLIE YONG: (*Very indignant*) You say Chinaman should marry sing-song girl? You no good Chinaman—and you no good friend of mine.

WONG: Well, I think you American Chinaman.

CHARLIE YONG: Oh sure. I dress American—speak English fine, but in heart I am true Chinaman. (*Patting himself over heart.*)

WONG: I hear you all American.

CHARLIE YONG: (*Takes off his hat, showing que in coil on his head under hat.*) Oh—fifty-fifty.

WONG: Then you no want Ming Toy because she sing-song girl?

CHARLIE YONG: Oh, yes—but no for wife.

WONG: I understand—all right. (*Rises from seat.*)

CHARLIE YONG: Wait—keep seat. If Ming Toy fine girl, why you want to give Ming Toy away? Passé to you?

WONG: (*Indignant*) Oh no! What you think?

CHARLIE YONG: That's all right—girl be passé to one man—and be frappe for another.[50]

WONG: You no understand. Ming Toy is like bud that has not blossomed—only sun kiss her.

CHARLIE YONG: You mean Ming Toy not your woman?

WONG: No! What you think?

CHARLIE YONG: She live here one year and she not your woman?

WONG: Ming Toy NOT my woman! Ming Toy no man's woman! Ming Toy good girl.

CHARLIE YONG: You got her on love-boat—how can you say she good girl? You lie!

WONG: (*Rising from his seat*) Charlie Yong, maybe you fifty-fifty—but you no call me lie!

CHARLIE YONG: (*Rising from seat*) Then you no try fool Charlie Yong. No man fool Charlie Yong. Charlie Yong wise guy. (*Pats himself with cane.*)

WONG: I don't try make you fool—but you try make me liar.

CHARLIE YONG: Why you tell me you give me new coat, when you know it is second-hand?

WONG: Well, I know it is new. I am at love boat when her father bring Ming Toy fresh like apple blossom just plucked from tree.

CHARLIE YONG: And all time she been with you?

WONG: Sure.

CHARLIE YONG: You swear?

WONG: (*Walks over to Joss.*) I swear. Ming Toy just as good as Joss.

CHARLIE YONG: All right. Sorry I make you mad. Wong Lo, my good friend, give me nice flower. Wong Lo, you pick out best man. Wong Lo, you almost as smart as Charlie Yong.

WONG: All right. (*Goes to door—opens it and calls.*) Ming Toy. (*During this business Charlie Yong rises and rearranges his dress, places flower in boutonniere, and struts up and down floor with hands in pocket puffing away on cigarette. Enter Ming Toy with Wong.*) Charlie Yong—Ming Toy. (*Ming Toy bows to Yong. Both scrutinize each other closely. Wong lights pipe.*)

MING TOY: Charlie Yong, I know you.

CHARLIE YONG: Everybody know Charlie Yong. (*Takes another puff of cigarette.*)

MING TOY: I see you always in Kelley's. You live there?

CHARLIE YONG: When you see me in Kelley's?

MING TOY: All time.

CHARLIE YONG: Any place Charlie Yong hang his hat is his home. (*Pats himself again with cane.*)

MING TOY: I see you in Kelley's with lots women.

CHARLIE YONG: Pretty girls—eh!

MING TOY: All kinds. One time I see woman slap you face.

CHARLIE YONG: Charlie Yong's face! Woman slap!

MING TOY: Maybe it was love pat.

CHARLIE YONG: All women give Charlie Yong love pat.

MING TOY: Why you got name Charlie Yong? Half Chinese-half American.

CHARLIE YONG: Fifty-fifty.

MING TOY: I see you dance nice at Kelley's. Sometime you take me to Kelley's to dance?

CHARLIE YONG: Alright. You dance?

MING TOY: I dance fine Shimmy Wiggle.

WONG: Charlie Yong, Kelley's no place to take Ming Toy.

CHARLIE YONG: I take finest ladies to Kelley's. White women glad to dance with me. I got Oriental motion.[51]

MING TOY: All these women I see you with—they love you?

CHARLIE YONG: All women love Charlie Yong.

MING TOY: All girls I see you with—they love you too?

CHARLIE YONG: Sure.

MING TOY: What you want little Ming Toy?

CHARLIE YONG: Charlie Yong got enough love spread all around everywhere.

MING TOY: Ming Toy no like spread out love. Ming Toy want her man to keep his love in one place—all for Ming Toy.

CHARLIE YONG: (*Walks over to Ming Toy, takes both her hands in his.*) If Ming Toy can collect Charlie Yong's love from all places and put it in one spot, all right. But it will be hard job for Ming Toy.

WONG: Ming Toy so smart—she make all other girl to Charlie Yong look like faded rose.

MING TOY: (*To Yong*) You got nice home—you take me there? I be there alone with you?

CHARLIE YONG: Three more girls—faded roses—get jealous of you and maybe try to kill you. But that's all right. All girls I have insured—you see; you be safe. I got nice home full of smoke—smelling fine—like home of Sultan.

MING TOY: What I have to do at your home?

CHARLIE YONG: Everything easy—just love Charlie Yong.

MING TOY: Is that all?

CHARLIE YONG: Oh no—lots more. You don't go sleep until I come home. Sometimes I come six in the morning—sometimes not at all. You must always have pitcher cold ice. Sometimes I come with headache—you got to fix me up. In my room, my private table—when I feel like it I eat. You bring everything to me. You watch me eat; when I get through you eat at same table Charlie Yong eat. (*Turning to Wong*) See Wong, I show you how I like Ming Toy! When I get more time, I tell you lots more things you do for me. Now I just tell you what you not do. You must not sit by window—no man must look at you. That show you how Charlie Yong like woman. You must not talk to anybody loud.

MING TOY: All right. I only speak to myself, but not too loud—neighbors listen.

CHARLIE YONG: All right—talk to yourself. When you talk to yourself always say Charlie Yong nice man. You say that loud, I don't care. Ming Toy listen to this—you give no man smile but Charlie Yong. If you do, and I catch you, you lose two teeth and one man and you cry for Charlie Yong but he no come back. Did you get all that?

MING TOY: Yes, it make Ming Toy so happy, she feel like crying now.

CHARLIE YONG: (*Turns to Wong*) All right—I take her tonight—eh!

WONG: All right—she go. Please, I ask you, Charlie Yong, treat her nice. If you treat her mean, she be like beautiful lily after storm goes by. Ming Toy like baby. Like baby, she not do everything right—sometimes she do mischief—but like baby she no do it with sense. I love Ming Toy just like Chinese father love honored son. You good to Ming Toy, I give you silk dress for your three faded roses.

CHARLIE YONG: Sure I be good to her. Only trouble with Charlie Yong—he too good to girls. What I pay you for Ming Toy?

WONG: I no sell girls. Just be good to Ming Toy—don't want no money for her.

CHARLIE YONG: Oh no—Charlie Yong don't take girls for presents. Girl man can get for nothing no good. Man like girl better when he pay for her. Charlie Yong, he know about that. How much I pay?

WONG: Charlie Yong—you not got enough money to buy Ming Toy from me but if she cost you something—make you like her better—you can give me what I pay for her on love-boat—only that.

CHARLIE YONG: All right. How much you pay?

WONG: I pay 3,000 yen.

CHARLIE YONG: All right—you give me paper written Ming Toy is mine, I give you check.

WONG: All right—I write paper for you. (*Wong starts for door right—Just before reaching door Charlie pulls out four different checkbooks.*)

CHARLIE YONG: What bank I give you check on?

WONG: All same to me. I take little check on each bank—sometime bank bust. (*Wong exits down right.*)

CHARLIE YONG: (*He lingers behind—quickly comes down to Ming Toy.*) You mine—give me a kiss. I buy you. (*Grabs Ming Toy and kisses her.*) No man kiss sweet like Charlie Yong! (*Exit right.*)

MING TOY: (*She wipes kiss away in disgust. Picks up Charlie Yong's cigarette holder from table and reads.*) "Charlie Yong to Lulu." (*Throws holder to floor—sits down and picks up shamisen and begins to play sadly until Billy Benson enters door back. Billy remains standing at door for a moment. Ming Toy looks around, sees Billy—drops shamisen—rushes toward him transported with joy and bows in Chinese fashion.*) Oh! Mr. Billy Benson—you come!

BILLY: Glad to see me, Ming Toy?

MING TOY: Every day I pray you come. First I pray to Joss—you no come. Then I pray to Buddha—you no come. I pray to Confucius you no come. Today, I pray to Christian God—and you come. If three Chinese Gods cannot do what one Christian God can do—then I stick to Christian God—three China Gods no good.[52]

BILLY: Did you want to see me that much?

MING TOY: I want to see you much and mucher. You look so fine, Mr. Billy Benson.

BILLY: And you—Ming Toy—you look like a beautiful Chinese doll.

MING TOY: You make nice compliments, Mr. Billy Benson.

BILLY: It's the truth. How do you like this country? Well—how are things with you?

MING TOY: (*Hesitatingly—half-sadly*) Oh—all right.

BILLY: Have you been happy?

MING TOY: Yes—I been very happy.

BILLY: Have you been here with Wong all the time?

MING TOY: Oh, yes—all time with Wong—he very nice to me. When Wong was made, China God must be awful busy and leave job to Christian God. You come back long?

BILLY: No—or I would have been here sooner.

MING TOY: To see Wong—eh!

BILLY: (*Draws.*) Yes—but more so to see you.

MING TOY: It makes me happy that you want to see little Ming Toy.

BILLY: You speak English well now.

MING TOY: Wong buy me big English books. He buy me insicklepedes.

BILLY: Encyclopedia.

MING TOY: Mr. Billy Benson, you go back to China soon?

BILLY: Perhaps—perhaps.

MING TOY: You take me back to China with you?

BILLY: Why—don't you like America?

MING TOY: Yes—if Mr. Billy Benson in China. Ming Toy no like America.

BILLY: That's very sweet of you, Ming Toy.

MING TOY: I wish, Mr. Billy Benson—you come here sooner before to-day.

BILLY: I could not, Ming Toy.

MING TOY: Too bad—now it is too late.

BILLY: Why?

MING TOY: Everything happen wrong for Ming Toy. Oh—well—no matter.

BILLY: Now Ming Toy, you must be happy to see me.

MING TOY: Oh—I am so happy—I am miserable.

BILLY: (*Laughs.*) You remember that little song you played on the love-boat?

MING TOY: Doodle Yankee?[53]

BILLY: That little Chinese love song you played that night when I first saw you.

MING TOY: You like that—eh?

BILLY: Yes. (*Picks up her shamisen and hands it to her. Ming Toy plays and sings song played on love-boat. Score.*)

CHARLIE YONG: (*He enters door right—has large paper in hand—stops dead short at door at sight of Billy. Stands watching scene until Ming Toy has finished song.*) That's a damn nice song.

WONG: (*Enters, and seeing Billy, walks over to him.*) Welcome, my most august friend, Mr. Billy.

BILLY: Glad to see you, Wong.

WONG: I am very glad to see you in my honorable house. I have honor to introduce you to my most honorable friend, Mr. Charlie Yong. Charlie Yong—Mr. Billy Benson.

BILLY: Glad to know you, Mr. Yong. (*They shake hands.*)

CHARLIE YONG: (*Takes from his pocket a large, gold plated-cigarette case. He opens it and offers Billy cigarette.*) Have cigarette.

BILLY: (*Taking cigarette*) Thank you.

CHARLIE YONG: (*Closing cigarette case with snap and replacing in his pocket.*) All right. (*Turning to Ming Toy*) Ming Toy—you go and pack. I go get my automobile. I take you to my house tonight. You travel like fine lady—lemonsine.[54] All right—go ahead.

MING TOY: Got lots time.

CHARLIE YONG: You got no time—when Charlie Yong says "go now."

WONG: (*To Billy*) Charlie Yong big man in town. Ming Toy go with him—he got nice home for her.

BILLY: Oh—I see.

CHARLIE YONG: You see and I see. Don't let me see Ming Toy play for you again. Charlie Yong girl only play to Charlie Yong.

BILLY: (*Apologetically*) I beg your pardon, Mr. Yong. I did not know Ming Toy's relation to you, but I meant no offense. You are getting a mighty fine little girl, and I want to congratulate you.

CHARLIE YONG: When Charlie Yong gets girl, girl to be congratulated.

BILLY: All right then—I will congratulate Ming Toy. (*Extends his hand to her.*) Very glad for your sake.

MING TOY: I cannot take your hand, Mr. Billy Benson. I am not so happy about it.

CHARLIE YONG: Maybe you not happy now because you never had Charlie Yong, but when you get him for a little time, you be more than happy.

BILLY: What's the matter, Mr. Yong? Is your press agent sick?

CHARLIE YONG: Charlie Yong need no pressing. Don't you be too smart with Charlie Yong.

MING TOY: (*Smiling to Billy*) Don't mind Mr. Yong—he don't know what sweet man you are.

CHARLIE YONG: You got short memory, Ming Toy. I tell you not to smile at other man.

MING TOY: You tell me you spread your love, I spread my smile—fifty-fifty.

CHARLIE YONG: Fifty-fifty all right—maybe. When you come to my house—it be 101-nothing.

MING TOY: You insult my nice friend, Billy Benson. Maybe I don't go to your house. I like Mr. Billy Benson better than any man.

BILLY: No—no, Ming Toy. You must not say that. You must like no man better than the man you are going to marry.

MING TOY: He don't marry me!

BILLY: (*To Wong*) I thought you found a nice husband for Ming Toy?

WONG: No Chinaman marry sing-song girl.

BILLY: What are you giving her to Mr. Yong for?

WONG: I got to give her away. Mission make bad talk about me. Charlie Yong, he be all right. Charlie Yong—he ask for her—say he be good to her —so I give her away.

BILLY: Yes, she's got something.

CHARLIE YONG: You bet! Now I go for my lemonsine. Ming Toy, I come for you—you be ready. Ming Toy, go and pack. (*She does not move.*) When Charlie Yong say you go—you go.

WONG: Go, Ming Toy. Chinese woman always obey Chinese man.

MING TOY: Charlie Yong—he no Chinese man—he fifty-fifty. (*Turns to Billy.*) Good-bye, Mr. Billy Benson—very sorry I see you no more.

BILLY: (*Takes her hand.*) Good-bye, Ming Toy. And the best of luck.

MING TOY: (*At door*) Good-bye, Mr. Billy Benson.

BILLY: Good-bye—don't feel sad.

MING TOY: All right. I no feel sad—I laugh. Sing-song girl must never feel sad. Sing-song girl always happy. (*Break—little cry—exit.*)

CHARLIE YONG: Maybe you see me—but you don't see Ming Toy again. You try to see her and—well, have a cigarette. (*Offers him cigarette.*)

BILLY: (*Refusing*) No thank you.

(*Charlie Yong exits.*)

POTTER: (*Entering through private entrance—sees Billy in room.*) Hello, Bill!

BILLY: Hello, Jim!

POTTER: (*To Wong*) I just came from the Mission. I told them what a very fine man you are, and they insist that you keep Ming Toy under your protection.

WONG: (*Coldly*) First they make trouble—now it is too late. I made arrangements with Charlie Yong to take care of Ming Toy.

POTTER: (*Surprised*) Charlie Yong!

WONG: Now people cannot talk any more about Wong Lo. (*Exits to store.*)

BILLY: How do you know Ming Toy?

POTTER: Do you know Ming Toy?

BILLY: I met her in China. Isn't she the cutest thing?

POTTER: Too bad that Charlie Yong should get her.

BILLY: Do you know Charlie Yong?

POTTER: Who doesn't know Charlie Yong? He is the Beau Brummel of Chinatown, or rather par excellence. He is the leader of a gang of fanatics—a very dangerous fellow. The Mission has more trouble with him about girls than any other Chink in Chinatown.[55]

BILLY: Why couldn't you land him?

POTTER: Land Charlie Yong! If you did, you could not convict him. He controls every vote in Chinatown. He even reaches the Governor.[56] Where is Ming Toy?

BILLY: She is packing. He is going to call for her.

POTTER: By Jove, Billy—I've got an idea.

BILLY: It's about time you had one.

POTTER: Listen—your sister asked me several times if I could not get her a nice little Chinese girl for her maid. Why not take Ming Toy?

BILLY: By Jove, that is a good idea. (*Billy knocks at door of Ming Toy's room. She enters dressed for the street with a little grip in her hand.*)[57]

MING TOY: Oh—Mr. Billy Benson—you no go away—I am so glad you still here.

BILLY: Listen, Ming Toy. Does it make you happy to go to Charlie Yong's house?

MING TOY: Well—I got no other place to go!

BILLY: Would you go to another place if I had one for you?

MING TOY: What place?

BILLY: To our house to be a maid for my sister.

MING TOY: Oh—Mr. Billy Benson—why you ask this? I can go to your house?

BILLY: Yes—if you want to go.

MING TOY: Oh—it would make me so happy! Oh, Mr. Billy Benson, if I could go to your house—I would go to Hell—

BILLY: Good—you shall go.

MING TOY: But Mr. Charlie Yong—he come for me right away.

BILLY: You stay here and I'll get you before he comes. I'll get a taxi. (*To Potter*) Jim, go inside and keep the old man busy. (*Potter exits to store.*) Keep your head, Ming Toy. I'll be back in a minute. (*He rushes off.*)

MING TOY: All right. (*Ming Toy goes to small door in back—opens same—reaches in—takes out cross she had formerly prayed with—comes down front stage.*) Christian God, you good to Ming Toy—I take you with me. (*Opens grip—places cross in grip. She hears footsteps on private entrance stairs—quickly looks down—quickly dives underneath table and hides.*)

CHARLIE YONG: (*Enters private entrance—goes to Ming Toy's door—opens door and calls.*) Ming Toy—Ming Toy. (*Goes to store back door and calls Wong.*) Pause. (*Wong enters.*) Wong, where is Ming Toy?

WONG: She is packing in her room.

CHARLIE YONG: She not there. (*Looks at him sternly.*)

WONG: Not there?

CHARLIE YONG: Isn't she in the store? (*Goes into store to look.*)

WONG: No. (*Goes to door of Ming Toy's room. Charlie Yong goes in store.*) Wait—I see. (*Opens door to her room—stands in front of door and hears Billy calling—Ming Toy says nothing—comes out of hiding place quickly. Wong sees it all but says nothing.*)

BILLY: Ming Toy.

MING TOY: (*In whisper*) All right. (*Exits. Re-enter Charlie Yong from store door.*)

WONG: Did you find her?

CHARLIE YONG: No!

WONG: Well, Charlie Yong—don't be mad. I give you back check.

CHARLIE YONG: I don't want check—I want Ming Toy. I got paper call for Ming Toy—I want Ming Toy. You see, Wong, I find Ming Toy—

WONG: I find Ming Toy, you get her, Charlie Yong—

CHARLIE YONG: And if you don't find her, I get her. (*Winks—walking to exit private entrance.*)

(*Curtain*)

## Act 2

SCENE: *Living room in Benson's home.*

*Door right leading to Benson's study. Door left leading to dining room. Glass French windows back left overlooking garden. Staircase leading to upper floors back right.* (*At opening Mildred discovered coming down stairs. She is petulant in manner; goes to table, picks up magazine, turns pages rapidly for a second, throws magazine down on table and goes to piano and starts to play. After a moment Potter comes down stairs. He goes over to piano and tries to put his head close to Mildred's, but she draws away and turns.*)

MILDRED: Good Heavens, can't you leave me alone for a minute?

POTTER: I'm not bothering you.

MILDRED: Oh, yes you are. You never leave me alone for a second. What is it you want this time?

POTTER: Just a slight favor. I want you to marry me.

MILDRED: (*Lightly*) What have you to offer beside love and money?

POTTER: Myself.

MILDRED: That counts for nothing.

POTTER: Well, my career.

MILDRED: Your career is just the thing I object to.

POTTER: What is your objection to my career? I am doing good work.

MILDRED: Yes—trying to make Christians out of heathen Chinese—a hopeless task.

POTTER: If the task is difficult—it shows how wonderful I am to undertake it. I think I have accomplished wonders here among the Chinese.

MILDRED: Well, I don't believe in this mission work. The Chinese have their own creed and customs. Let them keep them. Let each race work out their own destiny. I don't believe in interfering with other people's Gods.

POTTER: Self-determination—you with President Wilson.[58]

MILDRED: Self-determination in the individual as well as the state.

POTTER: I notice you're trying very hard to prevent me from having the privilege of self-determination. You are telling me what to do.

MILDRED: I'm not telling you anything. You can do anything you like.

POTTER: Anything I like. Well, I'd like to marry you.

MILDRED: Where were you last evening, Jim?

POTTER: Oh, I see. At last it has come out. I knew there was something on your sweet little heart. Well, I will tell you.

MILDRED: I know where you were. You don't have to tell me.

POTTER: Well, I'll wager you don't.

MILDRED: I'll wager I do. You were at the theatre with Harriet, and then you took supper at Tait's.[59]

POTTER: How did you guess it?

MILDRED: I didn't have to guess it. I saw you. I was to the same theatre with Jack and to Tait's to supper with Arthur.

POTTER: So you went out with Arthur? You might have shown better taste in compliment to me.

MILDRED: Well, you certainly weren't very complimentary to me when you went out with Harriet.

POTTER: Arthur is baldheaded—weighs two hundred and ten pounds.

MILDRED: Harriet is a poor little pigmy—a bag of bones protruding from every corner.

POTTER: It would have been in much better taste on the part of both of us had we been together.

MILDRED: Did you have a good time?

POTTER: Rotten. I'll never go out with that bag of bones again. How about you?

MILDRED: Don't mention it. It was all right when Arthur wasn't resting his weight on my toes. He one-steps like a walrus. There's a bandage on two of my toes now.

POTTER: Well, would you object to a ring on one of your fingers?

MILDRED: Are you going to show me that same ring again?

POTTER: Please take it this time.

MILDRED: Like a pill, I'm supposed to take it five times a day.

POTTER: Darling, please take it this time. If you don't, the diamond will get rusty.

MILDRED: No, I couldn't bring myself to accept a ring from a man who would go out with Harriet. You had better give me a little more time. I will let you know to-morrow.

POTTER: You said that yesterday.

MILDRED: Well, I am letting you know, am I not?

POTTER: (*Puts ring back in pocket.*) Back to the stable. We may take another ride to-morrow. (*Mildred turns around and resumes playing some Chinese song.*) That's Ming Toy's little melody, isn't it?

MILDRED: Yes—she's been trying to teach it to me. Do you know she's quite a talented little thing. And how she picks up our ways. I've never had a white maid so intelligent.[60] She is most unusual. Bringing Ming Toy here is the most useful thing your career has ever done for me.

POTTER: I'm not so sure it is going to turn out as usefully as you think.

MILDRED: What do you mean?

POTTER: Oh, nothing.

MILDRED: (*Mildred resumes playing same little Chinese melody.*) Isn't it quaint —and so plaintive?

POTTER: It is very plaintive.

MILDRED: (*Still playing*) Are the Chinese a sad people?

POTTER: Not at all. On the contrary, they are a humorous people; very good natured.

MILDRED: To me their faces seem to express nothing in particular—so immobile.

POTTER: It's another case of quiet waters running deep. (*Mildred continues playing, striking a few notes off key.*)

MING TOY: (*Comes down left; stands listening to Mildred playing piano—walks down.*) Beg your pardon, Miss Mildred. You strike wrong note and you don't mind I show you right one?

MILDRED: Certainly not, Ming Toy. I never can get that little part right in there.

MING TOY: (*Going over to Mildred who plays part of melody again.*) Now, see—you hit white note there—that's wrong. Hit black note two times—white note one time—black note three times—white note four time more—you hit white note half time—then black note half time—then you got it.

POTTER: See, Mildred, how simple that is?

MILDRED: How long have you been playing the piano, Ming Toy?

MING TOY: Only two weeks—since I am here.

MILDRED: Isn't it wonderful!

POTTER: (*Jokingly*) She's a born pianist—got it from her Chinese mother.

MILDRED: (*Plays tune correctly.*) Is that right?

MING TOY: All right.

MILDRED: You're a good little teacher, Ming Toy.

MING TOY: Now I tell butler to bring in cocktails for Mr. Jim—eh! I read in book all sweethearts drink cocktails. (*Exits door back.*)

POTTER: You will admit Ming Toy is a very good example of the work we are doing! (*Pause.*)

MILDRED: Isn't she the dearest thing? I am just wild about her. I can't put her in the same category with the ordinary Chinaman. She just takes to things naturally.[61]

POTTER: One little thing comes to me very naturally. (*Takes ring out of pocket—Mildred taps him over fingers.*) Back to the stable. (*He puts ring back.*) It's all right for us folks, but Billy should not pay so much attention to her.

MILDRED: Why should he be denied the same right?

POTTER: Well, Billy is a young, charming fellow and Ming Toy is a very naive little thing. She might fall in love with him, and it would break her heart.

MILDRED: Oh—he has more sense than that.

POTTER: Don't talk about sense when it comes to love. Look at me. (*Touching his pocket*)

MRS. BENSON: (*Enters door right. She is in afternoon gown.*) What are you children up to again? Well, Jim, is the horse out of the stable yet?

POTTER: No, it is in the stall, but I have hopes.

MRS. BENSON: Perseverance, my boy. Stick to it. Patience.

POTTER: Yes—I hope my patience lasts as long as the ring. The poor thing has been handled pretty roughly.

MING TOY: (*Enters door back with tray holding cocktails. She sees Mrs. Benson, puts tray on small stand, runs up stage quickly for foot stool and puts it under Mrs. Benson's feet.*) Your feet very tired.

MRS. BENSON: Thank you, dear. (*Ming Toy takes tray from stand, brings it to Potter. He drinks it, leaving cherry in glass on toothpick. Ming Toy takes glass, takes cherry out on toothpick, eats it and exits left.*) Isn't Ming Toy thoughtful? She seems to anticipate every little thought. Jimmey, I am so grateful to you—she is a find. If the Mission's influence is half as good on the other Chinese as it apparently has been on Ming Toy, it is certainly worth supporting.

MILDRED: Now, mother, I don't believe the Mission is responsible for Ming Toy—it's in her. I don't think anyone can change us fundamentally.

MRS. BENSON: Does environment count for nothing, my child?

MILDRED: Oh, yes—it counts in a way, but only externally; but it can't change one's blood—or one's soul. You can't put a cat in a birdcage and make it sing!

POTTER: (*Humorously*) That is it. You can't put a black man in a can of milk and make him white.

MILDRED: Or a white man in a barrel of pitch and make him black.[62]

MRS. BENSON: That may be so. Nevertheless, Ming Toy, though a Chinese, shows strong evidence of the characteristics of us, and that certainly is due to environment.

MILDRED: Do you think, mother, if I had been born and brought up among Chinamen, I could ever become a Chinese girl?

POTTER: (*Good naturedly*) You could become anything.

THOMAS (BUTLER): (*Enters.*) Beg pardon, Madam. May I be permitted to ask: who is the butler—me, or Ming Toy? She infringes upon my functions as a butler, but I should like to ask, does Ming Toy maintain the position of maid or mistress?

MRS. BENSON: Well, Thomas, she holds a unique position of both maid and mistress. When she is here she is one of us, and I hope when she is with you, you will make her one of you.

THOMAS: It is very trying to make a person one of us when she happens to be one of you. (*Mr. Benson enters from right.*) Thank you, ma'am. (*Thomas exits back door. Ming Toy enters. Butler bows graciously to her and exits. Ming Toy, after seeing Mr. Benson quickly scurries off again.*)

MR. BENSON: That little Chinese mouse is always moving. (*Sits down and reads newspaper.*) I see China is about to have another revolution. A good thing we left. It is very difficult for them to take to the new—even if it is for their betterment.

POTTER: They are very unprogressive people.

MR. BENSON: I don't agree with you. These very revolutions are evidence of the awakening of China.[63]

POTTER: Well, as an ex-Ambassador you should know.

MR. BENSON: I don't know everything! What do you think, mother?

MRS. BENSON: Use your own judgment, dear.

MILDRED: Father, don't you think if they intermarried it would be a great help to the race?

MR. BENSON: No, child. I don't believe in international assimilation, or internationalism in any form. Internationalism in any form is responsible for most wars. The moment you attempt to make an Austrian over to an Italian or a German out of a Frenchman, as in the case of Alsace-Lorraine, you sow the seed for trouble.[64]

MILDRED: Father, supposing you blot out all these indifferences by Internationalism.

MR. BENSON: You can't blot them out. History has shown that any attempt of blotting them out by one nation having world power, almost caused the destruction of the whole human race.

MILDRED: I am afraid, dad, I cannot agree with you. I believe in assimilation of individuals as well as nations.

MR. BENSON: It would be unnatural if you did, but I bet mother does.

MRS. BENSON: Yes, use your own judgment, and (*Ming Toy enters through back door holding tray of cocktails, comes down to Mr. Benson.*)

MING TOY: Mr. Benson—your cocktail. (*Benson takes glass—drinks same—hands glass back to Ming Toy.*) You no want cherry, Mr. Benson?

MR. BENSON: No, thank you.

MING TOY: I thank you, Mr. Benson. (*Takes cherry from glass, eats it, and turns.*) Anybody else want cocktail? (*Starts to go.*)

MR. BENSON: No, I think not. Come here, Ming Toy. Sit down. Ming Toy, what do you think about China?

MING TOY: What I think about China, I no say for ladies.

MR. BENSON: There has been another revolution in China.

MING TOY: Just like alarm clock to lazy man—make a noise, he go back to sleep.

MR. BENSON: They may set up a republic.

MING TOY: If they do, King knock it down. But all same to me what happens in China.

MR. BENSON: You don't love the country where you were born?

MING TOY: I born there—I die here.

MR. BENSON: You love America.

MING TOY: Sure—America fine place. Everybody dances here—make love, drink cocktails and no revolutions.

MR. BENSON: You don't drink cocktails, Ming Toy.

MING TOY: No—only like cherries. Mr. Benson, you want another cocktail?

MR. BENSON: No thanks, Ming Toy. But you may have cherries just the same. There must be a bottle of them out there.

MING TOY: Cherry no good unless he have bath in cocktail.

POTTER: Ming Toy, you said you love America. What do you think of American men?

MING TOY: Oh, American fine gentlemen. Chinese washing make them fine gentlemen.

POTTER: Is the American man as good looking as the Chinaman?

MING TOY: Chinaman, lemon. American man, peach. Chinaman get mad, he come home, beat his girls. American man get mad, he no beat girls—he make sour face and say—"Damn to Hell."

POTTER: Supposing an American man fell in love with you, would you marry him?

MING TOY: Mr. Potter, you ask a foolish question.

POTTER: Why?

MING TOY: You think Chinese girl ask any question if American man ask her THE QUESTION?

POTTER: Then, if an American man proposed to you, would you consider it?

MING TOY: No—I don't consider it—I grab him. (*Exits.*)

MILDRED: You see, father. Ming Toy does not agree with you. She believes in the intermixing of races.

POTTER: Yes, if we are not a little more careful, we might have an intermixing in this very household.

MRS. BENSON: (*Shocked.*) What are you intimating, Jim?

POTTER: Well, it may be just an unwarranted suspicion. But of course, we all of us here like Ming Toy, but there is one who likes her more than is good for us all or for himself.

MR. BENSON: (*Humorously*) Who is that? I hope you don't mean me, Jim.

POTTER: No, It's not so hard to guess.

MRS. BENSON: Billy?

POTTER: The very man, yes! You guessed it.

MILDRED: Jim Potter, do you know what you are saying?

POTTER: Well, I don't see why you should become excited. You believe in the mixing of bloods. You should not be shocked at the prospect of being aunty to a cute little Chink doll.[65]

MRS. BENSON: Now, don't joke. If there is any foundation to this, it is too serious.

MR. BENSON: There can be no foundation to that. Why, it's too ridiculous.

POTTER: Good people, I have no desire to cause you any anxiety, but in a way, I am responsible for Ming Toy's presence in this home. So it behooves me to see that no mischief results. I am very much afraid that there is more foundation for my suspicion than even I myself dare entertain.

MR. BENSON: Well, you must have some facts that lead you to any such conclusions.

POTTER: Well, I think I have. Of course you have all observed how much Billy admires Ming Toy.

MRS. BENSON: He admires her as he would a fine piece of art.

POTTER: Precisely. You notice that when Billy buys any antique or work of art, no one can get it away from him at any price. I am afraid he will refuse to part with this work of art.

MILDRED: Well, what are your facts?

MR. BENSON: Yes, I am a diplomat. I want facts.

POTTER: Well, when one takes an interest in an unfortunate creature, one does not buy her gifts as a man does his own sweetheart. I understand that he crowds Ming Toy's room every evening with all kinds of presents.

MR. BENSON: Has he done that?

POTTER: I believe he has, and he is very often in the garden with her until late at night, long after you are all asleep.

MR. BENSON: You are always in the house, mother. Have you seen anything like that?

MRS. BENSON: No, Andrew. I go to bed very early in the evening, and so often during the day. Of course, I know he is very fond of her.

MILDRED: Mother does not spy on anybody.

POTTER: Now listen, Mildred. This is a gratuitous remark. Entirely uncalled for. You know I am Billy's best friend, and you certainly know that I am a good friend of the family's. At least, I hope to be more than a friend when you get ready. I tell you, this is a very grave matter.

MR. BENSON: I mean to clear this up right away. (*Rings for Butler.*)

MILDRED: What are you going to do, dad?

MR. BENSON: Use a little diplomacy in my own home. (*Butler enters door back.*) Send in Ming Toy.

THOMAS: Beg pardon, sir. She is in her room dolling up. (*With malice*) She usually does about this time of the evening, sir.

MR. BENSON: Why this time?

THOMAS: Well, Mr. Billy generally comes in about this time, sir.

MR. BENSON: Well, you tell her that I want to see her immediately. (*Butler exits.*) If this little Chinese girl has taken advantage of our kindness, well (*Getting angry*)

POTTER: Will you do me a little favor? Let me handle her. I have known her longer than you, and I practically brought her here. She will tell me more than she will you.

MILDRED: That's right dad. Let Jimmey handle it. You must not excite yourself.

MR. BENSON: What do you think, mother?

MRS. BENSON: Use your own judgment, dear.

MR. BENSON: All right, Jim, I am a diplomat. I might become too excited and spoil it. Now you get all the facts from her.

POTTER: Leave everything to me. Just leave me alone with Ming Toy, and I'll get the truth.

MRS. BENSON: (*To Mildred*) Come, dear; we'll change.

MILDRED: As far as I am concerned, it doesn't make a bit of difference to me.

POTTER: Well, it does to me.

MILDRED: Wait until you are in the family. (*Exits.*)

MRS. BENSON: Go easy with her, Jim. Even though she is a little Chinese girl, remember: love has no race.

MR. BENSON: Would you approve of it, mother?

MRS. BENSON: No—no. (*Exits.*)

MR. BENSON: You get the truth and don't spare her. That's the first consideration.

POTTER: I will get the truth; don't worry. (*Mr. Benson exits. Ming Toy enters left all dolled up without any evidence of maid in her costume.*) My, how lovely you are looking.

MING TOY: Who want me?

POTTER: I do, Ming Toy. My, but you are dolled up, aren't you?

MING TOY: I always dress at this time.

POTTER: Ahem! Sit down.

MING TOY: All right.

POTTER: Would you like something? (*Ming Toy takes out handkerchief and rises.*) What's the matter, Ming Toy?

MING TOY: I forgot perfume. When I dress up, I always use perfume.

POTTER: I will get it. I will have the butler fetch it for you.

MING TOY: All right.

POTTER: (*Rings for Butler. Ming Toy sits on chair just occupied by Mrs. Benson and places foot stool cutely under feet.*) Wait, I will rearrange it for you. You are not comfortable.

MING TOY: You nice man. (*Potter places foot stool for her.*) Thank you. (*Butler enters.*)

POTTER: Thomas, will you go to Ming Toy's room and fetch her perfume?

THOMAS: (*Looks at Ming Toy and squirms.*) I beg pardon, sir. Did I hear you right? Did you say Ming Toy's perfume, sir?

POTTER: Yes. Ming Toy's perfume.

THOMAS: I beg your pardon, sir, but you will have to excuse me if I disobey; I cannot stand the odor of Ming Toy's perfume. (*Exits.*)

MING TOY: He got nose like pig. He no like nice smell. I use best perfume. I ask Billy to buy me best perfume.

POTTER: What perfume do you use?

MING TOY: Tar soap.[66]

POTTER: Tar soap a perfume? Since when?

MING TOY: Yes, I like it. I put in water, make suds, rub all over hands and face, wipe off, smell good. (*She sniffs.*) Mr. Billy want pay lot money for bad perfume in bottle. I no let him. Tar soap fine perfume and don't leak out.

POTTER: Mr. Billy buys you lots of things.

MING TOY: Oh yes. Billy want buy me whole world, but I can't put it in my room.

POTTER: What, for instance? Does he bring you flowers every day?

MING TOY: Oh yes, nice flowers.

POTTER: Orchids?

MING TOY: I no like orchids. I like daisies. All over my room everywhere is daisies.[67]

POTTER: That's very nice. What else?

MING TOY: Oh, he bring me nice stockings. Silk.

POTTER: Silk?

MING TOY: All silk—long ones. Come nearly half way on Ming Toy.

POTTER: Well, that is nice of Billy, and of course you get some nice jewels.

MING TOY: Oh yes, he give me ring, but I don't like wear jewelry. But he give me two nice gold diamond safety pins. I wear them here to hold up (*Pointing to shoulders*). Can't be seen. That's why I wear them. But the best present I like, he always bring me peanuts. I like peanuts.

POTTER: He hasn't given you an auto yet?

MING TOY: Don't like autos. I like to walk.

POTTER: You like to walk?

MING TOY: Oh yes, take nice walks with Mr. Billy in the garden. And when the moon shine, and Mr. Billy by my side, feel like soft silver cloud that floats in the sky. And when the sweet breeze blow my hair against my cheek, I feel as if God kiss Ming Toy. Nothing sweeter than that.

POTTER: Is there nothing sweeter than that?

MING TOY: I don't know, Mr. Jim. Do you?

POTTER: Well, I have never been in love.

MING TOY: Then you lie to Miss Mildred?

POTTER: Well, I have been in love with her so long, I don't feel it anymore.

MING TOY: When you in love long you don't feel it? I don't think so, Mr. Jim. The longer you love the better you like it.

POTTER: Is that your experience?

MING TOY: Yes.

POTTER: What do you love?

MING TOY: Oh, lots of things. I love music. I love moon, stars, daisies, Christian God and perfume.

POTTER: Don't you love people?

MING TOY: I love all American people.

POTTER: Don't you love any in particular?

MING TOY: Sure. Lots. I love Wong. I love Mr. Benson, Mrs. Benson, Miss Mildred, Mr. Billy Benson and Ming Toy.

POTTER: Don't you love me?

MING TOY: I don't think so.

POTTER: Why don't you love me?

MING TOY: I don't know. If I find out, I tell you.

POTTER: Is there anyone in the world you love best?

MING TOY: Mr. Billy Benson and Miss Ming Toy.

POTTER: Do you think it's all right to love Billy?

MING TOY: Sure, it's all right, he always do nice things for me.

POTTER: Well, you know sooner or later Mr. Billy might become engaged and then you'll feel pretty bad. It will break your little heart.

MING TOY: Mr. Billy Benson can't hurt me. Whatever he do, I love. (*Enter Billy from large glass door back, wearing light overcoat.*)

BILLY: Hello. Am I interrupting a nice little tete-à-tete?

POTTER: Not at all. Ming Toy and I are just having a little chat. What's the matter with those pockets, what have you got there? They're bulging out as if they are going to burst.

BILLY: Oh, I brought home some private papers. I've got a little work to do.

POTTER: Don't look like paper. (*Billy takes off coat and places on chair.*)

BILLY: Oh yes it is. Well, what have you been talking about?

MING TOY: Oh, Mr. Jimmey, he ask me lot foolish questions.

BILLY: Oh Jim always wants to know everything.

MING TOY: I tell him all nice things you bring me every day.

BILLY: Oh, is that what he asked you?

MING TOY: Oh everything, about love, kiss, moon, everything.

BILLY: Oh, he did. Jim's getting romantic.

MING TOY: Don't think Mr. Jim understand me. You do, Mr. Billy.

POTTER: I'll admit you're a Chinese puzzle.

MING TOY: You right. I am lot little pieces. Nobody but Mr. Billy ever put me together.

BILLY: I guess she's right, Jim. There are lots of Chinese puzzles you can't solve.

POTTER: What do you mean?

BILLY: Well, solve it. It's a Chinese puzzle.

POTTER: Well, I guess I have one puzzle of my own to solve. (*Takes ring from pocket.*) How to get this ring on the proper finger. (*Exits upstairs.*)

BILLY: I got a bunch of stuff in the coat for you.

MING TOY: Got tar soap?

BILLY: Two cakes.

MING TOY: Got peanuts?

BILLY: Got a bag full.

MING TOY: Quick, give me peanut. (*Gives her bag, and sits down besides her. She takes peanuts out of bag.*)

BILLY: Have you heard from Wong, Ming Toy?

MING TOY: No.

BILLY: Don't you want to see him?

MING TOY: Sure I want to see him. I like to see Wong, but if I go to see Wong, maybe Charlie Yong catch me there. You think Wong think about Ming Toy? I don't know whether Wong care to see me. Maybe Wong forget Ming Toy.

BILLY: Well, don't mind that. I have been thinking about you all day.

MING TOY: I know you think about me. (*Eats peanuts.*)

BILLY: How do you know?

MING TOY: Cause I think about you.

BILLY: What did you think about me?

MING TOY: I think too bad you got go down town. You can't stay here all day.

BILLY: I am sorry that you have to stay here all day.

MING TOY: Why don't you send Thomas down and you be butler, and then you stay here. Thomas good businessman. He borrow a dollar from me and not pay back. He good businessman. You make fine butler.

BILLY: Well, I don't quite fancy the job, but I might manage to take you down town.

MING TOY: Oh, that would be fine. Can you teach me how to play on letter machine like girl in your office do?

BILLY: It's called a typewriter.

MING TOY: All right, tripe whiter. You make girl go away. I do work for you. I work for you cheap. No, I'll pay you.

BILLY: How much?

MING TOY: Three bags peanuts.

BILLY: Oh, make it a barrel.

MING TOY: All right, a barrel.

BILLY: I'm afraid neither one of us would do much work if you were in my office.

MING TOY: Nice moonlight tonight.

BILLY: How do you know? It's daytime.

MING TOY: I feel it in my bones.

BILLY: You like the moon?

MING TOY: Yes, when it make your face brighter so I see you better.

BILLY: You'll meet me in the garden tonight?

MING TOY: If garden be there, Ming Toy will be. You know, I never feel so happy as when I walk with you in garden. You feel same way? How you feel?

BILLY: Happiness does not express it. I will have to get someone to invent a new word.

MING TOY: All right, I do it.

BILLY: What word would express my feelings when I walk with you?

MING TOY: All right, I invent a word for you. I find it in big book.

BILLY: Suppose I should have to go away?

MING TOY: If you go to bottom of ocean, I go too.

BILLY: What if you should have to leave here?

MING TOY: I don't leave here. Too nice. Feel too happy.

BILLY: Supposing the folks ask you to go.

MING TOY: I stay here with you and tell folks to go.

BILLY: But I hardly think they would accommodate you.

MING TOY: Why should they want me to go? Don't I make Thomas do his work? Don't I make Kate wash dishes before she goes out with her beau? Don't I make Maggie sweep carpet before she eat breakfast? And don't I bring your papa pills when he coughs in the night, and don't I fill hot water bottle for your mama? If they make me go away, this house all bust up.

BILLY: They appreciate that. And yet, there may be some trouble.

MING TOY: But I don't go away. They can make all trouble they like. I once stand in China when they shoot all around me, and I don't go away. For bullets I don't care this (*Snaps fingers of right hand*) for trouble I don't care this (*Snaps fingers of left hand*).

BILLY: You don't fear death? You are always ready to die?

MING TOY: If they send me away from you, I be glad to take bullets.

BILLY: And I'll do just as much for you, sweet little Ming Toy. (*Takes both her hands in his. Butler enters.*)

THOMAS: A distinguished looking Chinaman to see you, sir.

BILLY: It's Wong!

THOMAS: That sounds like it, sir.

BILLY: Let him come right in.

THOMAS: Yes, sir. (*Exits.*)

MING TOY: Oh, he is come. You see, he like Ming Toy. I knew Wong come sometime to see Ming Toy. (*Wong enters.*) Hello, Wong! (*Wong is elaborately dressed in heavily embroidered robe.*)

WONG: Hello, Ming Toy. You look fine. (*Takes her hand.*)

MING TOY: You look fine, too.

WONG: Hello, Mr. Benson.

BILLY: (*Shaking hands with Wong*) Hello, Wong. Mighty glad to see you.

MING TOY: We miss you. You miss Ming Toy much?

WONG: Sleep did not come to Wong's eyes for long time, he miss you so.

MING TOY: Ming Toy very sorry. You're not mad I run away?

WONG: No, I could not be mad with Ming Toy.

MING TOY: You look for me in police station?

WONG: No.

MING TOY: I see you and Charlie Yong look for me all over house.

WONG: And I see you when you run away. (*Smiles.*) You hide under table.

MING TOY: You didn't stop Ming Toy?

WONG: If Wong could help, he do nothing to stop the happiness of Ming Toy.

MING TOY: I guess Charlie Yong mad, eh?

WONG: Very mad. Yes.

BILLY: Has he tried to make trouble for you, Wong?

WONG: Every day Charlie Yong come and say, "Get me Ming Toy." I say I don't know where Ming Toy is.

MING TOY: You lie to Charlie Yong?

WONG: Yes, I lie for Ming Toy.

BILLY: That was fine of you, Wong.

MING TOY: He say no girl run away from him. He smart man, Charlie Yong, but Ming Toy show him.

WONG: Yes, you show him, Ming Toy, but Charlie Yong no man to be fooled always. Ming Toy, I come to take you back.

MING TOY: You want me back in your house?

WONG: Yes.

MING TOY: But I am very happy here. No more happiness could be anywhere.

BILLY: Wong, Ming Toy loves it here, and we all love to have her too.

MING TOY: Sure, I am whole boss here. This big house and I am more than boss. I see no Chinamen, only fine American ladies and gentlemen. I eat with nice silver knives and forks. I hear nice big words, and I pick them up. Mr. Benson teach me about diplomacy. He teach me when you mad you smile, and when you smile you mad. Oh, I like it here very much.

WONG: All the same you must come back with Wong. Two times every day I lie to Charlie Yong. He get mad, but now no more lies. He say you bring Ming Toy or my brotherhood men society make Wong no more. If you love Wong, you come back. If you don't care, Wong have to die.

MING TOY: Oh, this is awful.

WONG: Charlie Yong say he have no Ming Toy by today he send two brotherhood men to kill Wong tonight.

BILLY: Oh, he's a bully, Wong. That's only a threat.

WONG: Oh no. You do not know Chinese ways. When Charlie Yong say man must die, man die.

BILLY: Couldn't it be squared with money?

WONG: Charlie Yong got lots of money. He don't want money. He want Ming Toy.

BILLY: Well, he can't have her, Wong. Ming Toy won't leave this house. Not while I'm here.

MING TOY: No. (*Sits down defiantly on chair.*)

BILLY: Wong, don't you think little Ming Toy has been juggled around enough, thrown from place to place, bought, sold and resold? She has never been happy before. She has found a real home here. She is happy and she is going to stay happy. I will see to that.

WONG: Then Wong Lo must prepare to meet his ancestors. Wong Lo die tonight.

(*Thomas enters with card, hands same to Billy—he reads it.*)

BILLY: Tell Charlie Yong to come in.

MING TOY: Wait, Thomas. (*Thomas stops.*) Don't let Charlie Yong come in. He take me away.

BILLY: Don't worry, Ming Toy. He won't take you.

WONG: Charlie Yong follow me here. Don't let him in. He make trouble.

BILLY: I'm not afraid of him. I'm going to thrash this thing out right now. Show him in. (*Ming Toy tries to hide under table.*) What are you doing?

MING TOY: I hide under table while you talk to Charlie Yong.

BILLY: Stay right where you are.

(*Enter Charlie Yong.*)

CHARLIE YONG: Wong, you lie to Charlie Yong.

WONG: Did not know Ming Toy was here.

CHARLIE YONG: (*Looks at Ming Toy severely.*) This time you don't run away. This time you go with Charlie Yong. What you think, you take girl away from Charlie Yong? Eh!

BILLY: I didn't take her. She was perfectly willing to come.

MING TOY: Sure. I like always to be where Mr. Billy Benson is.

CHARLIE YONG: What you like not important. What Charlie Yong like, that goes. You're mine. I pay for you.

BILLY: Now listen, Charlie Yong. You might as well know this now, once for all. Ming Toy is here to stay. If you have any further business here, let us hear it. If not, goodbye.

CHARLIE YONG: I pay for Ming Toy. I got it written. She belong to Charlie Yong.

MING TOY: Ming Toy belong to nobody that she don't like. Ming Toy belong to herself. Why you come here, Charlie Yong, make me unhappy? Charlie Yong can't stand Ming Toy have a little happiness. Ming Toy never had chance. In China no happy home, one out of sixteen children—not much left for Ming Toy. I come here, Wong nice to me. Mission complain and Wong must put me out. Christian God send Mr. Billy, angel, to me. He do everything for me. Charlie Yong you again try to take away my happiness. You may have lots of Tong men. Ming Toy only little girl, but I tell you Charlie Yong, you don't let me alone, I kill you and all Tong men. That's what Ming Toy do.

BILLY: You paid for her, and that's the only claim you have, isn't it?

CHARLIE YONG: Charlie Yong have other claim. Charlie Yong love Ming Toy. First time Charlie Yong ever love.

BILLY: Well, I'm sorry, but you love the wrong girl.

CHARLIE YONG: Ming Toy not wrong—Ming Toy all right.

BILLY: Well, I know that.

CHARLIE YONG: I know you do. I know you love Ming Toy.

BILLY: Supposing I do?

CHARLIE YONG: Well, you have no right to love her. Ming Toy Chinese girl. Why you want Chinese girl?

MING TOY: Ming Toy no China girl. Ming Toy was American girl even when she was in China. Got nothing China. Don't speak China. Don't know what the hell God put me in China.

CHARLIE YONG: I know Chinese Mission take good Chinese girl, try to make them bad American girls. But you Chinese all right.

MING TOY: No, I say! Charlie Yong, don't you say again I'm China girl. (*Picks up vase threateningly.*)

CHARLIE YONG: I know why you say you don't want to be Chinese girl. You love American man, Mr. Billy Benson. Now you want to be American girl so he love you. You love him, don't you?

MING TOY: Yes, I love him. You try to take me away from him, you see, Charlie Yong, you see.

CHARLIE YONG: Charlie Yong get girl he want. Always get her, and will get you too.

(*Enter Mr. Benson right. He is surprised at gathering and goes to Wong.*)

MR. BENSON: Hello, Wong Lo. (*Shakes hands.*)

WONG: Hello, Mr. Benson. Haven't seen you for two years.

MR. BENSON: Still glad I advised you to come to this country?

WONG: Very grateful to my most august friend that he advise me to come to America.

MR. BENSON: (*Indicating Charlie Yong*) Is this a friend of yours?

CHARLIE YONG: (*Hands his card to Mr. Benson.*) Charlie Yong.

MR. BENSON: (*Looks at card.*) Oh! You're the famous Chop Suey magnate.

CHARLIE YONG: Yes, everybody all over the world know Charlie Yong's Chop Suey. When you buy Chicken Chop Suey from Charlie Yong, you get chicken.

MR. BENSON: I have always wondered what was in it. I'm glad you can pay your food such a compliment. What can I do for my distinguished visitors? Or is it with my son?

CHARLIE YONG: It is with your son. It has also to do with chicken.

MR. BENSON: Indeed!

CHARLIE YONG: Your son, he take my girl away from me. Ming Toy.

MR. BENSON: Oh, you know Ming Toy?

CHARLIE YONG: Sure; she is my property.

BILLY: You know, dad, the old practice in China. Well, Charlie Yong has a title to this girl. When she came here, it was to escape from him.

CHARLIE YONG: That's not true. I would treat Ming Toy fine, but they did not give me a chance. Your son, he stole her away from me.

MR. BENSON: Why should my son steal your girl? A Chinese girl.

CHARLIE YONG: Lots of white men love Chinese girl.

MR. BENSON: What do you mean?

CHARLIE YONG: You know, he want her for himself.

WONG: Not so, Mr. Benson. Mr. Billy Benson just feel sorry for Ming Toy. He try to help her.

MR. BENSON: Why, of course that's it. How could it be anything else? (*To Charlie Yong*) Ming Toy, that is your mission here.

CHARLIE YONG: Yes, I only come to take what is mine.

MR. BENSON: Could you love Ming Toy?

CHARLIE YONG: Yes, I do anything in the world for her.

MR. BENSON: Come here, Ming Toy. (*Ming Toy comes to him.*) Wouldn't you like to go with Charlie Yong? He says he is going to be very nice to you.

MING TOY: Charlie Yong got lots girls. He be nice to me for little while—just when I am very young. Then he throw me out like others.

BILLY: That's his reputation, dad! He will take Ming Toy, degrade her, and then throw her over.

CHARLIE YONG: Not Ming Toy. I will always love Ming Toy. Never throw her over. I give up all girls for her.

BILLY: Will you marry her?

MR. BENSON: Yes, will you marry her? (*Charlie Yong hesitates.*) If you do, I will see that you get her.

CHARLIE YONG: All right. I know every hour I love Ming Toy. I marry her. Ming Toy have honor of being first wife Charlie Yong ever married.

MING TOY: I don't want honor—don't want marry Charlie Yong.

MR. BENSON: Yes you do, Ming Toy. You can't be a maid always. Charlie Yong is a very prosperous citizen. He will take good care of you, and I think it is the best thing for you to do.

CHARLIE YONG: Thank you, Mr. Benson. Come on, Ming Toy, we go.

MR. BENSON: You've got to marry her now. I'll go right with you to be sure that you are sincere. I will take you to the Judge.

CHARLIE YONG: All right, I marry her.

MING TOY: (*Pleads.*) Oh, Mr. Benson, I don't want marry Charlie Yong. I don't want marry Charlie Yong.

MR. BENSON: You've got to.

MING TOY: I want to stay here.

MR. BENSON: You can't stay here any more; you've got to marry Charlie Yong. You may not like him now, but you will see, you will love him. Get ready. (*Ming Toy looks at Billy with a very sad pitiful expression, about to go to door left. Billy, unable to contain himself any longer, bursts out.*)

BILLY: Wait a minute, dad. Charlie Yong told you a moment ago that I love Ming Toy. He was right. I love her.

CHARLIE YONG: Charlie Yong never wrong. See, I told you.

BILLY: I love Ming Toy, and no man shall get her.

MR. BENSON: What do you mean, you love her?

BILLY: I mean that I love her, and that I'm going to marry her.

MR. BENSON: What? You marry Ming Toy?

BILLY: Yes. (*Pause.*)

MR. BENSON: (*To Charlie Yong*) Will you please step into my library? (*Opens door.*)

CHARLIE YONG: All right.

MR. BENSON: You will excuse me for a little while.

CHARLIE YONG: Sure, you got sense. I wait while you fix everything up for Charlie Yong. (*Offers cigarette case to Mr. Benson.*) Have a cigarette.

MR. BENSON: No thanks. (*Charlie Yong exits. Potter and Mrs. Benson enter, coming from upstairs.*)

POTTER: Hello, Wong!

WONG: How do you do.

MRS. BENSON: Hello, Mr. Wong.

WONG: How do you do, Mrs. Benson.

POTTER: (*Noticing the strained look on faces of all those present*) What's the matter?

MR. BENSON: You were right, Jim. My hat off to you.

POTTER: Billy, you can't be serious about this?

BILLY: I am darn serious.

POTTER: Are you going through with this idea?

BILLY: I certainly will!

POTTER: Do you realize what it means to your family? To you? Do you realize that it will cut you off from every possible chance in your life?

BILLY: Maybe, but I love Ming Toy.

MRS. BENSON: Billy, you know you will be ruined. You know you will be a laughing stock. You will be crushed.

BILLY: Maybe I will, mother, but I love Ming Toy. I love her! I love her!

MRS. BENSON: Do you know that she is a girl out of your class? Caste and color?[68]

BILLY: I know dad, but I love Ming Toy. I love her and don't care what anyone thinks or says. You may all be right. The whole world's ideas may be right. But I love Ming Toy.

POTTER: Just as well kill yourself as marry Ming Toy.

BILLY: Well, I'd rather do that than not marry Ming Toy. Now that's final, folks.

MRS. BENSON: Now let me reason with you, my boy. Now you know—

BILLY: Don't tell me. I thought it over. I appreciate all the difficulties. All the pains and sufferings that it may cause you, but I cannot help it, mother. I love Ming Toy. (*Almost trembling*) I love Ming Toy.

MR. BENSON: Now listen, Billy.

BILLY: I don't want to listen. I can't listen. Everything you ever told me to do I have done. I know what you are going to ask. I have asked and answered those things myself again and again and again, and maybe in your way, just as you would ask. But I can't help it. I love Ming Toy. (*Pause.*)

MR. BENSON: (*Goes to Ming Toy.*) You love my boy?

MING TOY: I love Mr. Billy Benson.[69]

MR. BENSON: So this is the gratitude you have shown us, Ming Toy. Why didn't you let my boy alone?

MING TOY: I can't say, Mr. Benson.

MR. BENSON: You love him because he is a fine, handsome white man.

MING TOY: I love Mr. Billy Benson if he was poor man in the street. I love Mr. Billy Benson if he was black, white, red, green. I love him. If stone have heart like Mr. Billy Benson, I love stone. If devil have soul like Mr. Billy Benson, Ming Toy love devil.

MR. BENSON: I think you're a little devil yourself, and you can't stay in my house another minute.

MING TOY: All right, Mr. Benson. I go tomorrow.

MR. BENSON: No, you go right now.

MING TOY: All right, I go now. (*Starts to go.*)

MILDRED: (*Comes from below table left center.*) You are not going to send Ming Toy off, father. It's no crime to love.

MR. BENSON: (*Crosses below Billy.*) She must go.

BILLY: Just a minute. I'll go with you.

MR. BENSON: What are you going to do?

BILLY: I am going with Ming Toy.

MR. BENSON: Where will you go with her? Where can you go with a Chinese girl? You will be barred here, and if you go to China you will be barred there, and every home will be closed to you here and there.

BILLY: I know dad, but I love Ming Toy just the same, and if the lands are closed to me, the seas are open to me!

POTTER: That's some love.

MR. BENSON: Wong, will you explain to Ming Toy what this means!

WONG: When girl loves man like Ming Toy loves Billy, Wong can say nothing to her.

BILLY: Come, Ming Toy, I'll marry you today.

MR. BENSON: Wait a minute. It is your life that you are staking, and after all, one has a right to one's own life. But one favor your dad will ask of you. I want you to wait, say, three months. Remain here, both of you. Think it over, and if at the end of that time you are both still of the same mind and same heart, you can marry with my blessing.

BILLY: Oh dad, it's no use. I shall love Ming Toy in three months or three years or in three hundred years.

MRS. BENSON: Then you won't do this little thing for your dad and me?

BILLY: Well, what's the use of it, mother? It won't make any difference.

MING TOY: Oh yes, Mr. Billy, we do what your papa and mama just ask. We wait.

BILLY: But it's useless, Ming Toy.

MING TOY: You do that for me! We wait. I want it, Billy.

BILLY: All right, we will.

MR. BENSON: Thank you, little Ming Toy. From now on, you need never do any work as a maid. You will be one of us.

MING TOY: I don't mind going in kitchen. I like to boss Thomas.

MR. BENSON: Well, suit yourself about it. (*Opens door of library and calls.*) Mr. Yong. Step in please.

CHARLIE YONG: Oh, hello, Mr. Potter!

POTTER: Hello.

CHARLIE YONG: You find everything all right, Mr. Benson?

MR. BENSON: Yes.

CHARLIE YONG: Come on, Ming Toy. We go.

MR. BENSON: Just a minute. Mr. Yong, you will have to be patient for a little while.

CHARLIE YONG: You try to trick Charlie Yong?

MR. BENSON: No, no, I am just asking you to be patient.

CHARLIE YONG: How long you want me to wait?

MR. BENSON: I don't know!

CHARLIE YONG: Well, just because you treat me decent, I wait about two weeks. But Ming Toy is mine. (*Turning to Ming Toy*) Ming Toy, you know Chinese custom. If you no come to me at the end of two weeks, my Tongs kill your Billy Benson.

MING TOY: Charlie Yong, you know if you kill my Billy Benson what happen to you? If all people in the world afraid of you, Ming Toy no afraid of you. If you hide away somewhere, Ming Toy find you, and Ming Toy kill you, Charlie Yong. Don't say to me again you kill my man. Now you heard what Ming Toy had to say. I don't say no more so that you remember what I say, and now Ming Toy is boss here, and I tell you to get the hell out. (*She runs to door.*) Go on out, Charlie Yong. Nobody send for you. Go on! (*Charlie Yong does not move. Ming Toy calls.*) Thomas!

CHARLIE YONG: I go, but you come to me.

MING TOY: Maybe I will, and maybe I won't but I can't hear you say you kill my man and speak to you much more. (*Thomas enters.*) Thomas, you put that Chink out. (*Charlie Yong exits.*) See, you all here great big men and little Ming Toy get him out. Thomas, you bring cocktail to Mr. Benson. I want cherry.

(*Curtain*)

## Act 3

(*Curtain rises. Mildred is at the piano. Ming Toy stands beside her, facing audience. All guests are gathered in the room grouped in different ways. Some are sitting, some standing. At rise of curtain there is applause and cry of "Encore" is heard by some of the guests.*)

MILDRED: Come on, Ming Toy. Give that little Chinese song.

MING TOY: Oh! I am so tired—I can't sing.

MILDRED: Oh yes you can. (*More applause by guests.*)

BILLY: Go ahead, Ming Toy.

MING TOY: All right, Billy.

(*Mildred plays. Ming Toy sings Chinese song of first act. When song is finished, there is applause. They all gather about her and congratulate her, offering a jumble of compliments. Music is heard outside playing Fox Trot. All guests exit right in couples, excepting Miss Claybrook, Mrs. Davis and Miss Fountain.*)

MISS CLAYBROOK: Well, it's been a wonderful evening.

MISS FOUNTAIN: Perfectly delightful! I never had such an exhilarating time in all my life. I didn't miss a dance but this one.

MRS. DAVIS: Well, I danced with every man except my husband.

MISS CLAYBROOK: Well, I must say the Bensons outdid themselves tonight.

MRS. DAVIS: Doesn't Mildred look beautiful? Only I don't think she is getting such a wonderful man.

MISS FOUNTAIN: Jimmey Potter has been rejected by every girl in town. He proposed to Elizabeth twice, and to me five times.

MISS CLAYBROOK: I wager Mildred will break the engagement before long. (*Enter Mildred.*) Oh Mildred! This has been a perfectly lovely evening. We were just saying what a wonderful catch you have made—the catch of the season. You certainly are lucky.

MILDRED: I'll know more about that next year.

MRS. DAVIS: There's no doubt about Jimmey—he is such an adorable boy. (*Enter Potter hastily.*)

MISS CLAYBROOK: Oh! There's Jimmey.

POTTER: I've been looking for you, Mildred. Why did you run away for?

MILDRED: I've been looking for you, too!

POTTER: Come on. (*Mildred and Potter exit right.*)

MISS FOUNTAIN: Poor Mildred. She has my sympathy. I just feel like telling her that Jimmey proposed to me five times.

MISS CLAYBROOK: Did he really ask you?

MISS FOUNTAIN: The very words he said: "Estelle, I don't intend to remain single all my life." Didn't that mean he wanted to marry me?

MISS CLAYBROOK: Indeed he did. Why, that was a direct proposal. (*Ming Toy enters.*)

MING TOY: Are you ladies not dancing?

MISS FOUNTAIN: Well, we wanted to give some of the other girls a chance.

MING TOY: I try to book up a man, and there is none loose.

MRS. DAVIS: You don't mean that such a cute little girl like you could not make some husband forget his wife?

MING TOY: Oh! But I don't want to make husband forget his wife. He might become happy.

MRS. DAVIS: Oh, then you are becoming more and more Americanized.

MISS FOUNTAIN: Miss Ming Toy, I understand that you are of Royal blood.

MING TOY: Oh yes, one of our dead Emperors is my second cousin.

MRS. DAVIS: How long have you been in this country?

MING TOY: Oh, a year and a half.

MRS. DAVIS: You speak perfect English.

MING TOY: No, not quite. I have what you call an accent.

MISS FOUNTAIN: Foreign accents are so piquant.

MING TOY: Pig-can't. You mean I speak like a pig?

MISS FOUNTAIN: Oh no, your foreign accents are delightful.

MING TOY: Oh! I see.

MISS FOUNTAIN: I love an accent. Where did you learn yours?

MING TOY: I get it in America.

MRS. DAVIS: I love China. I always wanted to go there, but the nearest I got to it was a kimona.

MISS FOUNTAIN: I am so fond of your native dish—chop suey.

MING TOY: What is chop suey?

MISS FOUNTAIN: Oh, I suppose it's only for the common people. Royalty don't eat it.[70]

MING TOY: Yes— that's why all Americans love it.

(*Enter Thomas from left with a tray filled with cocktails. He crosses right, passing very close to the three ladies. They look around, notice the butler and follow him off. Ming Toy takes a quick dive towards door, shakes her head and comes back. Enter Mr. and Mrs. Benson.*)

MR. BENSON: What are you doing here alone, Ming Toy?

MING TOY: (*Looking right*) Just watching things pass by.

MR. BENSON: I must say, little Ming Toy, that it is not for you to watch but the way you look tonight, it's for people to watch you.

MING TOY: Thank you, Mr. Benson.

MR. BENSON: You look like a little Chinese princess.

MING TOY: Don't I look like an American princess?

MRS. BENSON: Unfortunately, we have no princesses.

MING TOY: Have a revolution like in China. Princesses go with revolutions. (*Mr. and Mrs. Benson both laugh.*)

MR. BENSON: Well, Ming Toy, we must really be thankful to you for your contribution to the evening's success. You have proven yourself a clever little entertainer, and a perfect little lady.

MING TOY: It is so hard to be a lady when things pass by. (*Looks right.*)

MRS. BENSON: Why don't you go in and dance?

MING TOY: Oh! I dance five times the Shimmy Wiggle. (*Hastily correcting herself.*) I mean wobble. What's the difference between wiggle and wobble? The dance is the same.

MR. BENSON: No difference whatever.

MING TOY: You want to give me a dance, Mr. Benson?

MR. BENSON: You don't want to dance with an old man like me!

MING TOY: Oh, yes, I like to dance with old men—they don't move so fast, but you look better tonight than any other young man.

MR. BENSON: You little flatterer. Thank you; I don't dance with young girls. They are a little too fast for me.

MING TOY: I promise I go slow with you. Shall I write you in my book for the next dance?

MR. BENSON: No thank you. I will dance the next with Mrs. Benson. I only dance with Mrs. Benson.

MING TOY: Is that good style? Is it all right to dance with your wife? I see married men dancing tonight with cute little girls and all their wives sit around wagging their tongues about the cute little girls. Is that good style?

MR. BENSON: To most married men. But thank God, not to mother and myself. (*Butler enters right with empty cocktail glasses, several containing cherries on tooth picks. He crosses to left, turns, taking two cherries on toothpicks and shows them to Ming Toy.*)

THOMAS: Beg pardon, Miss Ming Toy, but there are several cherries left.

MING TOY: (*Ming Toy looks at Butler.*) No thank you, Thomas. (*Butler exits.*) It cost me so many cherries to be a lady.

MR. BENSON: You may have cherries and still be a lady.

MING TOY: Can I eat cherries and still be a lady? Thank you—you nice diplomat. (*Exits hurriedly left.*)

MR. BENSON: Well, at last we are alone. The evening has been a perfect success, and all credit to you, dear. (*Puts arm around Mrs. Benson. They kiss.*)

MRS. BENSON: Are you sure we have the right man for our darling Mildred?

MR. BENSON: A splendid boy.

MRS. BENSON: You are a diplomat; you ought to know.

MR. BENSON: He will make her a fine husband and you certainly have brought him up a very fine wife and me a dear child. (*Kisses her.*)

MRS. BENSON: Oh, Andrew, if only you could have arranged such a wonderful match for Billy.

MR. BENSON: Mother, I'd give my right hand if I could take my boy and hand him over to this sweet little Chinese doll.

MRS. BENSON: We can't help admiring her; she is adorable. They have all been wild over her tonight. If she were only one of our race. Do you know, dear, that the only thing Chinese I have so far observed about her is her Chinese accent? Why, without it, she could easily pass off as a white girl.

MR. BENSON: Yes, but she is Chinese just the same, and I know that our boy would suffer if we gave our consent.

MRS. BENSON: Are you sure about that? We have some of the best families here, and they all flocked around her tonight.

MR. BENSON: Yes, we will know very soon what they would think. The test will tell.

MRS. BENSON: Well, I am praying for poor little Ming Toy.

MR. BENSON: Not more than I. Now don't forget to take Ming Toy upstairs and do what I told you.

MRS. BENSON: I have everything ready.

MR. BENSON: Then you bring Ming Toy down at my signal.

MRS. BENSON: All right! (*Enter Billy.*)

BILLY: What are you folks having? A tete-à-tete?

MR. BENSON: Yes, a few reminiscences when mother and I were the sinecure of all eyes, but we are still the sinecures of each other's eyes.[71]

BILLY: Don't leave me out, dad! You're still for me a big gun, and mother, the sweetest girl here tonight. (*Kisses Mrs. Benson.*)

MING TOY: (*Enter Ming Toy with mouth full of cherries.*) Hello, Billy—

BILLY: What have you got in your mouth?

MING TOY: (*Still with mouth full of cherries.*) Half a dozen cherries.

MRS. BENSON: Come on, dear. I want to show you something.

MING TOY: All right! (*To Mr. Benson*) Be good. (*Mrs. Benson and Ming Toy exit upstairs.*)

BILLY: Well, dad. Some party tonight.

MR. BENSON: Yes, but the party has just begun.

BILLY: Really? Are you going to make a night of it?

MR. BENSON: Well, perhaps. I have a surprise for you, Bill.

BILLY: Well, it's about time someone sprang a surprise on me. You used to tell me that when I was a kid—then showed it to me in the wood shed.

MR. BENSON: (*Seriously*) This one I hope will turn out less painful.

BILLY: Well, shoot it!

MR. BENSON: Bill, while we are at your sister's engagement I have decided to announce your engagement to your best little girl.

BILLY: Now dad, you're kidding.

MR. BENSON: No, I am serious.

BILLY: You know my best little girl?

MR. BENSON: I know!

BILLY: Who?

MR. BENSON: Ming Toy.

BILLY: You don't really mean that dad?

MR. BENSON: I do—I do.

BILLY: (*Overcome*) If ever I felt like kissing you, I am going to do it now. (*Puts both arms around Mr. Benson, almost in tears—hysterically.*) Dad, I always knew you were a broad-minded man. (*Butler enters left with tray of cocktails walking through and about to exit right.*)

MR. BENSON: One moment, Thomas. Send all the guests in.

THOMAS: Yes sir! (*Exits right.*)

BILLY: God bless you, dad.

MR. BENSON: I even bought your ring.

BILLY: You are great.

MR. BENSON: When the guests come in, I'll make the announcement. And here. (*Handing him ring.*) I got this for you to give to Ming Toy. (*Hands Billy ring.*)

BILLY: (*Overcome*) God bless you, dad. I knew you'd come around to me. (*Enter guests right. When they are all in room, Mr. Benson announces engagement.*)

MR. BENSON: Ladies and gentlemen, permit me to announce my son's engagement to the finest little girl in the world. (*Applause.*)

MILDRED: Why, dad, this is news to me!

MR. BENSON: I wanted to give you a surprise.

MISS CLAYBROOK: Who is the lucky girl?

MR. BENSON: We shall see her presently. (*Steps to table center—presses button —a moment of suspense.*) You will see her in a moment. (*Mrs. Benson comes down steps alone, looking puzzled and some of the guests laugh. When Mrs. Benson reaches bottom step, Ming Toy, dressed gorgeously as a Chinese princess, enters. Mr. Benson walks over to Ming Toy, takes her hand, and says*) Here is the lucky girl. Ming Toy.

(*No one stirs—there is an awkward pause. Billy walks over to Ming Toy, places ring on her finger and kisses her. All stand still. After another pause, one elderly distinguished couple walk out by the street entrance. They are followed by another and still another couple until the only couple remaining is Mr. and Mrs. Davis.*)

MRS. DAVIS: I am sorry it is so late. Come, Ed, I have an acute longing for some chop suey. (*Exit.*)

MR. BENSON: (*Goes over to Billy*) My boy, there is nothing I can say that speaks as loud as the silence of our friends who have just left. It is late, and we are fagged out.[72] Mother and I will retire. Good night.

BILLY: Good night, dad.

MRS. BENSON: I'm so sorry, Billy. Good night.

BILLY: Good night, mother. (*Kisses her.*)

MILDRED: A lot of narrow-minded snobs, to say the least. They might have congratulated you.

POTTER: Snobs indeed! But you must give them credit for not being hypocrites.

MILDRED: Credit for what? For insulting the whole family? (*Goes to Ming Toy.*) Don't you mind, Ming Toy. We love you and what's important, Billy does.

MING TOY: For myself I don't care. My father in China used to have a lot of pigs. I am accustomed how pigs behave. Sometimes they run away just like that, but I am sorry for Billy.

BILLY: Oh! That doesn't annoy me, Ming Toy.

MILDRED: That's the spirit. That's the kind of love I hope Jimmey turns out, but I don't think he is capable of such love.

POTTER: Is that so? You running away from me for three years was much more embarrassing than a few people running away from Billy.

MILDRED: Well, good night, Ming Toy. You have been perfectly adorable tonight. Don't worry. (*Kisses her.*) I am for you, strong.

MING TOY: Thanks. Very nice of you to say that to me (*Pause*) tonight, and I love you. (*They kiss.*)

MILDRED: Good night, Jimmey.

POTTER: No good night at all.

MILDRED: Good night, Jimmey.

POTTER: We did not have a minute together.

MILDRED: All right. You shall have one minute. You can't keep me up. (*Exit Mildred and Potter.*)

MING TOY: You feel very bad, Billy. I am not to blame. God make me Chinese girl.

BILLY: Of course you are not. To hell with everybody. (*Grabs her and kisses her passionately.*) God thought the Chinese people good enough to make, so why should I object to his plan?

MING TOY: Oh! You got strong love. See, Ming Toy got strong love too. (*Embraces Billy.*)

BILLY: Ming Toy, how would you like to go back to China?

MING TOY: You say so, all right. When we start?

BILLY: Looks like we might have to start tomorrow.

MING TOY: Why you want to go away from here?

BILLY: Because no one shall embarrass you again.

MING TOY: Oh! I see, that make you feel bad. I know! You think your papa make me leave here now?

BILLY: I don't know and I don't care what he is going to do, but I have my own plans.

MING TOY: I don't want to make your mama cry, and I love your mama so. If you go away she will lose you.

BILLY: Well, if she has to lose me, she will lose me.

MING TOY: If we go to China she lose her nice boy, and your mama she love you oh so much.

BILLY: I know, but it can't be helped.

MING TOY: She did not tell me anything, but in her face I see her heart breaking, and that hurts Ming Toy. Why didn't God make all people white?

BILLY: Because God is a master painter. He uses in his creations many colors.

MING TOY: Well, why don't God's children like all his pictures?

BILLY: Because they haven't God's appreciation—his sympathy—his love.

MING TOY: But you have.

BILLY: Yes, I have. And I appreciate one of his best pictures, and nobody is going to talk me out of it. (*Kisses her.*)

MING TOY: I know your friends talk about me. Billy, could you learn to fly?

BILLY: Why?

MING TOY: Because you could buy a flying machine and live in the air. When people look up, all look alike and we can't hear people talk.

BILLY: Well, we may have to resort that. I wonder what course the folks will adopt now? I know they are feeling terrible.

MING TOY: I bet they can't sleep. It's a shame, Billy, we should make them so unhappy. Billy, I want to ask you something.

BILLY: Yes?

MING TOY: Now you don't get angry?

BILLY: Angry with you?

MING TOY: You promise you don't get mad? I think you should marry nice white girl—make all family happy and all your friends happy.

BILLY: Why? Don't you want to marry me?

MING TOY: I love you—I always love you—but don't want to marry you.

BILLY: Now what put that into your head?

MING TOY: I am afraid you will not be happy when you make your family and your friends unhappy. Maybe we marry—maybe we have little baby with pigtail—and that make your friends so unhappy.

BILLY: If I endeavor to please my friends, what about you?

MING TOY: Oh! I go far away to New York. I learn lots fine things here, and get fine position and forget.

BILLY: Forget me?

MING TOY: Forget you, never Billy. I always think about you. I never love another man—never. I always look in newspapers for your name. Some day maybe I see in paper Mr. Billy Benson marry to nice white girl, and then I say you no have baby with pigtail.

BILLY: Don't worry about the pigtails. We can always cut them off. No, Ming Toy, we will stick it out together no matter what happens. If father refuses his consent, why, we will marry without it.

MING TOY: I don't like to do that, Billy. Ming Toy make everybody unhappy. Better Ming Toy should die, and then everybody be happy.

BILLY: If you do, you'll make me very unhappy. You don't want to do that, do you?

MING TOY: No.

BILLY: Then I want you to do what I think is right.

MING TOY: All right. You come first always. (*Billy kisses her.*)

BILLY: Now you run along to bed. Good night.

MING TOY: Good night! (*Exits up stairs.*)

(*Billy lights cigarette and walks up and down for a moment in meditation. Potter enters down steps.*)

POTTER: Well, Bill, what have you and Ming Toy decided to do? You certainly don't intend to marry Ming Toy after tonight?

BILLY: I certainly do. What's tonight? A lot of darn fools who think a little color can separate two people.

POTTER: It's not color—it's blood.

BILLY: What about blood? Isn't the blood the same? All blood is red. They all have the same cells.

POTTER: Yes, it's not the same. It's yellow blood, and all that yellow blood suggests.[73]

BILLY: Yes, it suggests gold. It certainly suggests it in Ming Toy.

POTTER: I don't deny that Ming Toy as an individual is attractive, a sweet little soul, but you can't separate her from her race.

BILLY: Race prejudice is all rot. Each race has its good points and its bad points. We have bad ones, and lots of them.

POTTER: You are not maintaining that the yellow race is as good as the white?

BILLY: Will you tell me wherein we are superior?

POTTER: In brains.

BILLY: Have you ever tried to get the better of a Chinese merchant?

POTTER: Oh! They are shrewd.

BILLY: Shrewdness implies brains. A man can't be shrewd unless he has brains.

POTTER: You'll admit we are more civilized.

BILLY: Are we? What about the white German people?[74] Have you ever been in China? I have spent years there, and I love the Chinese people. They are a kindly, peaceful, lovely, moral people. I am not a sociologist now; I am a lover. No baneful race prejudices are going to interfere with my love.

POTTER: You're going to fight the world?

BILLY: I don't want to fight anybody. I only want to be left alone with the woman I love.

POTTER: Well, you won't be left alone.

BILLY: I will not permit anyone to interfere with my life.

POTTER: That's it; no one will interfere. No one will associate with you.

BILLY: Won't they? Ming Toy has such wonderful adaptability that in no time no white girl will be able to hold her own with her.

POTTER: She will always be a Chinese girl, no matter what her environment or what she assimilates. She will always be Chinese.

BILLY: No environment will change her! I see you have been studying Mildred.

POTTER: Perhaps—but just the same, you're wrong. You will discover that when it will be too late.

BILLY: Well, don't you worry about me.

POTTER: Well, I do worry. In the first place, you are my brother now, and in the second place, I suggested Ming Toy's coming here, and I don't want to have any tragedy bound to result on my conscience.

BILLY: Oh! You are just biased like the rest.

POTTER: Oh no! We wanted to give you a fair chance. We wanted to see how our friends would receive your engagement, and it was mighty embarrassing, and you saw what happened.

BILLY: What do you mean you wanted to give me a chance?

POTTER: Well, the sudden announcement of your engagement was a test.

BILLY: Oh! You had planned it?

POTTER: Yes, father and I.

BILLY: Father's diplomacy.

POTTER: No, it was my idea.

BILLY: The least I can say to you in the future is you keep your hands off my life.

POTTER: I did this for your good. Had our friends looked upon it as you do, you would have gotten father's consent. As it is, you can't expect it.

BILLY: My God! What a dastardly trick, Jim. I would not have played it on you. I don't want to have anything to do with you. Good night.

POTTER: Now just wait a minute. You have always been impulsive, but you are doing me a great injustice.

BILLY: I don't want you ever to talk to me. And as I am going to marry Ming Toy you probably would not want to talk to me, so good night, and good-bye.

POTTER: (*Follows Billy to door.*) Now listen, Bill, you have lost your heart—don't lose your head. Listen to reason.

BILLY: Your idea—good night. (*Exits right.*)

MILDRED: (*From top of stairs*) Are you still here, Jim?

POTTER: Yes. I have spoken to Billy.

MILDRED: I asked you not to.

POTTER: Well I did, and I got H—. Good night, dearest.

MILDRED: Serves you right.

POTTER: I have lost a brother, but I got you, so that's all right, sweetheart. (*Throws her a kiss.*)

MILDRED: Good night, dear. Don't forget to turn off the lights as you always do. (*Exits.*)

POTTER: All right.

(*He turns out lights and exits to street door. The stage is in darkness excepting one shaded lamp. Billy enters door, takes box of cigarettes from table, and exits. Three Chinamen and Charlie Yong appear at back window. Charlie Yong opens door and steps in.*)

CHARLIE YONG: (*To Chinamen*) You wait—I call you. (*Goes to door left, opens it a little bit and closes it. He goes to door right and listens. Ming Toy appears on top of staircase. Charlie Yong sees her and hides behind back of chair. Ming Toy comes down, opens bookcase, takes out book that we referred to in second act as "Sorrows of Love," and proceeds to staircase when Charlie Yong suddenly appears from behind and gets hold of her wrist.*)

MING TOY: What you want, Charlie Yong?

CHARLIE YONG: You holler, I kill anybody who come in. Three months today—you no come. I kill Billy Benson tonight if you no come, and Charlie Yong never disappoint.

MING TOY: You come now to kill Mr. Benson? Charlie Yong never do hard work.

CHARLIE YONG: Yes. See? My men here. (*She sees shadows of Chinese faces.*)

MING TOY: Remember what I say. I told you: you kill Billy Benson, I kill you, and Ming Toy never disappoint either.

CHARLIE YONG: Don't care what you do, but Charlie Yong always make good. (*Grabs her and pulls her to door.*) You come on.

MING TOY: Where?

CHARLIE YONG: My men hold you. We fix Billy Benson.

MING TOY: Wait—I want to tell you something.

CHARLIE YONG: What you want to say?

MING TOY: Sit down, Charlie, I tell you.

CHARLIE YONG: No—quick tell me.

MING TOY: What you gain if you kill Billy?

CHARLIE YONG: I get you, and he gone. You love Charlie Yong.

MING TOY: I never love anybody but Billy Benson.

CHARLIE YONG: Oh! You fool. What you want to love white man? You say you afraid, I throw you away. You marry white man, you see, he throw you away. You see all white women at Kelley's? White men throw them away.

MING TOY: They are not like Billy Benson.

CHARLIE YONG: Oh! You stick to your people. I know you try to be white, but you are fool. You never be white. You always be Chinese, and Chinese people best people in the world.

MING TOY: Can't believe it when I see you.

CHARLIE YONG: You marry me and I make you queen of Chinatown.

MING TOY: I marry Billy Benson or nobody.

CHARLIE YONG: All right. You no marry Billy Benson, that sure. I show you. (*Holding Ming Toy's wrist, he walks back and motions to two Chinks. They enter, pointing to door right.*) You know him—get him. (*They go to glass door.*)

MING TOY: Wait, Charlie Yong!

CHARLIE YONG: Hurry up—be quick.

MING TOY: Don't kill him—don't kill him.

CHARLIE YONG: You come home with me now, I let him alone.

MING TOY: I come to you to-morrow.

CHARLIE YONG: No! You come right away.

MING TOY: I go pack my things.

CHARLIE YONG: It's all right. I buy you all clothes you want. Hurry up.

MING TOY: Can I go to my room to put something on?

CHARLIE YONG: All right. I go with you.

MING TOY: All right. (*Charlie Yong motions to Chinaman.*)

CHARLIE YONG: You wait for me outside.

MING TOY: (*Goes up stairs—Charlie Yong with her.*) Charlie Yong, I hate you, but I love Billy Benson so much I didn't want no trouble to come to him and I go with you. (*They enter her room for a second. The phone rings two or three times. Enter Billy right.*)

BILLY: (*Through phone*) Oh! Hello, Wong—don't worry. (*Pause.*) Have they? Thank you, old man. (*Hangs up receiver. He starts to go right and almost reaches door when the door at the head of steps opens and he sees Ming Toy and Charlie Yong. Ming Toy is wearing an evening wrap. Ming Toy and Charlie Yong do not see Billy until they are on the first step. When Ming Toy sees him, she runs down staircase and stands in front of Billy as if to protect him*).

MING TOY: Billy—Billy!

CHARLIE YONG: You had no sense to sleep. Soon you will never awake. (*Rushes to door and calls to men.*) Come in. (*Billy quickly turns on switch light. Two Chinamen enter, one of whom is Ming Hop Toy.*) There is your man.

HOP TOY: (*Catching sight of Ming Toy, he stops short and scrutinizes her face for a second. Ming Toy does the same, recognizing Hop Toy*).

MING TOY: Good Heavens!

BILLY: What's the matter?

MING TOY: (*Pointing to Hop Toy*) My father.

BILLY: Hop Toy!

MING TOY: Yes.

CHARLIE YONG: (*To Hop Toy*) Well, why you stand? Go ahead.

HOP TOY: I no kill. (*Starts to go but Charlie Yong stops him.*)

CHARLIE YONG: She your daughter? Is that it?

HOP TOY: I don't kill because she not my daughter.

BILLY: What? Ming Toy is not your daughter?

HOP TOY: No! I steal her. Christian Mission come to China—take Chinese children—make 'em love Christian God. I steal Christian children—make them love Chinese God. I get even for my God and Buddha bless me. I steal Ming Toy, but cannot make her love Chinese Gods—can make her love nothing Chinese. Hard to make her learn speak Chinese good and she always like to do things like Christian child. I get mad she like Christian devils—no good, I sell her.

BILLY: Who were her parents?

HOP TOY: Her father American—her mother Spanish—Christian Missionary.

BILLY: She's a white child?

HOP TOY: Sure—only steal white child. Buddha bless me when I steal white child and make them love Chinese Gods. (*Billy rushes to door right, opens it and calls parents. Enter Wong from street door.*)

BILLY: Hello, Wong. Thank you very much for phoning.

WONG: Everything all right, Mr. Benson?

BILLY: It's all right—it's all right. (*Mr. and Mrs. Benson—he in robe and Mrs. Benson in kimona—enter.*)

CHARLIE YONG: (*To Hop Toy*) Is that why you don't want to kill him?

HOP TOY: Sure—she no Christian girl, and only I kill white man when he takes away Chinese girl from Chinese man. Buddha only bless me when I take away white girl from Chinese men.

MR. BENSON: Children! What is this?

MING TOY: Oh, Mr. Benson—this man (*Pointing to Hop Toy*) he steal me from nice white parents when I have no sense. I am of your race. I always knew it! I always felt it. Christian God Ming Toy's God now. Billy can love Ming Toy now, and nobody got right to say nothing.

MR. BENSON: (*Going over to Hop Toy*) When did you steal Ming Toy?

HOP TOY: When she was five weeks old.

MR. BENSON: What was the name of her parents?

HOP TOY: John-stone.

MR. BENSON: Was it Herbert? Herbert Johnstone?

HOP TOY: Yes—Herbert John-stone.

MR. BENSON: Christian Mission in Canton? Johnstone! I remember. Johnstone came to me to see if I could help him out as the Ambassador. (*To Hop Toy*) Do you remember her mother? What was her complexion?

HOP TOY: What that?

MR. BENSON: Color.

HOP TOY: Almost like Chinese.

MR. BENSON: Spanish?

HOP TOY: Yes.

MRS. BENSON: Oh! I am so happy, Ming Toy. You are one of us. You could not be anything else— such a sweet soul could not simply be anything not white. (*Kisses her.*)

WONG: (*To Hop Toy*) I understand now, Hop Toy, what you meant when you said on the love-boat that you sell your children for the sake of heaven. They were not your children.

HOP TOY: No—they were all white devils.

WONG: You steal for Heaven and you're even willing to kill for Heaven—that is not good Chinese religion, Hop Toy.

HOP TOY: Well, better than the Christian Mission who try to kill Chinese religion.

WONG: Only one good deed you ever do, Hop Toy. It shine like the China moon on the rice fields, and that deed was on the night you bring Ming Toy down to the love-boat on the Yangtze River.

MRS. BENSON: Oh, Mildred, congratulate Ming Toy—she belongs to the white race.

MILDRED: We are a conceited race aren't we? I don't see why Ming Toy should be complimented for that! I love her whatever she is.

MING TOY: (*To Charlie Yong*) Well, Charlie Yong, you still want me?

CHARLIE YONG: No! Don't want white woman. I say stick to your race and Charlie Yong say what he means. I would not take Ming Toy white for all yellow gold in the world.

MING TOY: You have very fine sense, Charlie Yong, but just the same Ming Toy get away from Charlie Yong.

CHARLIE YONG: But Ming Toy is white girl. I still say no Chinese girl ever get away from Charlie Yong. (*Turning to Mr. Benson*) Want cigarette?

MR. BENSON: No thanks. (*Charlie Yong exits with his men.*)

WONG: Mr. Billy Benson, Ming Toy is not of my people, but you do not know how close she was to Wong Lo's heart, and maybe sometime you don't mind if Wong should stop in when he is passing by.

BILLY: You're always welcome, Wong.

WONG: Good-bye, Ming Toy.

MING TOY: You know what I think, Wong? You have been so good to me, I never forget you. Always come to see me, and since Charlie Yong don't like white girls I can always come to see you. Thank you so much for being a good papa to me when people of no color had much use for Ming Toy. I hope some day you turn out to be white man too.

WONG: The color of a man's face is not the reflection of his soul. Good-bye, Ming Toy. Good evening, everybody. (*Exits.*)[75]

MR. BENSON: Now little Ming Toy, once I objected to your being my daughter. I am afraid that now you may object to having me as your father.

MING TOY: Why?

MR. BENSON: Because you are the daughter of some very distinguished parents. Your father, whom I knew, was one of the greatest scholars in America, and your mother comes from a highly artistic and distinguished Spanish family.

MING TOY: That don't make me a better Ming Toy. I don't have no objection to you.[76]

MR. BENSON: Yes, but your folks may have to my boy, and I think you want to consult them. Just a minute. (*Goes to phone.*) Give me 4137 Frisco.

BILLY: Who are you calling, dad?

MR. BENSON: Ming Toy's mother.

BILLY: But it's so late.

MR. BENSON: It's never too late to hear good news. Ming Toy's mother refused to go to bed many nights in the faint hope of hearing such news. Why should I not take her out of bed when the hope is realized—actually realized. (*Phone rings.*) Hello, I want to talk to Mrs. Johnstone. Oh! Is this you, Floretta? Yes—yes—Andrew— Oh! Just to meet a charming little person, just a minute— (*Hands phone to Ming Toy.*) Come here, Floretta, speak to your mother.

MING TOY: Floretta? I don't like it as well as Ming Toy. (*Speaks in phone.*) Hello, mama. (*Pause.*) This is Ming Toy. It's your Chinese daughter speaking to you. (*Billy puts his arm around her.*) Yes, I am little Floretta Ming Toy Johnstone Benson and beside me stands your son, Mr. Billy Floretta Ming Toy Benson. He is a naughty boy—he is kissing me so late in the night. I will sit up all night waiting to see you.

(*Curtain*)

# NOTES

## Introduction

1. Most work in scholarship on prostitution in American theatre focuses on the mid- to late nineteenth century. See Rosemarie K. Bank, "Hustlers in the House: The Bowery Theatre as a Mode of Historical Information"; and Claudia D. Johnson, "That Guilty Third Tier: Prostitution in Nineteenth-Century American Theaters." For depictions of white slavery in the early twentieth-century theatre, see M. Joan McDermott and Sarah J. Blackstone, "White Slavery Plays of the 1910s: Fear of Victimization and the Social Control of Sexuality." More recent work includes Kirsten Pullen, *Actresses and Whores on Stage and in Society*.

2. Rebecca Schneider, *The Explicit Body in Performance*, 24.

3. *The Traffic in Girls: White Slavery as Now Practiced in America*, 2.

4. For more information about brothel dramas, see Katie N. Johnson, *Sisters in Sin: Brothel Drama in America, 1900–1920*. While I draw upon some of that research for this introduction, it has been significantly revised and reworked for this book.

5. "Plays of Brothel Still Unchecked."

6. "Escaping *House of Bondage*," 583.

7. Kathleen Barry, *Female Sexual Slavery*.

8. Timothy Gilfoyle, *City of Eros: New York City, Prostitution, and the Commercialization of Sex, 1790–1920*, 20.

9. Michel Foucault, *The History of Sexuality, Vol. 1, An Introduction*.

10. Ruth Rosen, *The Lost Sisterhood: Prostitution in America, 1900–1918*, xi.

11. Committee of Fifteen, *The Social Evil, with Special Reference to Conditions Existing in the City of New York*, v.

12. Committee of Fourteen, *The Social Evil in New York City: A Study of Law Enforcement by the Research Committee of Fourteen*.

13. Chicago Vice Commission Report, cited in Clifford Griffith Roe, *Horrors of the White Slave Trade: The Mighty Crusade to Protect the Purity of Our Homes*, 382.

14. Review of *The Lure*, *New York Dramatic Mirror*, 20 August 1913, 6.

15. Reginald Wright Kauffman, *The House of Bondage*, iii. See also Kauffman's unpublished version of the play, Manuscript Division, Library of Congress.

16. James M. Metcalfe, "Here We Are Again, Mr. Merryman," 390.

17. James Shelley Hamilton, "The Sex Tangled Drama," 679.

18. "Sex O'Clock in America," 113–114.

19. The Page Act was the popular name for Clause 79 of the Inferior Courts Act of 1910, which required compulsory physical examinations for convicted prostitutes. The 1910 Mann Act prohibited the trafficking of women across state lines. See Gilfoyle, *City of Eros*, 258–259, 308–309.

20. J. Ellen Gainor, *Susan Glaspell in Context: American Theater, Culture, and Politics, 1915–48*, 10.

21. "Offending Plays."

22. George Lipsitz, *The Possessive Investment in Whiteness: How White People Profit from Identity Politics*, 3.

23. Ernest Bell, *Fighting the Traffic in Young Girls or War on the White Slave Trade*, 20.

24. McDermott and Blackstone, "White Slavery Plays," 150.

25. Sims quoted in Bell, *Fighting the Traffic in Young Girls*, 17.

26. See Gretchen Soderland, "Covering Urban Vice: the *New York Times*, 'White Slavery,' and the Construction of Journalistic Knowledge," 457 n. 2.

27. *The Traffic in Girls: White Slavery as Now Practiced in America*, 2.

28. "Over 50,000 Girls Disappear in This Country Yearly," SM9.

29. For more on the controversy regarding *The Lure* and *The Fight*, see Johnson, *Sisters in Sin*; and also John Houchin, *Censorship of the American Theatre in the Twentieth Century*.

30. "Immoral, Gross, Revolting, the Judge Calls *The Lure*," no pagination.

31. "Waldo's Censors Watch Two Plays of Underworld," no pagination.

32. "Police Stop Two Plays," 116.

33. "Decency and the Stage,"12.

34. Emma Goldman, "The Traffic in Women," 20. Josephine Butler had fought similar battles in England in the 1880s. She, like Goldman, did not separate her rescue work along racial lines; nor did she perceive white slavery as a special subset of prostitution. For a brief summary of Butler's work, see chapter 2 in Barry's *Female Sexual Slavery*.

35. See Egal Feldman, "Prostitution, the Alien Woman and the Progressive Imagination, 1910–1915." See also Mark Connelly, *The Response to Prostitution in the Progressive Era*.

36. Karen A. Keely, "Sexual Slavery in San Francisco's Chinatown: 'Yellow Peril' and 'White Slavery' in Frank Norris's Early Fiction," 129. See also Yu-Fang Cho's chapter on yellow slavery in *Uncoupling American Empire: Cultural Politics of Deviance and Unequal Difference, 1890–1910*.

37. Many of these titles can be found in the Manuscript Division, Library of Congress.

38. See Dave Williams, ed., *The Chinese Other, 1850–1925: An Anthology of Plays*; McDermott and Blackstone's essay "White Slavery Plays"; and my chapter on white slave plays in *Sisters in Sin*. I have revised and updated that discussion here.

39. Frank Norris, *The Third Circle*, 1. I thank Andrew Hebard for pointing this story out to me.

40. See William Brown Meloney, "Slumming in New York's Chinatown." For more about what I have called "slum voyeurism," see Katie N. Johnson, "The Salvation Lass, Her Harlot-Friend, and Slum Realism in Edward Sheldon's *Salvation Nell* (1908)"; and J. Chris Westgate, *Staging the Slums, Slumming the Stage: Class, Poverty, Ethnicity, and Sexuality in American Theatre, 1890–1916*.

41. Roe quoted in Bell, *Fighting the Traffic in Young Girls*, 108.

42. Krystyn R. Moon, *Yellowface: Creating the Chinese in American Popular Music and Performance, 1850s–1920s*.

43. Bernard Weintraub, "Play a Hooker and Win an Oscar."

## *The Web* by Eugene O'Neill

1. Arthur Gelb and Barbara Gelb, *O'Neill*, 126.

2. In the typescript of *The Web* at the Library of Congress Manuscript Division, O'Neill crossed out the original typed title—"Circumstance: a Play in one act"—and added a handwritten title, "The Web of Deceit." The last two words were then also crossed out and "play" was changed to "tragedy" for the final title, "The Web: A Tragedy in One Act." Princeton also has an eight-page manuscript. As Travis Bogard has observed, in the Library of Congress edition, O'Neill continued to edit his plays, even after they were performed or published. The version used here comes from *Thirst and Other One Act Plays*, which was published in Boston by Gorham Press in 1914 and also used for the Library of America edition.

3. The Comstock Act, named after moral crusader Anthony Comstock, was passed by U.S. Congress in 1873 as an "Act of the Suppression of, Trade in, and Circulation of, Obscene Literature and Articles of Immoral Use." Margaret Sanger was arrested under this statute for her birth control book *What Every Girl Should Know* in 1914.

4. Eugene O'Neill, *The Web*, in *Complete Plays, 1913–1920*, 28.

5. Katie N. Johnson, "'*Anna Christie*': The Repentant Courtesan Made Respectable."

6. "Yeggman" was an American slang term for criminal or burglar.

7. In the original typescript, O'Neill uses "isn't" instead of "ain't" in Rose's line. As he worked on the text, O'Neill emphasized Rose's lower-class accent. For example, he changed "God" to "Gawd."

8. The island referred to is Blackwell's Island, also known as "the Tombs," where prostitutes were often sent to do time.

9. "Con" is an abbreviation for consumption (tuberculosis). O'Neill himself was suffering from consumption when he wrote this play in 1913.

10. In the original typed manuscript O'Neill wrote this line somewhat differently, adding "but Tim and Rose are so close together he is afraid to fire." Upon revision, O'Neill removed Steve's concern for Rose, thus making Steve less sympathetic.

11. In the earlier typed manuscript, O'Neill wrote the following stage direction to accompany the policeman's final lines: "and says in the idiotic voice generally used in speaking to babies." This line does not appear in the 1914 published version.

## *Moondown* by John Reed

1. John Reed, *Moondown*, *Masses* 4 (September 1913): 8–9; reprinted in *John Reed for The Masses*, ed. James C. Wilson, 38–42.

2. A copy of *Moondown* can be found in the Manuscript Division of the Library of Congress. This version has the more positive ending (Sylvia leaving with her beau) and to my knowledge was never performed.

3. Frank T. Shay's one-act play *The Machine: A Commonplace Tragedy in One Act of Three Scenes*, which also appeared in the *Masses* in August 1913 next to Reed's *Moondown*, sketched three scenes of prostitutes summoned in front of the court. As far as I can tell, it was never performed.

4. "A Jury of Her Peers" was a short story written by Provincetowner Susan Glaspell in 1917. Her dramatic version of this story, called *Trifles*, preceded the short story and was performed by the Provincetown Players in 1916.

5. For more on the Provincetown Players, see Helen Deutsch and Stella Hanau, *Provincetown: A History of the Theatre*. See also Brenda Murphy, *The Provincetown Players and the Culture of Modernity*.

6. George Cram Cook and Frank Shay, eds., *The Provincetown Plays*, 5.

7. "Little Plays Again at the Bandbox," *New York Times*, 27 March 1915, 11. From the *Moondown* clipping file, Billy Rose Theatre Collection, New York Public Library for the Performing Arts.

8. Reed, *Moondown*, 8.

9. "Minute Visits in the Wings," *New York Times*, 1 September 1918, 36.

10. See chapter 1 of Leona Rust Egan, *Provincetown as a Stage: Provincetown, the Provincetown Players, and the Discovery of Eugene O'Neill*.

11. Walter Prichard Eaton, *Plays and Players: Leaves from a Critic's Scrapbook*, 400.

12. John S. Bak, "Eugene O'Neill and John Reed: Recording the Body Politic, 1913–1922."

13. When Reed sets the action of the play in the "present," he means the 1910s.

14. A "French Novel" had salacious and erotic content; the fact that Mame is reading such a tawdry novel, while smoking and wearing a "violently colored kimono," marks her as a loose woman.

15. "Puffs" are ringlets of curled hair that lined the face. These are clip-on ones.

16. A shirtwaist was a woman's blouse worn with a skirt in the nineteenth and early twentieth century.

17. The New York subway opened on October 27, 1904. In 1913, when Reed was writing *Moondown*, the subway was considered a modern form of transportation.

18. In the original manuscript that Reed submitted to the Library of Congress, he uses "White-light District" instead of "White-hot district." One newspaper described the "white-light district" as synonymous with Broadway, extending "from Fourteenth street to Fifty-ninth street along Broadway and for a block or two on either side" and as "the greatest amusement centre in the world." "Six Million Dollars for Pleasure," 2.

19. The Fifth Avenue Baptist Church was also known as the "Rockefeller Church" because of its benefactor and regular member, John D. Rockefeller. The church was on 46th Street near Fifth Avenue.

20. Washington Square, a central hub in Greenwich Village, was where the Provincetown Players made their new home. In referencing those "charity boys" from Washington Square, Reed is clearly poking fun at his penniless bohemian comrades who valued art over money.

21. 126th Street lies just on the other side of Harlem, typically marked by 125th Street. In the manuscript submitted to the Library of Congress for copyright, Mame references the Bronx, not Harlem, here.

22. Shanley's was a famous restaurant in Times Square.

## *Cocaine* by Pendleton King

1. As far as I can tell, *Cocaine* was never reviewed.

2. For an excellent summary of *Cocaine* and its relevance to the Provincetown Players, see Jeffrey Kennedy's website devoted to the Provincetown Playhouse, http://www.provincetownplayhouse.com/cocaine.html.

3. See Jeffrey Kennedy, "The Artistic Life of the Provincetown Playhouse, 1918–1922." See also Edna Kenton, *The Provincetown Players and the Playwrights' Theatre, 1915–1922*.

4. An unpublished typescript of King's manuscript (with a copyright date of 1916) can be found in the Edward Goodman Collection of the Billy Rose Theatre Division, New York Public Library for the Performing Arts. It differs slightly from the version that appeared in 1917 (edited by Frank Shay) and in a 1921 collection: Cook and Shay, eds., *The Provincetown Plays*.

5. Laura Mulvey, "Visual Pleasure and Narrative Cinema."

6. Constance D'Arcy Mackay, *The Little Theatre in the United States*, 52.

7. "Drug Traffic Lucrative," 24.

8. A "deck" refers to a bag of drugs. Today this term often is used when talking about heroin, but Joe is talking about cocaine.

9. Ida Rauh was known as the "Duse of the MacDougal Street," in reference to the great actress Eleonore Duse (1858–1924). See Deutsch and Hanau, *Provincetown*, 50–51.

10. The Bowery is part of lower Manhattan, which was often characterized by cheap tenement housing, poverty, and vice at turn of the twentieth century.

11. Camphor is an ointment used to treat itching or blisters. Nora uses it for her fever blister.

12. "Ta" is slang for "thanks."

13. The term "elevated" refers to an elevated urban rapid transit system. Later Joe refers to it as the "El," which is the abbreviation still used today.

14. "Sniff" is another slang term for cocaine.

15. Nora is quoting a poem by Oscar Wilde called "My Voice."

## *Ourselves* by Rachel Crothers

1. The version of *Ourselves* in this volume is dated 1917 and comes from Crothers's papers (including her revisions), found at the Rare Book and Manuscripts Library, the University of Pennsylvania. An earlier version of *Ourselves*, from the Shubert Archive, was used in Maggie Barbara Gale and Gilli Bush Bailey, eds., *Plays and Performance Texts by Women, 1880–1930: An Anthology of Plays by British and American Women from the Modernist Period.*

2. Colette Lindroth and James Lindroth, eds., *Rachel Crothers: A Research and Production Sourcebook*, 26. See also "*Ourselves* as Seen by a Woman," *New York Morning Sun*, 14 November 1913, no pagination.

3. Norman Hapgood, "Stage Notes," 12.

4. Review of *Ourselves* in *Everybody's Magazine* 30 (February 1914): 264.

5. Ibid.

6. "White Slave Still a Theatrical Asset."

7. Brenda Murphy, "Feminism and the Marketplace: The Career of Rachel Crothers," 82.

8. Although Rachel Crothers wrote the first—and only—white slave play that was produced by a woman, another female playwright, Rachael Marshall, co-wrote a short play called *The Traffic* with Oliver D. Bailey that had a limited run in 1913.

9. Portions of my discussion of *Ourselves* are taken from my lengthier essay, which I have revised here: "Rachel Crothers's *Ourselves*: Feminist Dramaturgy in the Brothel Drama."

10. See "Rachel Crothers," in Anne L. Fliotsos and Wendy Vierow, eds., *American Women Stage Directors of the Twentieth Century*, 134.

11. Gilfoyle, *City of Eros*, 276.

12. "Dramatic Outlook in New York Brighter," no pagination.

13. Ibid.

14. Ruth Rosen and Sue Davidson, eds., *The Maimie Papers*.

15. Ruth Rosen, *The Lost Sisterhood*, 62. See Rosen's chapter "The Lady and the Prostitute."

16. "More Underworld Put on the Stage," no pagination. Maude Miner and Jane Addams were key figures in Progressive-Era reform efforts. Miner was known for her 1916 treatise *Slavery of Prostitution: A Plea For Emancipation*.

17. "White Slave Still a Theatrical Asset," no pagination.

18. "*Ourselves* as Seen by a Woman," no pagination.

19. "Rachel Crothers," no pagination.

20. "Another Drama of Social Problem," *New York Herald*, no pagination.

21. "*Ourselves* Deals with That Old Dual Morality," no pagination.

22. Ibid.

23. Charles Darnton, "*Ourselves*: A Play That Goes Wrong," no pagination.

24. A. R., "What Is the Drama League Driving At?" 7.

25. Review of *Ourselves* (1913), no pagination.

26. Unidentified clipping from *Baltimore News*, 10 December 1913, no pagination.

27. The author erroneously calls Bedford "Bradford." "*Ourselves* at Bradford," no pagination.

28. Ibid.

29. "Reformatory Girls See Morals Drama," no pagination.

30. Ibid.

31. "*Ourselves* at Bradford," no pagination.

32. Throughout *Ourselves* Crothers underlined words for emphasis. They have been changed here to italics.

33. Serge is a type of ridged twill fabric that was often used for military uniforms because of its durability.

34. For more about working-class women and their entertainments, see Peiss, *Cheap Amusements*.

35. In the 1917 typescript Crothers has crossed out Beatrice's following lines: "Wilson's been with us twenty years and she says Molly's more square and good-natured than anyone who's been in the house all that time. I've told her all about Molly and she says she's worth saving—That's an awful lot for Wilson." These changes indicated Crothers's most recent thinking about the text are dated "06-27-17."

36. Crothers cuts Molly's stage directions at the end of her line, which makes her character stronger: "*(Leever does not reciprocate or show any feeling—Molly does all the loving.)*"

37. Leever is referring to the well-established practice of prostitutes who advertised themselves with promenades on Broadway.

38. The term "gay" at this historical moment was used to mean someone or something that was fun or easygoing.

39. Crothers cut some minor stage directions for Leever in the preceding lines. Additionally, before "Un?" Crothers has cut this direction for Leever to intimidate Molly physically: "(*Throws her hands down and stands over her.*)"

40. Crothers cuts Leever's following lines and action, signaling that she wished to diminish his physical abuse: "(*Suspicious—goes to her—takes her wrists.*)." Have you got another man? (*Whirls her by wrists to right of him.*)"

41. Dr. Abraham Flexner wrote one of the most influential studies on prostitution, *Prostitution in Europe* (1914). His book came out after Crothers's play premiered, demonstrating that she was at the forefront of such debates. Together with Kneeland (*Commercialized Prostitution in New York City*), Flexner was one of two researchers who shaped and redefined public debate on prostitution in the Progressive Era.

42. This last bit of action was handwritten in the manuscript by Crothers.

43. "Fagged" means tired.

44. Crothers cuts Bob's stage directions here: "(*Starts to take her hand, he starts to put hand on her shoulder.*)" This is the first of three bits of stage action in which Bob attempts physical intimacy with Irene. In revising the play, Crothers removed them, minimizing intimacy between the characters.

45. Crothers cuts a second bit of action that requires Bob to touch Irene, just before his lines: "(*Arms about her—standing above her.*)"

46. Crothers cuts a third physical action by Bob after his line: "(*kisses her head.*)"

47. Crothers also cuts this line about Bob speculating about the gender of the baby: "And what if it's a boy, Irene?"

48. Crothers cuts the following physically violent stage direction, suggesting that she wished to minimize how brutally Molly is treated: "(*Throws Molly to floor again.*)"

49. This last change in the script is significant. In the 1913 version Crothers writes that Molly "turns to Bob." In this revised script, however, she walks out the door, just like Nora in Ibsen's *A Doll's House*.

## *My Little Sister* by Elizabeth Robins

1. As Angela John has noted, the original idea for *My Little Sister* came from Maude Pember Reeves in 1907, who told Robins about the abduction case. Angela V. John, *Elizabeth Robins: Staging a Life, 1862–1952*, 185.

2. Elizabeth Robins, *My Little Sister*; and Elizabeth Robins, *Where Are You Going To . . . ?* Heinemann agreed to wait to publish *Where Are You Going To . . . ?* until the story appeared in *McClure's*.

3. Display advertisement for *My Little Sister*, *New York Times*, 8 February 1913, 11. See also John, *Elizabeth Robins*, 185.

4. S. M. Franklin, "When We Have Time to Read," 83.

5. Hildegarde Hawthorne, "*My Little Sister*: Miss Robins's Novel a Strong Plea for Our Invisible Neighbor," 62.

6. Harriet Burton Laidlaw, Review of *My Little Sister*, 201 (emphasis in the original).

7. Sue Thomas, "Crying 'the Horror' of Prostitution: Elizabeth Robins's '*Where Are You Going To . . . ?*' and the Moral Crusade of the Women's Social and Political Union."

8. Ibid., 207.

9. The Fifth International Congress for the Suppression of the White Slave Traffic was held in London from 30 June to 4 July 1913.

10. John, *Elizabeth Robins*, 184–185.

11. Elizabeth Robins, "My Little Sister," cover of unpublished play, Elizabeth Robins Papers (hereafter Elizabeth Robins Papers), MSS 002, Series 7, Box 75, Files 12–15, Fales Library and Special Collections, New York University Libraries.

12. Letter to Elizabeth Robins from "W" (likely William Archer), 29 July 1913, Elizabeth Robins Papers, Box 75, Folder 16.

13. Undeterred, Robins solicited help from a fourth collaborator, J. K. Jerome himself. It is impossible to know to what extent other collaborators shaped the dramatization of *My Little Sister*, but it remains clear that Robins represented this version as her own—and as distinctly different from, and superior to, Hamilton's.

14. The Syndicate was a group of booking agents and theatre owners that included Sam Nixon, Fred Zimmerman, Charles Frohman, A. L. Hayman, Marc Klaw, and Abraham Erlanger. They controlled virtually every theatre in New York from 1896 to 1916.

15. "New English Plays Here for Frohman," 6.

16. "The Stage," 1023. Other announcements about producing the play include articles in *Theatre Magazine* 13 (1913): vi; and *Field Illustrated* 23 (July–December 1913), 189.

17. "New Productions," 17.

18. In a letter to Jerome K. Jerome on 3 April 1914, Robins confirmed that Frohman had rejected Hamilton's dramatization. Letter to J. K. Jerome, 3 April 1914, Elizabeth Robins Papers. Box 75, Folder 16. Many thanks to J. Kerry Powell for sharing this letter with me.

19. Cecily Hamilton, "Where Are You Going To . . . ?" act IV, p. 15. Elizabeth Robins Papers, Box 75, Folders 8–11.

20. Letter to J. K. Jerome, 3 April 1914.

21. Katherine E. Kelley, "The Actresses' Franchise League Prepares for War: Feminist Theatre in Camouflage."

22. Letters to Elizabeth Robins from Inez Bensusan, 6 June 1914; 12 June 1914; 28 July 1914, Elizabeth Robins Papers, Box 75, Folder 16.

23. Robins was strategizing with Archer behind the scenes about approaching other producers like Harley Granville Barker.

24. Letter to Elizabeth Robins from G. Golding Bright, 5 August 1914, Elizabeth Robins Papers, Box 75, Folder 16.

25. Letter to Elizabeth Robins (likely from Tracy Stuart; the handwriting is difficult to read, but I believe that it is the writing of Bensusan's secretary), 25 July 1914, Elizabeth Robins Papers, Box 75, Folder 16.

26. Joanne E. Gates, "The Theatrical Politics of Elizabeth Robins and Bernard Shaw."

27. Thomas, "Crying 'the Horror' of Prostitution," 213. See also Powell and Johnson, "The Censoring of *My Little Sister*." While the paper was co-authored, Powell wrote this part.

28. See Emelyne Godfrey's second chapter, "Elizabeth Robins and the 'White Slave Trade' Panic," in *Femininity, Crime and Self-Defense in Victorian Literature and Society: From Dagger-Fans to Suffragettes*; Molly Hite, "The Public Woman and the Modernist Turn: Virginia Woolf's *The Voyage Out* and Elizabeth Robins's *My Little Sister*"; and Leslie Fishbein, "The Harlot's Progress in American Fiction and Film, 1900–1930."

29. Mark Sullivan, *Our Times: The United States, 1900–1925*, vol. 1, *The Turn of the Century*.

30. "White Slave Play of Some Grim Power," 7.

31. *My Little Sister*, directed by Kenean Buel, Scenario Films, 1919.

32. At the beginning of the first act Robins refers to this character as Bettina but then changes her name to Betty. I have used Bettina as the character's name throughout to make it consistent, although other characters sometimes refer to her by both names.

33. *Hein* is French for "huh?" or "eh?"

34. Lowndes Square is an upscale residential area of London known for its white stucco buildings.

35. Handwritten notes on Robins's manuscript indicate that she intended to write speeches for Bettina and Honor here but hadn't managed to do so.

36. Robins notes on the manuscript that she's contemplating cutting his lines here.

37. Patchouli is a scent that was often associated with prostitutes.

38. These are lyrics from a song "Where Are You Going To?" from *A Baby's Opera* by Walter Crane (1877). It was also a well-known nursery rhyme in Britain.

39. The scent is likely patchouli—another clue that the girls are in a brothel.

40. "That sort" is a phrase that refers to a fallen woman. It was also the name of a play about a fallen woman written by Basil MacDonald Hastings, which starred Alla Nazimova in a 1914 Broadway production.

41. "Tartar" referred to an ethnic group from what is now Russia. They are descendants from "Tartary," such as the Turks and Mongols. Here Robins is recycling the pervasive stereotype of Eastern Europeans as white slavers.

42. The colonel is referring to having bad luck in gambling on horses. His horse was scratched—removed from the race. Bettina in all her innocence takes the literal meaning of "scratched."

43. Maud Allan was a turn-of-the-century actress whose sultry performance of *Salomé* resulted in her being charged with obscenity in 1918. The court case equally tried her lesbianism and the performance of the play.

44. Bezique is a two-person card game developed during the nineteenth century in France.

45. In her manuscript notes, Robins wondered if these two last lines should be cut.

46. Robins marks the following four lines as "alternative" and lists them on a separate piece of paper.

47. "Gaol" is another spelling for "jail."

48. He is referring to Hull Harbour in London.

## "A Shanghai Cinderella" (*East Is West*) by Samuel Shipman and John B. Hymer

1. Samuel Shipman and John B. Hymer, "A Shanghai Cinderella" (unpublished play, 1918). After entering the script under this title with Library of Congress in 1918, the play title was changed to *East Is West*, and it was performed under this title. A somewhat modified version was published by Samuel French in 1924. *East Is West* opened on Christmas day in 1918 and played through August 1920.

2. "*East Is West*: Play of the Month," 66.

3. Review of *East Is West*, 78.

4. Samuel Shipman and John B. Hymer, "A Shanghai Cinderella," 47.

5. Review of *East Is West*, 78.

6. John Corbin, Review of *East Is West*, 9. Kipling's "Ballad of East and West" was first published in 1889.

7. Josephine D. Lee, *Performing Asian America: Race and Ethnicity on the Contemporary Stage*.

8. Robert Hood Bowers (words and music), "Chinese Lullaby."

9. "The Theatre in Review," 244–245.

10. Review of *East Is West*, 78.

11. *Ming Toy* (1949) was a musical comedy with book by Leslie Carter and lyrics and music by John Laurence Seymour. See also Moon, *Yellowface*, 127–128.

12. Quoted in Gerald Martin Bordman, *American Theatre: A Chronicle of Comedy and Drama, 1869–1914*, 95. Heywood Broun's review sparked a feud with playwright Samuel Shipman, who charged him to "use his penetrating brain to state his reasons for condemning the play," charging that a critic who could not clearly articulate dramaturgical faults "should quit his job." Samuel Shipman, "If a Critic Cannot Say Why a Play Is Bad, He Is No Critic," 104.

13. Corbin, review of *East Is West*, 9.

14. T. H. "Gold Bricks and Staple Goods," 104.

15. Anne Paul, "A Song of Success," 23.

16. Corbin, review of *East Is West*, 9.

17. Jill Lane, "ImpersoNation: Toward a Theory of Black-, Red-, and Yellowface in the Americas."

18. Karen Shimakawa, *National Abjection: The Asian American Body Onstage*, 3.

19. Ibid., 17.

20. In the 1924 version of this play Wong Lo is called Lo, whereas "A Shanghai Cinderella" refers to him as Wong. Charlie Yong is renamed "Yang."

21. The original manuscript ("A Shanghai Cinderella") uses the word "samisong" to refer to the instrument, but I have substituted "shamisen," which is a three-stringed Chinese musical instrument. The 1924 version of the script has the sing-song girls playing moon-harps.

22. The term "raiment," from Old French, was used to describe an article of female clothing at the turn of the twentieth century.

23. The term "sing-song girls" was widely used to describe "flower girls" (concubines) in nineteenth-century Chinese culture. Concubinage was legal until 1911 in China. While these women were companions, they were not always lovers. Sing-song girls were popularized in the 1892 fictional work by Han Bangqing called *Sing-Song Girls of Shanghai* (also known as *Flowers of Shanghai*). See Fan Boqun, "The Sing-Song Girls of Shanghai: The Pioneering Work of Modern Popular Fiction."

24. Although female infanticide was practiced throughout China during this period, it is also a stereotype that the play exaggerates.

25. The influence of Progressive-Era "pure race" theories and eugenics can be seen in lines such as these, in which characters value whiteness over other races and ethnicities.

26. Whereas in "A Shanghai Cinderella" Hop Toy speaks only in Chinese, in the 1924 script (*East Is West*) his character speaks both Chinese and broken English. In this version his English accent draws on Asian stereotypes, using comical words like "vely" for "very."

27. Foot binding, the long-standing traditional Chinese practice of binding upper-class women's feet, was perceived as increasing women's erotic value, though it caused extreme pain and disability. The practice began to be challenged in the early part of the twentieth century before being banned after the rise of the Republic of China in 1912.

28. The 1924 script uses the Chinese word "tzien" instead of yen. It also includes Chinese throughout the prologue (phonetically spelled out), whereas the original manuscript simply indicates that the characters say the lines in Chinese.

29. In the 1924 script the name Bing Bang Boo is changed to Chang Lee.

30. The Proprietor (or Merchant) in the 1924 version says he is selling Ming Toy "because you got Christian ways." Later Hop Toy says a similar thing. This version therefore aligns criminality with being anti-Christian.

31. This play contains many misconceptions of Buddhism and Asian culture, such as the idea that selling women would please Buddha.

32. The stage directions for Ming Toy in the 1924 version remove her mixing of the Chinese song with "Yankee Doodle." Instead, she sings "Ming Toy's Melody," a song especially written for *East Is West* that was a hit.

33. Benson's comment that Anglo-Americans did not participate in white slavery is misleading and racist. Traffic in women was a central concern of Progressive-Era culture, and racialized others and immigrants were often falsely charged as white slavers.

34. This Chinese drink is not specified in the original manuscript.

35. A punk stick is a scentless incense stick used in traditional Chinese religious rituals.

36. Ming Toy has the final lines in the prologue of the 1924 version, not Bing Bang Boo, as here. "A Shanghai Cinderella" ends with Ming Toy and Billy waxing about America as the "Land of the Free."

37. In the 1924 version of the script a Chinese servant announces Mr. Potter, making Wong appear more dignified. Wong is using a Chinese counting machine.

38. Joss is a spirit of the Chinese household who brings luck and protection. A joss stick is a traditional Chinese incense stick.

39. In the 1924 version the joke "credit to your razor" (in response to showing a "clean face") excludes the next phrase ("and your morals") to pack more of a punch; it is also laughed at by Lo in that version but not in this one, thus making him complicit in the racist humor.

40. A hatchet man was a Chinese assassin who typically carried a handleless hatchet. The term "coolie" refers to a laborer or slave of Asian origin; it was also used as a racial slur.

41. "Chicken" was slang referring to women as pieces of meat.

42. The lines about Charlie Yong being fat were cut from the 1924 script, probably because the actor who played him was not fat.

43. In the 1924 script Ming Toy also prays that God will send her a "nice American man, she see in China" by the name of Billy Benson to set up the scene when they reunite (31).

44. In the 1924 script Potter calls Ming Toy a "bad girl" (31) rather than Ming Toy calling him a "bad man" in the 1918 typescript.

45. The 1924 script calls this dance "shaking the shimmy" instead of Shimmy Wiggle (32). Deriving from African American dance forms, the shimmy was one of the most popular dances in the United States during the 1920s and was initially perceived as sexually provocative. See Rebecca A. Bryant, "Shaking Things Up: Popularizing the Shimmy in America."

46. This line is missing from the 1924 script. Tellingly, the line conveys Ming Toy's sense of identifying as American and thus the performative nature of identity not being fixed.

47. The term "Beau Brummel" was used to describe a man of high fashion.

48. Originally French in origin, "que" is another word for a man's ponytail, typically worn by the Chinese.

49. The Big Tong Society was made up of Chinese criminal organizations involved in the import and export of heroin. The 1924 script omits this reference entirely.

50. This is a laugh line. "Frappe" is French for "wrap." This joke was cut in the 1924 script.

51. The lines about dancing—including Yong dancing with white women—are deleted in the 1924 script, perhaps due to anxieties about miscegenation.

52. Ming Toy is referring to three figures in Chinese culture: Good Fortune, Prosperity, and Longevity, regarded as Fu Lu Shou (the three stars). See Emily M. Ahern, *Chinese Ritual and Politics.* These lines about the futility of praying to Chinese gods were cut from the 1924 script.

53. As before, the reference to "Yankee Doodle" is missing from the 1924 script.

54. Yong's use of "lemonsine" is a laugh line; it occurs twice in this play. The 1924 script spells "limousine" correctly.

55. "Chink" is a derogatory term for Chinese people. The 1924 script removes this word.

56. The line about Charlie Yong controlling the governor is deleted from the 1924 script.

57. The 1924 script uses "basket" instead of "grip."

58. Woodrow Wilson, president of the United States from 1913 to 1921, was an advocate of self-determination, a political theory that proclaimed that every nation had the right to its own sovereignty. This reference to Wilson was deleted from the 1924 script, because Wilson was no longer in office.

59. Tait's at the Beach was one of San Francisco's lively restaurants in the 1920s and was the place for socialites and celebrities to be seen. The reference to the couple going out with other people to Tait's was cut from the 1924 script.

60. The line "I've never had a white maid so intelligent" was cut from the 1924 script.

61. These two lines about Ming Toy not being like other Chinese, and taking to white ways, were cut from the 1924 script.

62. This exchange about not being able to change one's racial categorization was changed in the 1924 script. Instead of casting the problem in terms of black and white, Potter says, "Once a Chinese, always a Chinese. I mean, once a canary, always a canary" (55).

63. Mr. Benson is referring to the Xinhai revolution in 1911 (one year after this play's dramatic present, 1910), which was responsible for overthrowing the Qing Dynasty. This section about the Chinese revolution was cut from the 1924 script, although the subsequent discussion was kept.

64. Alsace-Lorraine is a region in eastern France with a history of being conquered by both the French and Germans. The 1924 script omits France as a case study and instead mentions the shifting borders of Poland.

65. "Chink doll" was revised as "China doll" in the 1924 script.

66. Ming Toy's preference for tar soap as a scent is a joke. Tar soap was sold as an antiseptic cleanser and had a distinct odor like cleaning supplies.

67. Ming Toy's love of daisies is another joke. Not only were they seen as simple flowers, but "daisy" was also another word for a loose woman. This line was not in the 1924 script.

68. Mrs. Benson's racist comment here was deleted from the 1924 script.

69. The original 1918 manuscript notes that a scene for Mildred should be inserted here, but it never was. I have included one of Mildred's lines from the 1924 script, as it likely conveyed those sentiments.

70. This opening scene with these women, including the double entendres and references to Ming Toy's blue blood lines, were cut from the 1924 script.

71. A sinecure is an office or position with little or no work. Here it is used to mean that the couple was the envy of everyone else.

72. "Fagged out" is a colloquialism that means to be tired or exhausted. This scene announcing the interracial engagement was cut from the 1924 version.

73. This eugenics-infused discussion of race in terms of blood type was cut from the 1924 script.

74. Billy is referring to Germans as enemies in the recently fought First World War.

75. Wong's final speech in the 1924 version paraphrases Kipling's well-known quotation: "In the infinite, Ming Toy, whence all things come, there is not East, there is no West. West is East, and East is West. Good evening, everybody" (89).

76. The 1924 script ends with this line. It leaves out the phoning of Ming Toy's parents.

# BIBLIOGRAPHY

*For additional brothel dramas and related material on the staging of sex work in the Progressive Era, see brotheldrama.lib.miamioh.edu.*


Ahern, Emily M. *Chinese Ritual and Politics*. Cambridge: Cambridge University Press, 1981.

"Another Drama of Social Problem." *New York Herald*, 14 November 1913.

A. R. "What Is the Drama League Driving At?" *New York City Tribune*, 6 December 1913, 7.

Austin, J. L. *How to Do Things with Words*. Ed. J. O. Urmson and Marina Sbisà. Cambridge, MA: Harvard University Press, 1962.

Bak, John S. "Eugene O'Neill and John Reed: Recording the Body Politic, 1913–1922." *Eugene O'Neill Review* 20.1–2 (Fall/Spring 1996): 17–35.

Bank, Rosemarie K. "Hustlers in the House: The Bowery Theatre as a Mode of Historical Information." In *The American Stage: Social and Economic Issues from the Colonial Period to the Present*, 47–64, ed. Ron Engle and Tice Miller. Cambridge: Cambridge University Press, 1993.

Barry, Kathleen. *Female Sexual Slavery*. Englewood Cliffs, NJ: Prentice-Hall, 1979.

Belasco, David. *Madame Butterfly: A Tragedy of Japan*. 1900. In *Six Plays by David Belasco*, 9–32. Boston: Little, Brown and Company, 1929.

Bell, Ernest. *Fighting the Traffic in Young Girls, or the War on the White Slave Trade*. Chicago: G. S. Ball, 1910.

Bogard, Travis. *Contour in Time: The Plays of Eugene O'Neill*. New York: Oxford University Press, 1972. Rev. ed., 1988.

Bogard, Travis, and Jackson R. Bryer, eds. *Selected Letters of Eugene O'Neill*. New Haven: Yale University Press, 1988.

Boqun, Fan. "The Sing-Song Girls of Shanghai: The Pioneering Work of Modern Popular Fiction." *Frontiers of Literary Study in China* 2.3 (2008): 472–490.

Bordman, Gerald Martin. *American Theatre: A Chronicle of Comedy and Drama, 1869–1914*. Oxford: Oxford University Press, 1994.

Bowers, Robert Hood. "Chinese Lullaby." New York: G. Schirmer, 1919.

Brooks, Peter. "The Mark of the Beast: Prostitution, Melodrama, and Narrative." *New York Literary Forum* 7 (1980): 125–140.

Bryant, Rebecca A. "Shaking Things Up: Popularizing the Shimmy in America." *American Music* 20.2 (Summer 2002): 168–187.

Bynner, Witter. *Tiger: A Play of the Tenderloin.* In *A Book of Plays*, 101–144. New York: Knopf, 1922.

Cho, Yu-Fang. *Uncoupling American Empire: Cultural Politics of Deviance and Unequal Difference, 1890–1910.* Albany: State University of New York Press, 2014.

Committee of Fifteen. *The Social Evil, with Special Reference to Conditions Existing in the City of New York.* New York: Putnam and Sons, 1902.

Committee of Fourteen. *The Social Evil in New York City: A Study of Law Enforcement by the Research Committee of Fourteen.* New York: Andrew H. Kellog Company, 1910.

Connelly, Mark. *The Response to Prostitution in the Progressive Era.* Chapel Hill: University of North Carolina Press, 1980.

Cook, George Cram, and Frank Shay, eds. *The Provincetown Plays.* Cincinnati: Stewart Kidd & Co., 1921.

Corbin, John. "East Is West" (review). *New York Times*, 25 December 1918, 9.

Crothers, Rachel. "Ourselves." Unpublished play. 1913. Annenberg Rare Book and Manuscript Library, University of Pennsylvania.

Darnton, Charles. "*Ourselves*: A Play That Goes Wrong." Otherwise unidentified clipping from the Shubert Archive, New York City.

"Decency and the Stage." Editorial. *New York Times*, 7 September 1913, 12.

Deutsch, Helen, and Stella Hanau. *Provincetown: A History of the Theatre.* New York: Farrar & Rinehart, 1931.

"Dramatic Outlook in New York Brighter." *Louisville Courier*, 23 November 1913.

Dreiser, Theodore. *Sister Carrie.* 1900. Reprint, New York: Literary Classics of the United States, 1987.

"Drug Traffic Lucrative." *New York Times*, 7 December 1916, 24.

Dumas, *fils*, Alexandre. *Camille.* 1852. Trans. Edith Reynolds and Nigel Playfair. New York: Hill & Wang, 1957.

*East Is West.* Directed by Sidney Franklin. Performed by Constance Talmadge. New York: Associated First National Pictures, 1922.

*East Is West.* Directed by Monta Bell. Performed by Lupe Vélez. Burbank, CA: Universal Films, 1930.

"*East Is West*" (review). *Dramatic Mirror of Motion Pictures and the Stage* 80 (11 January 1919): 47.

"*East Is West*" (review). *Theatre Magazine* 29 (February 1919): 78.

"*East Is West* at the Lyric." *Illustrated London News*, 26 June 1920, 1114.

"*East Is West*: Play of the Month." *Hearst's Magazine* 35 (16 June 1919): 46–47, 66.

Eaton, Walter Prichard. *Plays and Players: Leaves from a Critic's Scrapbook.* Cincinnati: Steward & Kidd Company, 1916.

Egan, Leona Rust. *Provincetown as a Stage: Provincetown, the Provincetown Players, and the Discovery of Eugene O'Neill.* Orleans, MA: Parnassus Imprints, 1994.

"Escaping *House of Bondage*." *Munsey's Magazine* 51 (April 1914): 583.

Feldman, Egal. "Prostitution, the Alien Woman and the Progressive Imagination, 1910–1915." *American Quarterly* 29 (1967): 192–206.

Fishbein, Leslie. "The Harlot's Progress in American Fiction and Film, 1900–1930." *Women's Studies: An Interdisciplinary Journal* 16.3–4 (1989): 409–427.

Flexner, Abraham. *Prostitution in Europe*. Introduction by John D. Rockefeller Jr. New York: Century Company, 1914.

Fliotsos, Anne L., and Wendy Vierow, eds. *American Women Stage Directors of the Twentieth Century*. Urbana: University of Illinois Press, 2008.

Foucault, Michel. *The History of Sexuality, Vol. 1, An Introduction*. Trans. Robert Hurley. New York: Pantheon, 1978.

Franklin, S. M. "When We Have Time to Read." Review of *My Little Sister*. *Life and Labor* 3 (March 1913): 83–84.

Gainor, J. Ellen. *Susan Glaspell in Context: American Theater, Culture, and Politics, 1915–48*. Ann Arbor: University of Michigan Press, 2003.

Gale, Maggie Barbara, and Gilli Bush-Bailey, eds. *Plays and Performance Texts by Women, 1880–1930: An Anthology of Plays by British and American Women from the Modernist Period*. Manchester: Manchester University Press, 2012.

Gates, Joanne E. "The Theatrical Politics of Elizabeth Robins and Bernard Shaw." *Shaw* 14 (1994): 43–53.

Gelb, Arthur, and Barbara Gelb. *O'Neill*. New York: Harper & Row, 1962.

Gilfoyle, Timothy. *City of Eros: New York City, Prostitution, and the Commercialization of Sex, 1790–1920*. New York: W.W. Norton & Company, 1992.

Glaspell, Susan. "A Jury of Her Peers." *Every Week* 5 (March 5, 1917): pages unknown. Reprinted in *Best Short Stories of 1917*, ed. Edward J. O'Brien, 256–282. Boston: Small, Maynard & Company, 1918.

Godfrey, Emelyne. *Femininity, Crime and Self-Defense in Victorian Literature and Society: From Dagger-Fans to Suffragettes*. London: Palgrave Macmillan, 2012.

Goldman, Emma. "The Traffic in Women." In *Anarchism and Other Essays*, 183–200. 2nd rev. ed. New York and London: Mother Earth Publishing Association, 1911.

Grimm, Henry. *The Chinese Must Go*. San Francisco: A. L. Bancroft & Co., Printers, 1879.

Hamilton, Cecily. "Where Are You Going To? . . . " Unpublished play. 1913. The Elizabeth Robins Papers. MSS 002, Series 7, Box 75, Folders 12–15, Fales Library and Special Collections, New York University Libraries.

Hamilton, Clayton. "Timely Topics in the Theatre." *Bookman* 38 (October 1913): 133.

Hamilton, James Shelley. "The Sex Tangled Drama." *Everybody's Magazine* 29 (October 1913): 676–684.

Hapgood, Norman. "Stage Notes." *Harper's Weekly* 58 (December 1913): 12–13.

Hawthorne, Hildegarde. "*My Little Sister*: Miss Robins's Novel a Strong Plea for Our Invisible Neighbor." *New York Times*, 23 February 1913, 62. Reprinted in *Theatre Magazine* 13 (1913): vi.

Heap, Chad. *Slumming: Sexual and Racial Encounters in American Nightlife, 1885–1940*. Chicago: University of Chicago Press, 2010.

Hite, Molly. "The Public Woman and the Modernist Turn: Virginia Woolf's *The Voyage Out* and Elizabeth Robins's *My Little Sister*." *Modernism/modernity* 17.3 (September 2010): 523–548.

Houchin, John. *Censorship of the American Theatre in the Twentieth Century*. Cambridge: Cambridge University Press, 2003.

Ibsen, Henrik. *A Doll's House: A Play in Three Acts*. Trans. William Archer. London: T. F. Unwin, 1889.

"Immoral, Gross, Revolting, the Judge Calls *The Lure*." *New York World*, 9 September 1913.

John, Angela V. *Elizabeth Robins: Staging a Life, 1862–1952*. London: Routledge, 1995.

Johnson, Claudia D. "That Guilty Third Tier: Prostitution in Nineteenth-Century American Theaters." *American Quarterly* 27 (1975): 575–584.

Johnson, Katie N. "'*Anna Christie*': The Repentant Courtesan, Made Respectable." *Eugene O'Neill Review* 26 (2004): 87–104.

———. "Rachel Crothers's *Ourselves*: Feminist Dramaturgy in the Brothel Drama." *Journal of American Drama and Theatre* 15.3 (2003): 101–121.

———. "The Salvation Lass, Her Harlot-Friend, and Slum Realism in Edward Sheldon's *Salvation Nell* (1908)." *Theatre History Studies* 26 (2006): 88–107.

———. *Sisters in Sin: Brothel Drama in America, 1900–1920*. Cambridge: Cambridge University Press, 2006; paperback 2009.

Kauffman, Reginald Wright. *The House of Bondage*. New York: Grosset & Dunlap, 1910.

———. "The House of Bondage." Unpublished play. 1913. Manuscript Division, Library of Congress.

Keely, Karen A. "Sexual Slavery in San Francisco's Chinatown: 'Yellow Peril' and 'White Slavery' in Frank Norris's Early Fiction." *Studies in American Naturalism* 2.2 (Winter 2007): 129–149.

Kelley, Katherine E. "The Actresses' Franchise League Prepares for War: Feminist Theatre in Camouflage." *Theatre Survey* 35 (1994): 121–137.

Kennedy, Jeffrey. "The Artistic Life of the Provincetown Playhouse, 1918–1922." Diss. New York University, 2007.

———. "Cocaine." Provincetown Playhouse.com. http://www.provincetownplayhouse.com/cocaine.html.

Kenton, Edna. *The Provincetown Players and the Playwrights' Theatre, 1915–1922*. Ed. Travis Bogard and Jackson R. Bryer. Jefferson, NC: McFarland & Company, 2004.

King, Pendleton. *Cocaine: A Play in One Act*. Vol. 5 of *The Provincetown Plays*. Ed. Frank Shay. New York: Frank Shay, 1917.

Kinser, Suzanne L. "Prostitutes in the Art of John Sloan." *Prospects* 9.1 (1984): 231–254.

Kneeland, George J. *Commercialized Prostitution in New York City* (1913). Reprint, Montclair, NJ: Patterson Smith, 1969.

Laidlaw, Harriet Burton. Review of *My Little Sister*. *Survey* (8 May 1918): 199–202.

Lane, Jill. "ImpersoNation: Toward a Theory of Black-, Red-, and Yellowface in the Americas." *PMLA* 123.5 (October 2008): 1728–1731.

Lee, Josephine D. *Performing Asian America: Race and Ethnicity on the Contemporary Stage*. Philadelphia: Temple University Press, 1997.

Lindroth, Colette, and James Lindroth, eds. *Rachel Crothers: A Research and Production Sourcebook*. Westport, CT: Greenwood Press, 1995.

Lipsitz, George. *The Possessive Investment in Whiteness: How White People Profit from Identity Politics*. Philadelphia: Temple University Press, 2006.

"Little Plays Again at the Bandbox." *New York Times*, 27 March 1915, 11.

Luhrmann, Baz. *Moulin Rouge!* Twentieth Century Fox Home Entertainment, 2001. DVD.

"The Lure" (review). *New York Dramatic Mirror*, 20 August 1916, 6.

Mackay, Constance D'Arcy. *The Little Theatre in the United States*. New York: H. Holt & Company, 1917.

Mantle, Burns, and Garrison P. Sherwood, eds. *The Best Plays of 1909–1919*. New York: Mead & Company, 1933.

Marshall, Rachael, and Oliver D. Bailey. "The Traffic." Unpublished play. 1913. Manuscript Division, Library of Congress.

McDermott, M. Joan, and Sarah J. Blackstone. "White Slavery Plays of the 1910s: Fear of Victimization and the Social Control of Sexuality." *Theatre History Studies* 16 (June 1996): 141–155.

Meloney, William Brown. "Slumming in New York's Chinatown." *Munsey's Magazine* 41 (1909): 825.

Metcalfe, James M. "Here We Are Again, Mr. Merryman." *Life Magazine*, 4 September 1913, 390.

Miner, Maude E. *Slavery of Prostitution: A Plea For Emancipation*. New York: Macmillan, 1916.

"Minute Visits in the Wings." *New York Times*, 1 September 1918, 36.

Moon, Krystyn R. *Yellowface: Creating the Chinese in American Popular Music and Performance, 1850s–1920s*. New Brunswick: Rutgers University Press, 2005.

"More Underworld Put on the Stage." *New York Herald*, 14 November 1913.

Mulvey, Laura. "Visual Pleasure and Narrative Cinema." *Screen* 16.3 (1975): 6–18.

Murphy, Brenda. "Feminism and the Marketplace: The Career of Rachel Crothers." In *The Cambridge Companion to American Women Playwrights*, ed. Brenda Murphy, 82–97. Cambridge: Cambridge University Press, 1999.

———. *The Provincetown Players and the Culture of Modernity*. Cambridge: Cambridge University Press, 2005.

*My Little Sister*. Directed by Kenean Buel. Scenario Films, 1919. "New English Plays Here for Frohman." *New York Times*, 16 August 1913, 6.

"New Productions." *New York Dramatic Mirror*, 26 February 1913, 17.

Norris, Frank. *The Third Circle*. New York: John Lane, 1909.

"Offending Plays." *New York Herald*, otherwise unidentified clipping from *The Lure* clipping file, Museum of the City of New York.

O'Neill, Eugene. "*Anna Christie*." 1921. Reprint, *Complete Plays*. Vol. 1. Ed. Travis Bogard. New York: Library of America, 1988.

———. *Thirst and Other One Act Plays*. Boston: Gorham Press, 1914.

———. *The Web*. In *Complete Plays, 1913–1920*. New York: Library of Congress Edition, 1988.

"*Ourselves*" (review). *New York City Review*, 6 December 1913.

"*Ourselves*" (review). *Everybody's Magazine* 30 (February 1914): 264.

"*Ourselves* as Seen by a Woman." *New York Morning Sun*, 14 November 1913.

"*Ourselves* at Bradford." *New York City Tribune*, 7 December 1913.

"*Ourselves* Deals with That Old Dual Morality." *New York Telegram*, 14 November 1913.

"Over 50,000 Girls Disappear in This Country Yearly." *New York Times*, 21 September 1913, SM9.

Partridge, Eric, Tom Dalzell, and Terry Victor, eds. *The New Partridge Dictionary of Slang and Unconventional English*. London: Routledge, 2006.

Paul, Anne. "A Song of Success." *Shadowland* 1 (September 1919): 23–25, 74.

Pegler, Arthur James, and Arthur Rose. "Little Lost Sister." Unpublished play. 1913. Sherman Theatre Collection. Southern Illinois University Special Collections Research Center. Box 39, Folder 1186.

Peiss, Kathy. *Cheap Amusements*. Philadelphia: Temple University Press, 1987.

"Plays of Brothel Still Unchecked." *New York Herald*, 6 September 1913.

"Police Stop Two Plays." *Theatre Magazine* 18 (September 1913): 116.

Powell, J. Kerry, and Katie Johnson. "The Censoring of *My Little Sister*: Elizabeth Robins's Lost Feminist Play." Presentation at the American Comparative Literature Conference, University of Colorado, 20–22 April 2001.

"The Process of Dry-Cleaning." *Munsey's Magazine* 51 (February 1914): 124.

Puccini, Giacomo. *Madama Butterfly*. No. 4. Columbia Records, 1906.

Pullen, Kirsten. *Actresses and Whores on Stage and in Society*. Cambridge: Cambridge University Press, 2005.

"Rachel Crothers." *Woman's Journal* 16 (May 1931). Otherwise unidentified clipping from the Rachel Crothers clipping file, Shubert Archive.

Reed, John. *Moondown: A Play in One Act. Masses* 4 (September 1913): 8–9. Reprinted in *John Reed for The Masses*, ed. James C. Wilson, 38–42. Jefferson, NC: McFarland & Co., 1987.

———. "Moondown: A Play in One Act." Unpublished play. 1915. Manuscript Division, Library of Congress.

———. "A Taste of Justice." *Masses* 4 (April 1913): 8. Reprinted in *John Reed for The Masses*, ed. James C. Wilson, 20–22. Jefferson, NC: McFarland & Co., 1987.

"Reformatory Girls See Morals Drama." *New York City Tribune*, 3 December 1913.

Robins, Elizabeth. Letter to J. K. Jerome, 3 April 1914. The Elizabeth Robins Papers. MSS 002, Series 7, Box 75, Folder 16, Fales Library and Special Collections, New York University Libraries.

———. "My Little Sister." *McClure's Magazine* 40 (December 1912), 121–145; and (January 1913): 253–260.

———. "My Little Sister." Unpublished play. 1913. The Elizabeth Robins Papers. MSS 002, Series 7, Box 75, Folders 8–11, Fales Library and Special Collections, New York University Libraries.

———. *My Little Sister*. New York: Dodd, Mead and Co., 1913.

———. *Where Are You Going To . . . ?* London: Heinemann, 1913.

Roe, Clifford Griffith. *Horrors of the White Slave Trade: The Mighty Crusade to Protect the Purity of Our Homes*. London: n.p., 1911.

Rosen, Ruth. *The Lost Sisterhood: Prostitution in America, 1900–1918*. Baltimore: Johns Hopkins University Press, 1982.

Rosen, Ruth, and Sue Davidson, eds. *The Maimie Papers*. Old Westbury, NY: Feminist Press, 1977.

Scarborough, George. "The Lure." Unpublished play. Shubert Archive, 1913.

Schneider, Rebecca. *The Explicit Body in Performance*. New York: Routledge, 1997.

Schrecker, John E. *The Chinese Revolution in Historical Perspective: Contributions to the Study of World History*. New York: Greenwood Press, 1991.

"Sex O'Clock in America." *Current Opinion* 55.2 (August 1913): 113–114.

Shaw, George Bernard. *Mrs Warren's Profession: A Play* (1898). Reprinted in George Bernard Shaw, *Plays Unpleasant*. Harmondsworth: Penguin, 1983.

Shay, Frank T. *The Machine: A Commonplace Tragedy in One Act of Three Scenes. Masses* 4.11 (August 1913): 9.

Shimakawa, Karen. *National Abjection: The Asian American Body Onstage*. Durham: Duke University Press, 2002.

Shipman, Samuel. "If a Critic Cannot Say Why a Play Is Bad, He Is No Critic." *New York Dramatic Mirror*, 1 April 1922, 103.

Shipman, Samuel, and John B. Hymer. *East Is West: A Comedy in Three Acts and a Prologue*. New York: Samuel French, 1924.

———. "A Shanghai Cinderella." Unpublished play. 1918. Manuscript Division, Library of Congress.

"Six Million Dollars for Pleasure," *[Nashua, NH] Telegraph*, 15 April 1907, 2.

Soderland, Gretchen. "Covering Urban Vice: the *New York Times*, 'White Slavery,' and the Construction of Journalistic Knowledge." *Critical Studies in Media Communication* 19.4 (December 2002): 438–460.

"The Stage." *Munsey's Magazine* 49.6 (September 1913): 1023.

"The Story You Can't Forget." Display advertisement. *New York Times*, 23 February 1913, 62.

"A Successful Playwright's Hardships." *Stage* 50 (November 1915): 297.

Sullivan, Mark. *Our Times: The United States, 1900–1925*. Vol. 1, *The Turn of the Century*. New York: Scribner's, 1926.

Taylor, Diana. *The Archive and the Repertoire: Performing Cultural Memory in the Americas*. Durham: Duke University Press Books, 2003.

"The Theatre in Review." *Forum* 61 (February 1919): 244–245.

T. H. "Gold Bricks and Staple Goods." *Nation*, 18 January 1919, 104.

Thomas, Sue. "Crying 'the Horror' of Prostitution: Elizabeth Robins's '*Where Are You Going To . . . ?*' and the Moral Crusade of the Women's Social and Political Union." *Women: A Cultural Review* 16.2 (2005): 203–221.

*The Traffic in Girls: White Slavery as Now Practiced in America, Including Detailed Descriptions of the Customs and Manners of the White Women Slaves and Wives of Asia, Turkey, Egypt*. Chicago: Garden City Publishing House, 1912.

Turk, Roy, Bert Grant, and Cecil Bernard. "Ming Toy." New York: Waterson, Berlin & Snyder Co., 1919.

"Waldo's Censors Watch Two Plays of Underworld." *New York Word*, 5 September 1913.

Walkowitz, Judith R. *City of Dreadful Delight: Narratives of Sexual Danger in Late-Victorian London*. Chicago: University of Chicago Press, 1992.

Walter, Eugene. *The Easiest Way: An American Play Concerning a Particular Phase of New York Life, in Four Acts and Four Scenes*. New York: printed for the author, 1909. Reprinted in *Best Plays of the Early American Theatre: From the Beginning to 1916*, ed. John Gassner. New York: Crown Publishing, 1978.

Weintraub, Bernard. "Play a Hooker and Win an Oscar." *New York Times*, 20 February 1996, C13.

Westgate, J. Chris. *Staging the Slums, Slumming the Stage: Class, Poverty, Ethnicity, and Sexuality in American Theatre, 1890–1916*. New York: Palgrave, 2015.

"White Slave Play of Some Grim Power." *New York Times*, 15 August 1917, 7.

"White Slave Still a Theatrical Asset." Otherwise unidentified clipping from the Rachel Crothers clipping file, Normal Public Library, Normal, Illinois.

Williams, Dave, ed. *The Chinese Other, 1850–1925: An Anthology of Plays*. Lanham, NY: University Press of America, 1997.

"Women to Run Theatre." *New York Times*, 23 October 1913, 11.

# INDEX

*Actors and American Culture, 1880–1920*
By Benjamin McArthur

*The Age and Stage of George L. Fox, 1825–1877: An Expanded Edition*
By Laurence Senelick

*American Theater in the Culture of the Cold War: Producing and Contesting Containment*
By Bruce McConachie

*Athenian Tragedy in Performance: A Guide to Contemporary Studies and Historical Debates*
By Melinda Powers

*Classical Greek Theatre: New Views of an Old Subject*
By Clifford Ashby

*Czech Theatre Design in the Twentieth Century: Metaphor and Irony Revisited*
Edited by Joseph Brandesky

*Embodied Memory: The Theatre of George Tabori*
By Anat Feinberg

*Fangs of Malice: Hypocrisy, Sincerity, and Acting*
By Matthew H. Wikander

*Fantasies of Empire: The Empire Theatre of Varieties and the Licensing Controversy of 1894*
By Joseph Donohue

*French Theatre Today: The View from New York, Paris, and Avignon*
By Edward Baron Turk

*From Androboros to the First Amendment: A History of America's First Play*
By Peter A. Davis

*The Jewish Kulturbund Theatre Company in Nazi Berlin*
By Rebecca Rovit

*Jews and the Making of Modern German Theatre*
Edited by Jeanette R. Malkin and Freddie Rokem

*The Making of Theatrical Reputations: Studies from the Modern London Theatre*
By Yael Zarhy-Levo

*Marginal Sights: Staging the Chinese in America*
By James S. Moy

*Melodramatic Formations: American Theatre and Society, 1820–1870*
By Bruce A. McConachie

*Meyerhold: A Revolution in Theatre*
By Edward Braun

*Modern Czech Theatre: Reflector and Conscience of a Nation*
By Jarka M. Burian

*Modern Hamlets and Their Soliloquies: An Expanded Edition*
By Mary Z. Maher

*Molière, the French Revolution, and the Theatrical Afterlife*
By Mechele Leon

*The Most American Thing in America: Circuit Chautauqua as Performance*
By Charlotte M. Canning

*Music for the Melodramatic Theatre in Nineteenth-Century London and New York*
By Michael V. Pisani

*"Othello" and Interpretive Traditions*
By Edward Pechter

*Our Moonlight Revels: "A Midsummer Night's Dream" in the Theatre*
By Gary Jay Williams

*The Performance of Power: Theatrical Discourse and Politics*
Edited by Sue-Ellen Case and Janelle Reinelt

*Performing History: Theatrical Representations of the Past in Contemporary Theatre*
By Freddie Rokem

*The Recurrence of Fate: Theatre and Memory in Twentieth-Century Russia*
By Spencer Golub

*Reflecting the Audience: London Theatregoing, 1840–1880*
By Jim Davis and Victor Emeljanow

*Representing the Past: Essays in Performance Historiography*
Edited by Charlotte M. Canning and Thomas Postlewait

*The Roots of Theatre: Rethinking Ritual and Other Theories of Origin*
By Eli Rozik

*Sex for Sale: Six Progressive-Era Brothel Dramas*
By Katie N. Johnson

*Shakespeare and Chekhov in Production: Theatrical Events and Their Audiences*
By John Tulloch

*Shakespeare on the American Yiddish Stage*
By Joel Berkowitz

*The Show and the Gaze of Theatre: A European Perspective*
By Erika Fischer-Lichte

*Stagestruck Filmmaker: D. W. Griffith and the American Theatre*
By David Mayer

*Strange Duets: Impresarios and Actresses in the American Theatre, 1865–1914*
By Kim Marra

*Textual and Theatrical Shakespeare: Questions of Evidence*
Edited by Edward Pechter

*Theatre and Identity in Imperial Russia*
By Catherine A. Schuler

*Theatre, Community, and Civic Engagement in Jacobean London*
By Mark Bayer

*Theatre Is More Beautiful Than War: German Stage Directing in the Late Twentieth Century*
By Marvin Carlson

*Theatres of Independence: Drama, Theory, and Urban Performance in India since 1947*
By Aparna Bhargava Dharwadker

*The Theatrical Event: Dynamics of Performance and Perception*
By Willmar Sauter

*The Trick of Singularity: "Twelfth Night" and the Performance Editions*
By Laurie E. Osborne

*The Victorian Marionette Theatre*
By John McCormick

*Wandering Stars: Russian Emigré Theatre, 1905–1940*
Edited by Laurence Senelick

*Writing and Rewriting National Theatre Histories*
Edited by S. E. Wilmer